Spenser's Life and the
Subject of Biography

Spenser's Life and the Subject of Biography

Edited by

JUDITH H. ANDERSON

DONALD CHENEY

DAVID A. RICHARDSON

University of Massachusetts Press / *Amherst*

Copyright © 1996 by
The University of Massachusetts Press
All rights reserved
Printed in the United States of America
LC 96–19287
ISBN 1–55849–050–7
Set in Adobe Garamond
Printed and bound by Braun-Brumfield, Inc.

Library of Congress Cataloging–in–Publication Data
Spenser's life and the subject of biography / edited by Judith H.
Anderson, Donald Cheney, David A. Richardson.
p.   cm. — (Massachusetts studies in early modern culture)
Includes bibliographical references.
ISBN 1–55849–050–7 (alk. paper)
1. Spenser, Edmund, 1552?–1599—Biography.
2. Poets, English—Early modern, 1500–1700—Biography—History and criticism.
3. Biography as a literary form.   4. Poets in literature.   5. Self in Literature.
I. Anderson, Judith H.   II. Cheney, Donald, date
III. Richardson, David A.   IV. Series.
PR2363.S65   1996
821'.3—dc20
[B]
96-19287
CIP

British Library Cataloguing in Publication data are available.

Table of Contents

CONTENTS

Contributors and Editors

Judith H. Anderson, professor of English at Indiana University, is the author of *The Growth of a Personal Voice: "Piers Plowman" and "The Faerie Queene"* (1976), *Biographical Truth: The Representation of Historical Persons in Tudor-Stuart Writing* (1984), and *Words That Matter: Linguistic Perception in Renaissance English* (1996). She has also coedited *Will's Vision of Piers Plowman* (1990) and has written more than twenty articles on Spenserian texts. She is now working on historicized metaphor in early modern England.

Jean R. Brink, professor of English at Arizona State University, has published in the area of Elizabethan biography and bibliography. She is currently working on a biography of Spenser that will contextualize documentary sources for his life and works.

Vincent P. Carey, assistant professor at the State University of New York at Plattsburgh, teaches early modern European history. He is editor with Clare Carroll of an annotated edition of Richard Beacon's colonial tract *Solon His Follie* (1996). He is currently working on a study of Gerald, the eleventh earl of Kildare, and Tudor rule in Ireland, as well as the relationship between government policy and atrocity in sixteenth-century Ireland.

Clare L. Carroll, associate professor of comparative literature at Queens College and the Graduate Center, CUNY, has with Vincent Carey edited Beacon's *Solon His Follie* (1996). Her current work includes a book on Ariosto, *"Orlando Furioso," A Stoic Comedy*. She is also editing Spenser's *View of the Present State of Ireland* and the Early Modern section of the *Longman Anthology of British Literature*.

Donald Cheney, professor of English at the University of Massachusetts, Amherst, is author of *Spenser's Image of Nature: Wild Man and Shepherd in "The Faerie Queene"* (1966), "Spenser's Fortieth Birthday and Related Fictions" (*Spenser Studies*, 1983), and other essays on Spenser. He is senior coeditor of *The Spenser Encyclopedia* (1990) and is working with Brenda Hosington on an edition and translation of Elizabeth Jane Weston.

Jay Farness, professor of English at Northern Arizona University, teaches ancient and Renaissance literature, literary criticism, and writing. His publications include *Missing Socrates: Problems of Plato's Writing* (1991), "Festive Theater, Restive Narrative in *Don Quixote* I" (*PMLA*, 1992), and *College Writing Skills* (with Peder Jones, 1991).

F. J. Levy is professor of history at the University of Washington and the author of *Tudor Historical Thought* (1967) as well as articles on Sidney, Greville, Bacon, and their contemporaries. He is completing a book on the literature and politics of the 1590s and has another underway on print culture in England from Caxton to the early eighteenth century.

Joseph Loewenstein is associate professor of English at Washington University in St. Louis. He is finishing a book called *The Authorial Impression*, on the development of Renaissance intellectual property. His scholarly publications treat of Jonson, Shakespeare, Sidney, Guarini, Gascoigne, Milton, the book trade, and the evolution of monopolistic practices in the cultural sphere.

David Lee Miller is professor of English at the University of Kentucky. He is the author of *The Poem's Two Bodies: The Poetics of the 1590 "Faerie Queene"* (1988) and editor with Alexander Dunlop of *Approaches to Teaching Spenser's "Faerie Queene"* (1994). His work in progress concerns the motif of filial sacrifice in Virgil, Shakespeare, Freud, and other writers.

Anne Lake Prescott, professor of English at Barnard College, is author of *French Poets and the English Renaissance* (1978) and a number of scholarly essays. She contributed to *The Spenser Encyclopedia* (1990) and is editor with Hugh Maclean of the Norton Critical Edition of *Spenser's Poetry* (1993). She has completed a book on Rabelais and Renaissance England.

Jon A. Quitslund is professor of English at the George Washington University, Washington, D.C. He has published a number of articles on Sidney and Spenser, among them the entries on "Platonism" and "beauty" for *The Spenser Encyclopedia*. His next publication will be a book, *Spenser's Supreme Fiction: Natural Philosophy in "The Faerie Queene."*

Richard Rambuss, associate professor of English at Emory University, is the author of *Spenser's Secret Career* (1993) as well as essays on Chaucer, Donne, Herbert, and Crashaw. He is completing *Closet Devotions*, a study of religious devotion, affect, and the body.

David A. Richardson is professor of English at Cleveland State University. He initiated "Spenser at Kalamazoo" (1976–) and *The Spenser Encyclopedia* (1990), of which he was managing editor, and has edited *Sixteenth-Century British Nondramatic Writers* for the *Dictionary of Literary Biography* (vols. 132, 136, 167, 172). His essay "Fair Allurements to Learning: The Legacy of a Professing Teacher" is a reflection on O. B. Hardison, Jr. (in *Acts of the Imagination,* ed. Arthur F. Kinney, 1996).

Foreword

JUDITH H. ANDERSON

Although Edmund Spenser is the major nondramatic poet of the Tudor period, less is known about his life than about that of Sir Philip Sidney or even of William Shakespeare, the contemporary artists whose achievements are comparable to his. Few personal documents such as letters written by him survive, and the traces of his life in other kinds of records are meager and often ambiguous. Spenser's life, far more than Sidney's, affords a situation in which we confront with unusual clarity the issues that the death of an author presents and the problematics of biography.

In Spenser's case, the most basic problems include historical reference (both the few "facts" and their many interpretations) and the relations of his voluminous writing (his fiction) to his sparsely documented life. Although little has been added to the record since Judson's biography in 1945, even a limited reexamination of his factual sources suggests how extensively dated his interpretation is and not merely his more obvious embroidery of the "facts." Both the factual and interpretative contexts in which we should be reading such records of Spenser as do exist have changed dramatically since Judson's review of them, yet these changes have barely been registered on the actual accounts of Spenser's life. From the standpoint of history, we need both to verify the claims made about this life (e.g., about Spenser's "exile" to Ireland) and to experiment with a variety of approaches to them, including the illumination available from recent social and political histories and from the better documented lives of relevant contemporaries, such as Gabriel Harvey or Spenser's colonial associates in Ireland.

While several of the essays we have invited for this volume directly address such historical questions in various ways, our major focus concerns the most vexing question of all about Spenser, one that involves fundamental biographical theory: precisely what bearing might the poetry have on his biography? Here the relation of life to writing and fiction to history

ix

is critical. Spenser's poetry (often dated interpretatively) is to an extraordinary extent the basis of Judson's biography, and it still remains the major trace, however elusive, distanced, and fictionalized, of the hand and the mind that history calls Edmund Spenser. But *what* the poetry means biographically, there's the rub, and there will be a good deal of attention to it in the essays that follow.

In them, the focus is not on coverage. We do not address, for example, Spenser's early years and education, his frequently examined relationship to Ralegh, or his problematic death. Our volume is not meant to substitute for a comprehensive life of the poet or for a complete methodology of life-writing. Instead, it has been gathered and largely written in the twin convictions that we must seriously question the problematics of biography and the biographical bases of Spenser's life before undertaking a major biography and that any credible biography of him will be characterized by openness and ambiguity rather than by closure. In accord with these convictions, we have declined to adjudicate or mask valid differences in emphasis on and interpretation of the biographical materials that delineate Spenser's life. Instead, we have exhibited them openly, seeing them as a means of highlighting the interpreter's aims and methods.

The essays that follow focus on two issues in Spenserian biography, the facts and the poetry, to our minds the most urgent and basic ones. Choosing among several possible factual points of entry, we have selected representative essays that concentrate either on Spenser's initial posting to Ireland, one of the most complexly nuanced events of his career, or on the relation of his writing to the fact of its publication. Both these problems are variously informed by recent scholarship on early modern patronage, on the Sidney circle, and on Spenser's friend Harvey, and also on publishing history, the material production of culture. By contrast, to accentuate the assumptions and methods that inform such historical issues, we have looked for alternative approaches that are largely skeptical of a (traditional) biographical project. These challenging approaches manage, if somewhat elliptically, to construct the suggestive ghost of an author whose decentered lineaments look persuasively postmodern: our own eyes always meet us in the mirrors. Their emphatic presence in the volume asserts our own belief that exploration and interrogation of the relationship between Spenser's writing and his life must *precede* any effort to write a psychological biography of Spenser or a persuasive critique of his ideology, which in the absence of adequate or even pertinent historical records will rest on his fiction.

The first essay, by Richard Rambuss, offers a provocative review of twentieth-century biography of Spenser, compared to that of Shakespeare. Examining the overlap between new and old historicists' versions of Spenser, Rambuss urges "a strategic decentering of 'the poetic Spenser'" in favor of the literally historicized figure to be found in colonial and bureaucratic contexts. Only in this way, he suggests, can we "begin to account for the . . . cultural work performed" by the persistent image of Spenser as poet's poet. The second essay is paired as a complementary Other to Rambuss's persuasive call for studies of Spenser centrifugal to the poetry. In it, Jay Farness looks at *The Faerie Queene*'s potential for biographical truth and finds in "the poet's life-writing" of figures like Colin, Malfont, and Artegall both an anticipation of the political diagnoses of Greenblatt and Montrose and the distinct "feel for a Tudor anthropology." Critiquing old- and new-historical readings from assumptions that differ markedly from Rambuss's, he argues effectively for an "internal distantiation" of the Tudor myth that is usually denied Spenser's epic romance, and he cautions against the rush to history when we "are not yet sure just what Spenser's literary text is or what it is capable of doing."

The essays of both Rambuss and Farness exhibit a heightened sensitivity to the fifth book of *The Faerie Queene*, almost an inevitability in engaging the historical politics of Spenser's writing. Accordingly, the three historically focused essays that follow them feature centrally Spenser's initial engagement with Ireland, each invoking his poetry where pertinent to buttress or supplement historical knowledge. Although the assumption that Spenser was exiled to Ireland colors numerous readings of his life and poetry, its validity has received little attention recently, in sharp contrast to many rereadings of events influencing his life once on Irish soil. Clare Carroll and Vincent Carey, specialists in literature and history respectively, therefore collaborate to examine "the historical question of how Spenser was sent to Ireland in 1580" and the literary question of how his "responses to the events and . . . affiliations formed during 1579 and 1580" are reflected in his poetry. They emphasize the role of Arthur, Lord Grey de Wilton, in Spenser's appointment as secretary in Ireland, and they also explicitly address the interplay of history with narrative and of literature with historical documentation and interpretation: more exactly, "the relation between biographical fiction and court faction, between Spenser's poetry and life, and between poetic and historical" mythmaking.

While similarly concerned with the question of whether Spenser's appointment as secretary to Grey meant preferment or exile, Jean Brink devotes much of her essay to the self-presentation of Spenser and Gabriel

Harvey in England. She seeks to illuminate the circumstances of Spenser's appointment by examining the image of an ideal courtier in Spenser's verse, the values of the Sidney circle, and finally and crucially the records of Harvey's attempts to gain preferment, much better documented in his case than in his friend Spenser's. Harvey's attempts intersect revealingly at various points with Spenser's, for example, in Spenser's gaining access to Leicester House (between September 1578 and April 1579, according to Brink) or in Harvey's mixed feelings about Spenser's successes, which in turn reflect adversely on Harvey's reliability in publishing "private" letters passed between himself and the poet. In the scantness of the actual record of Spenser's posting to Ireland, Brink's argument-by-association affords historically suggestive access to Spenser's immediate context.

Casting the interpretative net still more widely to encompass "the peculiarly English version of Italian civic humanism in its late, courtly phase" and "the underlying ideology of the whole generation of which Spenser was part," F. J. Levy also seeks "to make sense of Spenser's career—and especially its Irish component—by seeing it in terms of other men." Levy's impressive grasp of the nuances of late Elizabethan history allows for some memorable conclusions: for example, "Spenser never understood the political system at court well enough to manipulate it." Throughout, Levy's evaluation of Spenser's career balances realistic appraisal of the poet's opportunities and accommodations against the humanistic disillusionment they implied.

Jon Quitslund turns to a characteristically humanistic mode of expression and publication, ostensibly private but actually public correspondence, and examines the five heterogeneous *Letters* between Spenser and Harvey that were published in 1580, the same year that Spenser became Grey's secretary in Ireland. Quitslund's doubts about the evidentiary value of his documents rivals Farness's sense of the unsteadiness of Spenser's poetic text, yet when Quitslund reviews the contents of the *Letters* for their bearing on Spenser's life, he also finds "the remaining traces of his subjecthood" within them. Insofar as Quitslund stresses that Spenser's biography, especially in the liminal stages of his career, "took shape in the public domain, through deliberate moves in which courtiership and service were combined with publishing in pursuit of an author's status," his essay leads readily into Joseph Loewenstein's capacious study of "Spenser's Retrography," in Loewenstein's own gloss of this title, "a contribution to the intersecting historiographies of authorial subjectivity and of the institutions of print." Loewenstein's concern is "the material history of autobiography" as it is shaped by print, particularly in the instance of Spenser's printed sonnets, which offer a form of writing traditionally associated with self-expression, however social or private its nature and source. For Loewenstein, the dedicatory sonnets displaced from front to back matter in *The Faerie Queene* became a site in which "the poet experienced himself bibliographically" through a dialogue conducted "between manuscription and printing." This is a dialogue that enables the writing hand to wrest "a fiction of privacy from the facts of book culture."

Loewenstein's view that *all* Spenser's sonnets in some way recall du Bellay serves as a bridge to another unconventional biographical perspective, Spenser's methods of reading, which Anne Prescott explores through Spenser's debt to du Bellay in *The Shepheardes Calender*, the *Amoretti*, and the *Mutabilitie Cantos*. Basing her contribution to Spenser's intellectual biography on intertextual relations, yet recognizing the inevitable instability of any intertextual study, she seeks to elude this unsteadiness by focusing on the shape and chronology of Spenser's debt. She observes that, as Spenser's poetic career progresses, it is sometimes "a nice psycho-philosophical question" as to whether the traces of du Bellay in Spenser's writing indicate that he is still reading du Bellay or now, more simply, reading himself or, for that matter, in what sense the self that has absorbed du Bellay is still his. Here Prescott's poised essay touches the social self—the subjecthood—of Quitslund's. Both writers, like the majority of those in this volume, look for "Spenser" in Spenser's writing, but both also acknowledge the instability—the fictive nature—of this figure.

The final essay, by David Miller, teases out the considerable implications for biography of a six-verse epigram on the earl of Cork's lute that was attributed to Spenser in Ware's 1633 edition of *A View of the Present State of Ireland*. Taken as a metonymy for the author (and the author's death), these verses show "why his life cannot be written." Miller's essay credibly re-creates the "*mise en abîme* of [the poet's] speaking voice," which he describes as "a pervasive feature" of *The Faerie Queene*. While the texture—the "feel," if you will—of Miller's "signifying lute" differs distinctively from the tonality of Farness's "Disenchanted Elves," it comes full circle in demonstrating the "fictionality of [the] pretextual origins" of literary texts, whether called "life, history, or politics," and thus in questioning the possibility of biography based in any fundamental sense on a poet's fictions. Put simply, biographical conclusions so grounded ignore "the indeterminacy of texts."

But the indeterminacy of texts, in which the present writer believes profoundly, pushed to its extreme would finally leave us with nothing to do except to repeat this perception. Unless we construct and unless we historicize constructively, there will be nothing for us to deconstruct. And it is finally to construction, but to hypothetical construction, that we must always return. Even in what I have already described as the construction of ghostly postmodern lineaments, there is a figure to work with, and if this volume has a single driving purpose, it is to provoke further and perhaps more revisionary work on the questions surrounding Spenser's elusive life and on those inhering in the thoroughly ambiguous subject of biography. This is the subject to which Donald Cheney returns in his Afterword to the volume, which reflects on the "dialogic intertextuality" of *The Shepheardes Calender* as the paradigm of a life whose features are "not merely doubtful" but deliberately so: repeatedly, "the evidence for Spenser's life," whether fictive or ostensibly factual, calls "its own authority into question and [demands] that we question it." Today, perhaps, this is exactly what the face of Edmund Spenser looks like.

Spenser's Lives, Spenser's Careers

RICHARD RAMBUSS

> What wonder therefore, if our curiosity is excited to get
> some kind of intimacy with those, whom from their
> writings we cannot but esteem, and that we listen to every
> tale told of them with any degree of probability, or even
> suffer ourselves to be imposed on by invented stories?
> John Upton, in *"The Faerie Queene."* A New Edition

Prince of poets, "Englands Arch-Poet," "our new Poete," the poet's poet: despite garnering a host of epithets that appear to grant this poet and his poetics a status apart from and above the practices of his literary contemporaries, Edmund Spenser earned his living and made his place in the world, like so many other multiply employed poets of his time, by pursuing a career of dual humanist service.[1] For along with his laureate ambitions Spenser sought advancement by means of a sustained career as a secretary and bureaucrat—a career conducted principally in the context of colonial Ireland. In *Spenser's Secret Career*, I have argued that his works and biography cannot be adequately addressed outside the terrains of a double career. In this essay, which proceeds from that account, I review Spenser studies from the early decades of this century, in order first to note how scholarship on Spenser remained persistently biographical against a general redirection of literary study toward thematic analysis. Second, by looking even farther back to the *Spenser* volume in John Morley's formative nineteenth-century English Men of Letters series, I identify and interrogate a set of enduring critical tropes that, by effacing aspects of his biography and career, have effected the fashioning of Spenser as a great man of letters according to modern, not Renaissance, notions of authorship. These are figurings of Spenser as the poet's poet, as a lover of natural (Irish) beauty, as the representative new voice of his age, as an emergent modernist, as the formulator of a new notion of authorship, as well as the poet who ultimately retires from the public sphere into a private, Acidalean domain of pure poetic contemplation. In the final section of this essay, I turn to more recent critical treatments of Spenser to show that these clichés of Spenser criticism are as likely to occur in seminal new-historicist accounts of Spenser's poetic career as they are in positivistic, "old-historicist" accounts of his biography. I thus argue that, although our interest in Spenser is (at least in the first place) posited on his remarkable poetry, it is only by means of a strategic decentering of "the poetic Spenser"—a decentering to be achieved by placing him in other contexts, namely the colonial and the bureaucratic—that we can begin to account for the kinds of cultural work performed by this abiding incorporation of Spenser as the poet's poet.

Marking one in a still unfolding series of ideologically charged cultural "reinventions" of Shakespeare (and thus metonymically of literature), Gary Taylor fixes on the 1930s as the time of a major reorientation in critical practice. Through the influential endeavors of such critics as T. S. Eliot, G. Wilson Knight, and L. C. Knights, the chief objective of Shakespeare criticism was becoming (in a phrase meant to retain its musical overtones) the exposition of theme (Taylor 1989, 239).[2] Moreover, as Knights's facetiously entitled essay *How Many Children Had Lady Macbeth?* makes derisively clear, the animus of this vanguard critical practice was particularly directed against "character criticism" in its various permutations—from what was seen to be the misguided adulation of Shakespeare as a genius for creating true-to-life individual characters and psychologies, to the related impulse for devising extratextual biographies for the dramatis personae of his plays, to efforts to extrapolate the nature of Shakespeare's own character from his literary works. One can thus see how the repudiation of character study would entail a shift away from biographically oriented criticism as well, for "when you say good-bye to character," Taylor remarks, "you say good-bye to biography too" (240). As evidence for this attendant redirection of Shakespeare studies he points to E. K. Chambers's landmark 1930 study of Shakespeare's life. Noting that Chambers does not subtitle his tome "A Biography" but rather *A Study of Facts and Problems*, Taylor reminds us that Chambers allots just two chapters to an account of Shakespeare's life and career—an opening chapter on "Shakespeare's Origin" and another on "Shakespeare and His Company." The rest of Chambers's two-volume *William Shakespeare* is parceled out into discrete chapters providing information on such topics as the history of the stage, conditions in the printing houses, and possible chronological orderings of the plays, or into bibliographies and reproductions of pertinent documents. Significant here is Chambers's refusal to offer any narrativization of the life of Shakespeare based on what he terms "the scanty biographical *data* from records and tradition" (1930, ix). Instead of a life story, that is, Chambers presents an encyclopedic compendium of archival materials, bibliographies, and essays on literary and cultural topics pertaining to Shakespeare. As Taylor wryly notes, "You do not read Chambers' *William Shakespeare;* you use it" (244).

How different the situation looks when we turn from Shakespeare to contemporaneous Spenser scholarship. Still taking their cues from the inaugural work of Spenser criticism—the crypto-biographical introduction and annotation E. K. supplies to *The Shepheardes Calender*—as well as from the enticing autobiographical set pieces that continue to recur throughout Spenser's poetry, the Spenserians of this period were combing public records offices and manuscript collections in a sustained effort to decipher veiled personal allusions in the poetry, to rectify problems of scanty source material, and to close up the many significant lacunae that yet existed in the scholarly production of the "Life" of this poet. The questions that sent these scholars to the archives ranged from the determination of such basic biographical matters as the precise year and place of Spenser's birth, when and whom he married, and when and how he died, to more specialized topics of interest like where he resided at any given time, what properties he held, and the nature of his relations to other important figures of the period. The archival endeavors of these researchers led to an array of biographically focused Spenser articles that continued to appear throughout the first three decades of this century and beyond in the pages of *PMLA*, *Modern Philology, Studies in Philology, Modern Language Notes*, and *Review of English Studies*, not to mention *Notes and Queries*. "Biographical Notes on Spenser," "Spenser's Marriage," "Spenser's Rosalind: A Conjecture," "Another Spenser Portrait," "Spenser's Visit to the North of England," "Edmund Spenser's Family," "Spenser: The Uncertain Years, 1584-1589," "Did Spenser Starve?": these titles indicate a good deal about some of the prevailing concerns of Spenser studies at a time when Shakespeare studies, along with work on a number of other early modern literary figures, were undergoing a significant critical reorientation. I do not mean to suggest that the emerging enthusiasm for thematic criticism made no inroads in Spenser scholarship, though it is arguable that *The Shepheardes Calender* and *The Faerie Queene* were to prove rather more resistant to the critical protocols advocated by Knight, Eliot, and their formalist posterity than, say, the works of Shakespeare, Donne, or (in time) Milton. I am rather calling attention to the fact that a substantial amount of scholarship on Spenser remained persistently engaged in the endeavor of framing a "Life" of the poet.

Indicative of the efflorescence of Spenserian biographical criticism in this period is the work of Raymond Jenkins, who over the course of the 1930s published an important series of essays on Spenser that I want to consider here in some detail. Like a substantial amount of historically informed Spenser scholarship from the period between the wars, Jenkins's attentions are principally directed toward Spenser's life and career as they took shape in Ireland, not only during his important tenure there as Lord Grey's secretary but also afterward.[3] (Interestingly, this focus on "the Irish Spenser" is not fully revived when Spenser criticism turns historicist once again in the 1970s and 1980s—a point I will take up later.) Following the lead of H. R. Plomer, who had identified Spenser's secretary hand and presented facsimiles of some letters featuring it in a 1923 *Modern Philology* essay, Jenkins's work on Spenser is launched from the archives, particularly the State Papers of Ireland. There he uncovers some seventy additional letters either wholly penned or at least signed and addressed by Spenser, as well as a number of other documents and references that pertain to his professional and entrepreneurial affairs in Ireland (1937, 338). Whereas Plomer seems to have been satisfied with the accomplishment of definitively identifying Spenser's handwriting and simply bringing to light some newly uncovered historical materials, the archival work undertaken by Jenkins is, however, clearly in the service of composing biography: "What biographical facts do these new letters reveal?" is the first question he asks of his findings (1938, 350). Accordingly, he does not offer a handbook presentation of discrete biographical and bibliographical data, inferences, and problems about Spenser along the lines of Chambers's contemporaneous Shakespearean *Facts and Problems* or even Frederic Ives Carpenter's *Reference Guide to Edmund Spenser* of 1923. Tracking in detail Spenser's successive bureaucratic appointments and commissions, his various professional and financial dealings, and his travels, Jenkins instead aims to fashion a relatively continuous, traditional biographical *narrative*.[4] And it is to be the narrative of Spenser, in Jenkins's terms, "not only as a great poet but also as an actor in many roles on this world's stage" (1932a, 121).

Although Jenkins confidently reports that the letters he has found "naturally reveal much regarding the life of Spenser" (1937, 340), it needs to be pointed out that these documents are almost exclusively letters Spenser took down as dictation at someone else's hand—whether Grey's or those of the brothers John and Thomas Norris, whom he also served as secretary in his capacity of clerk of the Council of Munster. This is to say that the letters are not, strictly speaking, Spenser's own letters, and thus they reveal little direct information about his individual affairs. Qualifications of this sort hardly temper Jenkins's biographical sleuthings, however, and he assures us that "All of these letters and addresses in the poet's autograph are, of course, a very definite means of determining his primary concerns and whereabouts" (1937, 341). Equipped as he is with such "very definite means," Jenkins, like every Spenser biographer, nonetheless must construct his life of the poet with a substantial reliance on informed surmise and inference. Inference is crucial to this project because, with relatively little additional direct biographical material on Spenser forthcoming from the archives, any narrative of his life in Ireland depends on what can be pieced together from what is known or can be found out about his employers, patrons, and associates there—Grey and the Norrises, as well as Lodowick Bryskett, John Perrot, and Walter Ralegh, among others. Thus Jenkins's lead-off question—"What biographical facts do these new letters reveal?"—is immediately and necessarily refracted through a consideration of the "concerns and whereabouts" not of Spenser but of someone else: "By tracing the career in Ireland of Sir John and Sir Thomas Norris from 1584 to 1589, I shall now recount Spenser's experiences" (1938, 350).

A good deal of Spenser's own experiences can indeed be reliably surmised in this manner since, as Jenkins rightly contends, "Spenser was not a modern secretary who sat comfortably at the home office and communicated with his chief by telephone but rather a companion who suffered the moving accidents of flood and field" (1938, 355). Thus Jenkins is no doubt correct, for instance, in ascertaining Spenser's presence in attendance of Grey at the brutal Smerwick massacre in 1580, when the surrender and pleas for mercy of 600 besieged papal troops did not forestall the lord deputy's ordering their summary execution (1937, 343). Similarly creditable are Jenkins's trackings of Spenser's experiences by means of what we know about Grey's or the Norrises' various travels and campaigns across Ireland—experiences which, he notes, kept Spenser "at the centre of the Irish political arena" (1937, 341). But an outline of Spenser's whereabouts is only a portion of the promised yield from Jenkins's researches. They also serve, it will be remembered, as "a very definite means of determining [Spenser's] primary concerns," in addition to his whereabouts. Consequently, Jenkins is given to speaking in terms not only of Spenser's travels but also of what Spenser perceived, felt, and desired. Writing biography and not simply delineating an extended chronology, Jenkins purports to deliver more than facts and problems; he wants to tell the story of Spenser's "primary concerns"—his aims and motives, his ambitions and personal allegiances, his responses to and investments in what was occurring in Ireland, in what he himself (literally) had a hand in performing there.

The question, of course, is what constitutes Jenkins's access to the nature of Spenser's "primary concerns"? Interestingly, in construing this aspect of Spenser's life and career in Ireland, Jenkins does not turn to the archives, nor does he attend as much as one might expect to *A View of the Present State of Ireland* or the *Briefe Note of Ireland*, Spenser's two prose tracts on the "Irish problem." In a move indicative of most biographically oriented Spenser criticism, Jenkins instead turns to the poetry as the site at which Spenser's "primary concerns" are made manifest for us. To be sure, Spenser is shown by Jenkins—who matches him on this account with Shakespeare as another model self-starting, middle-class entrepreneur—to be ever vigilant for opportunities of career and financial advancement.[5] This is to say (though Jenkins himself cannot quite say it) that Spenser was wholly committed to the project of subjugating and administering Ireland as an English colony, however exorbitant, however brutal the costs. Those costs might begin to be measured in terms of such matters as the Smerwick massacre (of which Spenser offers a defensive account in *A View*), or in the sustained, sometimes even induced incidences of Irish famine (also in *A View* he advocates further usage of mass starvation to cripple Irish resistance), or even in the kangaroo court headed by Grey that convicted and executed Chief Justice Nicholas Nugent on unfounded charges of treason (as Grey's secretary Spenser probably helped prepare the case).[6]

I cite these particular instances of Spenser's deep enmeshment in the work of Irish colonization because they are all recorded in Jenkins's "biographies" of Spenser, though in contexts that eerily match these terroristic maneuvers with blithe talk of such matters as Spenser's love of beauty and appreciation of the picturesque qualities of the Irish landscape, Spenser's "confidence" that "his humane ideals would outlast the plots and schemes of all politicians" (1938, 362), or Spenser's abiding sympathies for the "poor, hard-working Irish tenants" (359). Thus Jenkins opens his narration of Spenser's presence at Smerwick with some lines cited from *The Faerie Queene* on the majestic Irish river the English troops had to cross to reach the fortress, and he concludes it with a cheery account of Spenser pausing on his return journey for a preview glimpse of "the picturesque surroundings of Kilcolman which Dr. A. C. Judson has so vividly described in his delightful volume, *Spenser in Southern Ireland*" (1937, 343-44). Similarly, Jenkins remarks that, while accompanying Grey on a number of further military forays and retaliatory strikes aimed at breaking the back of Irish resistance, Spenser "may have beheld, in addition to frequent surprise attacks and executions, some of the beautiful lakes of West Meath as on the previous [expedition] he had seen the lakes of Killarney" (1937, 344). A profound, poetic appreciation of natural beauty, along with a poet's attendant "humane ideals," is, in short, what Jenkins routinely privileges throughout his essays as Spenser's "primary concerns." And how does the biographer know that the natural majesty of the Irish fields, streams, and ruined abbeys is what chiefly occupied Spenser's thoughts as he rode to and from numerous scenes of counsel, trial, execution, and battle? He knows it from the poetry, which is amply, if selectively, cited throughout Jenkins's essays—cited in such a way that Jenkins's "Spenser" comes to appear less the colonial bureaucrat and rather more like a Renaissance Wordsworth on a tour of the (Irish) lake country. The unspoken conviction underwriting this account of the life of Spenser is that the poetry of *The Faerie Queene* could not have been dreamed up but by someone who valued beauty and humane ideals above all else: "Considering that Spenser during these hectic years was both witness and actor in some of the world's sternest work, we marvel," Jenkins remarks reverentially, "that the poet in him was never killed" (1938, 362). The poet in Spenser—Spenser as the poet, *as the poet's poet*—this is what endures; this is what the biography is written to produce and secure. And produced as such, biography then corroborates an aestheticizing critical reading of the poetry.

It should be evident that the construction of Spenser as an aficionado of the beautiful, of what is inherently "poetic" in the sweeps of Irish landscape and seascape he is thought to know so well, does service in Jenkins's essays as a distancing device. With regular recourse to Spenser's appreciation of the wild beauties of Ireland, always mediated through proof-text citations of the poetry, Jenkins can keep *the poet* at a protective distance from the brutalities of war and the English colonial enterprise, can set him at an aesthetic remove apart from the fray.[7] The trope-like declaration of Spenser's wonder at the "rugged grandeur" of Ireland is similarly employed, though on a larger scale, in the 1945 book-length *Life* A. C. Judson produced for the Spenser Variorum. Reliant on Jenkins's work on Spenser in Ireland for more than newly uncovered archival material, Judson's biography likewise evokes a Spenser who is "moved . . . profoundly" by the "rugged beauties and natural advantages" of his new home (1945, 99-100). Accordingly, Judson, like Jenkins, adorns his own account of Spenser's presence at Smerwick with the requisite mention of the poet's "love of beauty" and how he was "touched" by "this strange land" and "its mountains, rivers, and towns," which he had viewed by way of this grim expedition (1945, 93). Judson then goes on to provide some specific examples of the sights that so moved Spenser, conjuring them (again according to precedent) as they are described in his poetry: "'spacious Shenan spreading like a sea,' 'the gentle Shure' flowing by 'sweet Clonmell,' and the marble city of Kilkenny amid its orchards," and so on. Judson moreover adds to the now refrain-like recitation of Spenser's love of beauty a related appreciation of the antique, remarking on a number of occasions how the ancient island answered Spenser's "antiquarian taste" (1945, 93; see also 104, 185, 195). What thus emerges in Judson's and Jenkins's narrations of Spenser's tenure as Grey's secretary and his tours of Ireland as the lord deputy's right-hand man is not so much an account of Spenser's career as a colonialist bureaucrat or even a consideration of the interstices between this career and the poetic one. Rather, it is a portrait of the artist as the incipient creator of an epic, as though Spenser's principal reason for relocating to Ireland was to write *The Faerie Queene*: "Already the landscape of Ireland, sprinkled with castles and possessing a rugged grandeur by virtue of its forests and 'deserts' and mountains, must have begun to print itself sharply on his memory, ready to be drawn on later for subtle suggestions when he came to picture faeryland" (Judson 1945, 93). With insistent, even fantasmatic, recourse to the trope of him as "a lover of beauty" (195), Spenser's biographers are able to displace politics with poetics, able implicitly to justify the colonial enterprise (and interestingly they do register an anxious requisite that it needs some justifying) by the poetry that results from it.

Thus, although in these accounts we find Spenser wearing the hats of secretary, civil servant, planter, and possibly even soldier, the biography always concludes with a redaction of this multiply employed Spenser to Spenser-the-poet:

> But the *Faerie Queene* reflects most fully the influence upon his creative imagination of these trying years under Grey. Irish scenes and Irish figures gleam through the elfin allegory. . . . Under Grey Spenser had felt the long weariness of the wars, and could therefore write from the heart:
>
> > Sleepe after toil, port after stormie seas,
> > Ease after warre, death after life does greatly please.
>
> These active years unquestionably modified his conception of the virtues most essential to a complete gentleman as well as his vision of life. Their horrors and spiritual struggles intensified his temperamental melancholy, his longing for peace, and his fear of change which became an obsession.
>
> (Jenkins 1937, 352-53)

The pattern of Spenser's moral perceptions, longings, and temperament (terms Jenkins prefers above the predication to Spenser of anything as hard-edged as a "politics") is then spun into the gossamer fabric of *The Faerie Queene*. Moreover, it is the poem—and once again not Spenser's prose writings on Ireland—that "reflects most fully the influence . . . of these trying years under Grey." The story of Spenser's ambitions and careerism is, as presented here, thus matched and ultimately superseded by another story, a more poetic one: the story of Spenser's deepening and ennobling melancholy—a melancholy that precipitates his gradual withdrawal into the private, aloof, idealistic domain of the literary, a sphere carefully cordoned off from "the plots and schemes of all politicians."

This story of the poet's unfolding worldly detachment, his retreat into an apolitical contemplative literary realm, is one that continues to be told of Spenser, especially in accounts of his late poetry. Though the second installment of *The Faerie Queene* is even more ostensibly politically engaged than the first, one still finds the final phase of Spenser's career construed in terms of "his inclination to withdraw from the active world into an inviolate and wholly contemplative center" (Bernard 1989, 163) or of "signs of withdrawal, finally, from direct engagement with the historical world" (Miller 1983, 216), so that "[h]e comes to look on poetry as private and contemplative rather than as a form of public action" (Miller 1979, 174). Ultimately ensconced at a position above the public and the political, Spenser, whatever else he is or did, remains first and foremost—in a phrase that still obtains in Spenser criticism—"the poet's poet," an entitlement that tends to reify his achievement of a measure of transcendence over the historical world, over his determining social context and historical circumstances, over his own deeply personal and financial stakes in the successful colonization of Ireland.

What I am arguing here is that much Spenser scholarship, whether judged outmoded or updated in its approach, has effaced aspects of the biography in an endeavor to present a portrait of literary greatness along clearly modern notions of the "man of letters." Spenser was in fact one of the first Renaissance authors to be accorded a place and a volume in the highly successful Macmillan English Men of Letters series. Begun in 1877 under the editorship of John Morley, these sturdy, compact volumes were produced as much to form as to answer a new demand for textbooks. Morley was a leading figure in the campaign to secure a place for English literature in the university curriculum, as well as an advocate of extension lectures and evening classes for the acculturation of the masses.[8] His educational programs aspired to make "industrial England a sharer in the classic tradition of the lettered world" (cited in Gross 1969, 108). The English Men of Letters series was thus offered to equip "those who have to run as they read," the "immense class [that] is growing up, and must every year increase, whose education will have made them alive to the importance of the masters of our literature, and capable of intelligent curiosity as to their performances."[9] Morley's series became an institutional as well as a commercial success, garnering for itself and its literary subjects official, canonical status almost immediately (Gross 1969, 107).

Interestingly, in order to launch his new series properly, Morley thought it judicious to include in his crew of literary critics—among whom were T. H. Huxley writing on Hume, Leslie Stephen on Johnson, John Addington Symonds on Shelley, and Trollope on Thackeray—"*one* recognized divine. . . . We need that for respectability's sake" (cited in Morgan 1944, 116). Rev. R. W. Church, dean of St. Paul's, was thus recruited, and after hesitating among Dryden, Jeremy Taylor, and Spenser, he eventually chose to write on the last. Church's *Spenser*, which appeared in 1879, duly commences by framing English history in terms of the Reformation, matching Spenser, "the earliest of our great modern writers in poetry," with Richard Hooker, who, "born about the same time," is correspondingly "the earliest of our great modern writers in prose" (1879, 1). Ignoring much that is ostentatiously "antique" about Spenser, Church presents him as an emergent modernist, rising heroically above his own age and its murkiness of thought and clumsiness of expression (3) to inaugurate a new beginning of English literature, producing in his epic "The first great English poem of modern times" (87).[10]

Beyond his insistence that Spenser was too "keenly alive to all beauty," too much naturally inclined to a "passionate appreciation of every charm and grace" (16-17) to be a Puritan, there isn't much Church can do with his curious pairing of Spenser and the cleric Hooker, and soon this comparison gives way to the business of fashioning Spenser—in terms that were to accrue the force of catechism in biographical accounts of him on through the twentieth century—as an originary English man of letters. This is the same Spenser we find in Jenkins and Judson—a poet who is in the world but not of it; for while Church devotes a fairly detailed and informative biographical chapter to Spenser's civil service career in Ireland ("no one in those days could live by poetry," this biographer correctly recognizes), we are still exhorted to bear in mind that always "Spenser's heart was set on poetry" (52). Whatever the material or political circumstances he found himself in, Spenser maintained "the tastes and faculties of a poet, and the love not only of what was beautiful, but of what was meditative and dreamy" (15). But lest this portrait of the artist as a dreamy-eyed, Renaissance lover of beauty sound too ephemeral—or worse, too effeminate—Church repeatedly insists that our appreciation of Spenser turn on a recognition of his manliness along with his modernity. "We still think with Spenser," he instructs, "about the paramount place of manliness, as the foundation of all worth in human character" (153); thus "[a]ll Spenser's 'virtues' spring from a root of manliness" (152). For Church, "the poet of poets," as he terms him (103), is also the man's man, his Spenser volume setting in gendered relief the title of Morley's series: these are, after all, the English *men* of letters.

I have dwelt at some length on the critical practices of Church, Jenkins, and Judson because their incorporations of Spenser as a great man of letters still retain a shaping, though unacknowledged, force in Spenser studies. This is evident in the first wave of what might be broadly termed new historicist Spenser scholarship. Programmatically resisting "a traditional opposition of the privileged individual—whether an author or a work—to a world 'outside'" (Montrose 1986a, 304), this critical project replaced (or reconstituted) a much earlier generation of historicists' concern with the poet's *life* with a more politically attuned focus on the cultural dynamics of the poet's *career*. As David Lee Miller remarks in "Spenser's Vocation, Spenser's Career," "A poet, then, is a maker of texts that in turn 'make' him," so that "what we call 'Spenser' is a cultural artifact" (1983, 197).

Nonetheless, seen within the context of the criticism we have been reviewing, the "Spenser" produced in these unquestionably groundbreaking new historicist accounts bears some striking if unexpected resemblances to the "Spenser" handed down to us from the endeavors of an old school historicism and the positivistic attributions of an old-fashioned biographical scholarship.[11] This is especially the case, I would argue, in criticism that situates Spenser's careerism within a master context of his aspiration for poetic laureateship. Hence Richard Helgerson's much admired, much cited treatment of Spenser's career in *Self-Crowned Laureates* points to the poet's seminal, highly individual role in "bringing into existence an essentially new configuration of what Michel Foucault has called 'author-functions'" (1983, 3). Louis Adrian Montrose, citing his indebtedness to Helgerson's work on Spenser, echoes this claim: "Spenser synthesizes a new Elizabethan author-function" (1986a, 319). In Helgerson's account, Spenser is able to redirect the course of English poetry first by distancing himself from his "amateur" coevals—those writers who coyly trivialize their verse efforts as youthful distractions or leisurely toys—and then by "redefin[ing] the limits of poetry, making it once again (if in England it ever had been) a profession that might justifiably claim a man's life and not merely the idleness or excess of his youth" (1983, 60). As in Church's 1879 account, which nominates Spenser as the first modernist poet on the basis of his transcendence of the age's conventions governing poetic practice, the new historicist Spenser stands alone in, even above, his own literary moment: "Among his immediate contemporaries, Spenser was doubly unique," Helgerson writes. "Not only was he the best poet . . . , he was the only poet of distinctly laureate ambition" (55).

This exhilarated sense of Spenser as individualistic, forward-pointing, originary powers a good deal of new historicist work on the poet.[12] Yet, however dynamic and enabling we find this work to be, it is important to recognize that its "reinvention" of Spenser bears more than a passing resemblance to the Spenser of earlier critical generations, especially in terms of the recurring critical trope of Spenser transcending his epoch. Helgerson sees Spenser engaged in an unprecedented renegotiation of the current system of available authorial postures, a virtuosic effort to privilege the literary as a domain altogether apart from other career pursuits. In doing so, Spenser inaugurated a new path for the future laureate endeavors of Jonson, Milton, and possibly Dryden as well—men who, like Spenser in Helgerson's account, moved beyond the limitations of prevailing notions of authorship in order to establish their literary enterprises as the chief work of their lives and not only as a means to various careerist ends. In setting up this argument, Helgerson articulates Spenser's originary accomplishment in terms that speak in much the same key as Church's late-nineteenth-century efforts to canonize Spenser as an emergent modernist and the first English man of letters: "Before Spenser occupied it, the role of the great English poet was repeatedly said to be vacant. The system thus recruited the man, but it remained for the man to show that he met the requirements of the system. Could he pull this particular sword from its stone?" (6). Pulling the sword from the stone: cast in these terms, Spenser's efforts are not only seminal, they are positively heroic. The immediate resonance of Helgerson's Arthurian metaphor may be with the knightly matter of *The Faerie Queene*; but by figuring Spenser's literary accomplishment in terms of an individualistic feat of chivalric male bravura, his articulation uncannily reiterates the positivistic biographical attribution to Spenser of the "strong and resolute manliness" we find in Church's English Men of Letters volume (1879, 152).

I have seized upon this chivalric casting of Spenser's poetic accomplishment not only to remark a continuance of a certain tradition of Spenser scholarship, but also because Helgerson's Arthurian metaphor points up how court- and queen-centered early new historicist work on Spenser tends to be. The drive in this work to endow Spenser as the court poet he never quite managed to be stands in marked contrast to the figurations of Spenser as a kind of frontier poet or as a poet/bureaucrat we find in the old biographical criticism. That work insisted upon locating Spenser and his writing in the context of a colonized Ireland, however reticent critics like Judson and Jenkins may have ultimately proved to be in facing the political consequences of their own contextualizations. Given new historicism's shaping concern with situating literary production in relation to other cultural and political formations, it is surprising that only fairly recently has the renewal of historical Spenser scholarship also entailed a revived interest in a colonial Spenser.[13] Yet I would suggest that the effacement of a Spenser who is colonial, "Irish," and bureaucratic in favor of a Spenser who is courtly and "poetic" is a predictable effect of the erasure of the poet's poet's extrapoetic identity. "How then did he manage to distinguish himself as laureate from his amateur coevals?" Helgerson asks. The answer, he tells us, is that Spenser "publicly abandon[ed] all social identity except that conferred by his elected vocation. He ceased to be Master Edmund Spenser of Merchant Taylors' School and Pembroke College, Cambridge, and became Immerito, Colin Clout, the New Poet" (1983, 63). Abandoned in this account of Spenser's career formation (the new-historicist version of literary biography) is more than his identity as a Cambridge graduate; also jettisoned is Spenser's identity as a secretary, a civil servant, and a plantation maker—in short, effaced here is any identity or career pattern except the one that crowns Spenser the poet's poet. Like Judson's claim that "being a poet was the primary business of his life" (1945, 129), Helgerson refers to Spenser's other career as "all the years of minor civic occupation" (82). Likewise, Stephen Greenblatt—who does treat Spenser in relation to Irish colonialism, though in the service of an argument that in the end is not much concerned with colonialism per se—sets up his discussion in *Renaissance Self-Fashioning* by placing Spenser under the heading of the new possibility for "a small number of men to conceive of literature as their primary activity" (1980, 161).[14] Even Arthur Marotti suggests that Spenser considered himself as a kind of "professional man of letters" (1981, 208), despite Marotti's awareness of how another celebrated poet of the period, John Donne, regarded literature not as his vocation but more as an avocation to be used in the pursuit of mainly social rather than artistic patronage.

Such gestures work to hypostatize Spenser's poetic career as his only career, and to do so in ways that either set Spenser above his own cultural moment as a new kind of poet, or, worse, accord his verse varying measures of poetic transcendence over more material and political exigencies. But of course Spenser's poetic career was not his only career of significance. For much of the time from his Cambridge graduation to his death while on a courier mission for Thomas Norris that took him back to England for the final time, Spenser pursued a career as a secretary and civil servant (Rambuss 1993, 6-9). Indeed, Spenser appears in many of the documentary materials from which we would need to compose our biographies or career studies of him *not* as a poet but as a bureaucrat, investor, planter, and colonial litigant. Moreover, had Spenser aspired to a singular career as a poet (and we have no evidence that this was ever his ambition), one might expect him to have been more pleased than he apparently was with the fifty-pound pension the first installment of *The Faerie Queene* earned him—which was at that time a relatively lucrative behest for a poet. But instead of gratitude and the continuation of his laureate project extolling queen and country, Spenser published a whole volume of *Complaints* to intervene between installments of *The Faerie Queene.* That volume is an expansive articulation of what I take to be Spenser's own frustration at "Still wayting to preferment up to clime" (*Mother Hubberds Tale,* line 76; see Rambuss 1993, 80-82), a complaint about, among other matters, the tardiness of his further advancement in careerist spheres including but not limited to the poetic.

Given Spenser's social and presumably financial ambitions, I would suggest that the possibility of a single-track career as a poet might not have appealed or even occurred to him. Instead, Spenser's laureate aspirations were inscribed within an established career track which projected advancement through dual service as a poet/bureaucrat, eventually leading to higher offices. Seen in this light, Spenser's appointment as Lord Deputy Grey's secretary would thus be anything but "minor" for this son of a cloth worker. As Clark Hulse (one Spenserian who does not underplay the significance of Spenser's secretaryship) notes, Edward Waterhouse, who served as secretary to Henry Sidney when he was lord deputy, had been in time knighted and granted a seat on the Privy Council of Ireland (1988, 320). Perhaps Spenser was at last on his way to a similar course of ascension when he was nominated sheriff of Cork County in September of 1598. This position, Ruth Mohl suggests, might eventually have led to knighthood for him as well (1990, 670)—a rank, I'd add, Spenser's poetic endeavors, however celebrated, never earned him. Why then should we assume that Spenser necessarily would have cared more about his poetic career than his advancement along these other lines? Or, for that matter, why assume that because he is most important *to us* as a poet that Spenser himself had more invested in the literary success of *The Faerie Queene* than he had in the success of the Munster Plantation scheme, to which he no doubt had dedicated a good deal of his energies and financial resources?

14

Reinventing Spenser, Political Spenser, Spenser Left and Right, Spenser Reproduced, Puzzling Spenser, Alternative Spensers: these are the titles of Spenser books that have not been written, though of course they do allude to some important recent studies of a near contemporary of the poet's poet. As I have tried to show, the fact that current, theoretically informed and politically situated Renaissance criticism has successfully wrought new and alternative Shakespeares but has yet to achieve same for Spenser has to do with more than Shakespeare's unrivaled centrality to the canon and the curriculum. First-generation new-historicist work was, after all, as likely to direct its attentions to Spenser as it was to Shakespeare. In doing so, it has opened up rich, sometimes dazzling, new ways to read Spenser's texts and their careerist negotiations for patronage, the enhanced cultural status of English poetry, and the power to shape what Montrose has termed "the Elizabethan subject," understood to be both the poet himself and the queen as the subject of the poet's fictions (1986a, 323). I would nonetheless contend that neither new historicism nor the other recent critical approaches being brought to bear on early modern literature and culture have been able to effect—or have perhaps not wanted to effect—in Spenser studies what has been achieved in Shakespeare studies.[15] That is, we have new readings of Spenser but arguably no new or alternative "Spensers." One reason this is so involves a continuing ossification of the criticism around tropes of Spenser as the poet's poet, of a Spenser larger than his own cultural moment, of a poet who virtuosically stands above the impingements of determining social and political realities. Whether formulated in terms of his incipient "modernism," or his inauguration of a brand-new author function, or his final contemplative withdrawal to a private Acidale cordoned off from the historical world, the inevitable but deeply misguided next step for any critical or biographical account that abstracts Spenser and his poetry from other careerist pursuits—including those attendant upon his service as a colonial bureaucrat in Ireland—is the proffering of a transcendent Spenser.

No doubt Spenser himself had something to do with the enduring legacy of such approaches to his works, life, and career. *The Shepheardes Calender* inaugurates his poetic career by fashioning an authorial self for him as "our new Poete," England's Virgil, the nation's emerging laureate. Spenser sets up his career as the work of an essentially new kind of Elizabethan poet (though one who, at the same time, looks back intently to the precedents of Virgil, Petrarch, Marot, and the doubly employed English poet/bureaucrat Chaucer), and critical accounts of his work have been reiterating and troping on those very terms ever since. Spenser's presentation of himself as a kind of prince of poets may indeed be the single most successful achievement of a career of mixed and limited successes, even if the singular position he claimed as England's "Arch Poet" never earned him quite the degree of social advancement and enhancement he sought with it. His fashioning of himself as the principal poet of his time was of such abiding force that it seems to have traveled directly from the *Calender*'s opening tome to Spenser's tombstone inscription, continually being reinscribed in just about every account of his life and career from Camden's to those of our own time.

For the very reason of their unchallenged perpetuity, I think we need to scrutinize codifications of Spenser (including his own) as the new poet, the prince of poets, the poet's poet less as simply aesthetic valuations and more as what Upton terms, in the epigraph with which I began, "invented stories." From here we then should consider how these codifications have been produced and to what ends they have been deployed, by both Spenser and his professional readers. What is needed now in Spenser scholarship is, if not necessarily a full-scale cultural history of "Spenser" and Spenser studies, at least an interrogation of the relations between Spenser and the interests of the scholarship that has guarded and reiterated his status as the poet's poet. Such an interrogation might begin, as I have suggested here, with the coincidence of the rise of English literature as a university subject and the fashioning of Spenser as one of its first great men of letters. We also need to learn more about the various contexts—especially the Irish colonialist ones—in which his texts and careerist identities were formed and from which they were disseminated. In doing so, rather than following the usual practice of launching Spenser into an orbit apart from or above his contemporaries, we may want to draw him back into the spheres of Elizabethan authorial practice. Establishing more fully the relations between Spenser's authorial projects and those of other multiply employed poets like Gascoigne, Daniel, and Drayton would give finer texture to our understanding of how sixteenth-century literary careers were pursued in tandem with the other modes of employment available to humanists as, for instance, tutors, secretaries, bureaucrats, statesmen, and even colonizers. In Spenser's time, and even for the prince of poets, poetry was seldom considered an end in itself, but was instead routinely tied to other forms of intellectual service and cultural work.

If not an end for Spenser, perhaps his poetry should then no longer be the starting point for our critical and biographical approaches to him, especially given the obfuscating force of the critical tropes that have champi-

16

oned the poetical Spenser by effacing other aspects of his life and career. Nor is what I am suggesting here a critical endeavor whose energies and investments are primarily negative, debunking ones. Rather, decanonizing Spenser as the poet's poet may be productive of new sets of terms, new frameworks both historical and contemporary, in which we would continue to read (and to teach) him—perhaps as a colonial Spenser, or as a Renaissance figure of cultural hybridity, or as an author who produces literature in English from a position in the Empire outside England: Spenser, an early modern anglophone poet. This is to say that the kind of decanonization I have in mind here could both open onto the means for Spenser's recanonization and play some part in refashioning the premises of the English canon itself.

Disenchanted Elves:
Biography in the Text of *Faerie Queene* V

JAY FARNESS

Let me conjure up a crucial moment in *The Faerie Queene* for discussions of Spenser's temperament and, by extension, Spenser biography. In this familiar passage, the narrative places us with Sir Calidore watching strange events on Mt. Acidale, a scene shortly to be dispelled when the knight tries to breach privileged circles. Unlike Calidore, however, we readers drop backstage where the narrative poet takes two stanzas to explain the spectacle of dancers, identifying the Graces, alluding to the shepherd's lass, then naming Colin Clout, whose music moves this scene: "That jolly shepheard, which there piped, was / Poore *Colin Clout* (who knowes not *Colin Clout?*)" (VI x 16). When I come upon this question—"who knowes not Colin Clout?"—rhetorical in force and phrasing, ensconced within parentheses that denote the exchange of confidences between writer and reader, I must confess that I don't know how to answer it. The question wants to sweep me along, but I find myself resisting.

For one thing, Calidore, whose point of view we have been inhabiting, doesn't know Colin Clout, a fact that already skews the question's rhetorical transparency. But other obstacles also impede my trying to figure out whether I know Colin Clout or not. There are mediations that obscure for me—and for others—the disingenuous immediacy of this question. I would like to move through three responses to the who-knows-not-Colin-Clout question as a way of suggesting an unnerving latitude in what *The Faerie Queene* tells us about Edmund Spenser. My motive is, at least in part, constructive: I am wondering how these three approaches to fictional character—approaches that will implicate Artegall, Britomart, and others as well as Colin—can collaborate, or even communicate, in a biographical enterprise. At several points I would like to refer this survey of responses to the close approach of fiction to actuality in Book V, to the "almost comic doggedness of the poet's fidelity in pursuing the actual" (O'Connell 1977,

154-55). In doing so, I will try to resist the temptation that Books V and VI offer to biographically minded readers to coalesce the disappointments they suspect in Spenser's own life with those written into the poem.

There are many readers, I know, who don't have a problem fielding the text's question about the poor piping shepherd. These readers know Colin Clout, and knowing Colin, they vouch for the rhetorical question. I think I understand their position. At the risk of some injustice, let me broadly align this take on the question with our older historicism and its commonsensical rendering of formal subtleties. "Colin Clout," in this perspective, obviously impersonates Spenser himself in one of his accustomed guises, and the epic narrator's question cues and expects my recognition of this fact. Colin intrudes here, one supposes, because Spenser has something more he wants to say than the epic fable allows. And so Colin's interruption invites inferences about a poet and his "lasse," about the breakdown of epic and other decorum in this passage, about the pertinence here of *Colin Clouts Come Home Againe*, as well as about an implied retreat of the poor, still-piping author from epic to pastoral ambitions. This is all evidence for Spenser's supposed disenchantment with public life and public poem that has become a commonplace in biographies of Spenser, a disillusionment at this point exemplified by Calidore as well as by Colin.

For some, this disappointment has been frankly embarrassing: the "naturally high-minded" Spenser "reveals here and there in his verse, under the sting of disappointment, a petulance, somewhat unmanly, that his most radical admirers would fain argue away" (Dodge 1936, xxi). Dodge's "here and there" surely includes the conjuncture of Books V and VI as read in these more extreme terms by Roger Sale: "Spenser is naked and alone now, powerless beside a powerless Artegall, near the end of his vision of history and near the end of everything. And so he gives us the Blatant Beast, his most terrifying vision of evil" (1968, 179). Such an end to illusory historical vision—a literal disillusionment—gives us one sense of Spenser's alleged disenchantment, which is ambivalently manifested both in the terrorism and in the plaintive idealism of Books V and VI. This reading of a disenchanted author, that is, dominates even sympathetic accounts that see the poet laboring to fashion poetic, idyllic, or personalistic refuges from a still-worsening world.[1] If one takes Colin Clout for this Spenser, the shepherd's refuge among the Graces might offer a precise instance of compensatory escape from a world that has lost other charms.

If we come at the who-knows-not-Colin-Clout question from a different direction, however, we encounter trickier problems with such easy reasoning from text to biographical subject. To appreciate these problems, let me put on a different thinking cap, trading my old-historical Stetson for a "new-historical" beret. From this perspective, the question about knowing Colin is complicated by general questions of identity, individuality, and self-knowledge. "Colin Clout" is no longer a relatively transparent designation that common sense can decode. Who, after all, "knows" a fictional person? But even as a literary impersonation of an author, "Colin Clout" is an effect of multiple determinations within intersecting systems of court politics, patronage, pastoral conventionality, literary production, intertextuality, and so on. The equivalence of this effect to the term "Edmund Spenser," which functions in some of these and other systems, is not at all easy to see. This is the Spenser who is a product not just of his time but of a certain discursivity. To come at this more elusive, "subjected" subject, criticism has tried to define "Spenser" against narrower institutional specifications, first reconstituting the backdrop, so to speak, then trying to infer the actor from the stage and its scripts. Here we might expect Spenser to emerge from the institutional scene of the courtier or of the poet laureate or of the colonial official or of the professional "secretary."[2]

Related interpretations of Spenser's situation, also deeply involved with the new-historical temper of recent criticism, cite the problem of voicing as a factor in further perplexing the biographical subjects of the poem. These interpretations ask who or what speaks in *The Shepheardes Calender* or in *The Faerie Queene*, particularly in the poems' direct and oblique appeals to the queen. And with what authority are such passages voiced? Does a kind of ventriloquism govern the poem's enunciation? Is the poet a mouthpiece of discourses of an "other" in the different senses of Jonathan Goldberg or Louis Montrose?[3] Is Spenser's real distinctiveness the way he becomes a medium for the discourses of Tudor myth or of a corporate or social will? Or are those voices caught up in a circuit of exchanges whereby audiences and speakers displace and exchange authorities, here the poet metaleptically ascribing to the queen, as to a Muse, those attributes by which he claims to be influenced (Montrose 1986a, 318ff.)? "Loe here *thy Artegall*," as one line memorably puts it (V proem 11, my emphasis on *thy*). The poet's voicing of Colin's words on Mt. Acidale—especially in VI x 28, where the voices cohabit—offers another such case in point.

This view of the text as a voicing of authority is further complicated by the fact that we critics, who purport to speak for the text as well, also enter the circuit of discursive exchanges, both voicing our author and getting voiced by our author. Bakhtin, Derrida, Roland Barthes, and others have suggested how routinely, how pervasively utterance is pieced together with virtual quotation, citation, indirect and doubled discourse. It has fallen to a new kind of textual criticism to try to indicate suppressed quotation marks and to attribute utterances anew. This is an activity of particular importance to biography and its embattled hold on the notion of an individual self or of a relatively autonomous subject. Any ventriloquism in the voicing of discourses is crucial for biography to adjudicate, in other words, lest a biographer, to put it crudely, mistake a dummy for the ventriloquist.[4]

This choice is not, however, so easy for us postmoderns as my crude phrasing suggests. In the skeptical view of recent writing, neither Colin nor Edmund Spenser knows himself; such knowledge or self-possession as is implied by the question and scene on Mt. Acidale is a misrecognition. The disarming ease with which the text poses the question about Colin Clout should actually make conspicuous how difficult but how tempting it is to answer. To explore this difficulty in a little more detail, I would like to focus briefly on an especially valiant and justly celebrated response to such temptation: Stephen Greenblatt's answer to the author question in *Renaissance Self-Fashioning*, an answer that holds out the promise of a dazzling new biographical sophistication.

Greenblatt describes a Spenser who, through Guyon, despoils the Bower of Bliss in terms that anticipate a Freudian insight (in *Civilization and Its Discontents*): "the extent to which civilization is built upon the renunciation of instinct." Freud writes, "Civilization behaves toward sexuality as a people or a stratum of its population does which has subjected another one to its exploitation" (Greenblatt 1980, 173). Guyon exemplifies instinct violently disciplining its projections in order to aggrandize civilization. Greenblatt persuasively argues that this episode justly represents a crucial tendency in Spenser's whole poem. Then, in a stunning analysis prompted by Freud's analogy to social subjection, he parallels Guyon's actions with those of New World colonizers, of English undertakers in Ireland, and of Protestant iconoclasts.

This apparent detour through examples of Elizabethan subjection and exploitation impeccably answers to dominant themes of Spenser biography—the poet's alleged Puritanism, his offices in Ireland, his advocacy of the imperializing, colonizing faction at Elizabeth's court. Similarly, the Bower of Bliss episode is a well-established crux for biographical speculations about the temperament of poet and man. It's the episode that Lamb, Lowell, Yeats, and others, working the older biographical vein, turn to in trying to specify the distinctive complexion of Edmund Spenser's personality.

And yet, for all its power and interest, it seems to me that Greenblatt's marvelous new fashioning of Spenser only gives us more of what we already had: not a biography but another allegory of Edmund Spenser. True to its principles, Greenblatt's description of Spenser is as an effect, not a cause, of forces arrayed in his essay—modern as well as Elizabethan forces. The author, the originator, the subject, vanishes into a web of mediations constituting the historicist's text. Put another way, Greenblatt's Spenser is a personification—a type, a concept of what Guyon and Spenser are supposed to share, a concept that is reconstructed from selected circumstances of the text and, incidentally, represented with such energy, conviction, and likelihood that Greenblatt's Spenser has probably become more popular than its primary text. There is an affinity between this new-historical biography and the conclusion of Judson, Spenser's old-historical biographer, who asserts that Spenser's "distinction probably consists . . . in his remarkably complete embodiment of the spirit of his age" (1945, 212). For Judson, too, both in the poems and in the life, Spenser figures—he personifies—a type. Such writing conforms to Aristotelian poetics in valorizing general concepts rather than the anomalous particulars that distinguish history-writing and life-writing.[5]

Of course, Greenblatt stands an idealizing Sidneyan poetics on its head: for this newer biography, which has shown us the demons in "the spirit of the age," *The Faerie Queene* presents symptoms in a pathological field, symptoms that call for a diagnosis of some kind. Greenblatt's citation of Freud is itself more a symptom than a cause of this approach, merely making the fact of pathology more visible in this case. In contrast, note how different is this view of the text from a more conventionally literary one, which would have a poem not presenting symptoms for diagnosis but representing meanings for an understanding of some kind, the author more an actor than a patient.

This reflection on self-fashioning is meant to lead up to the third approach to the who-knows-not-Colin-Clout question, which will try to redraw the lines between text and author, reclaiming for the poem and its characters much of what has been alienated to Spenser. It happens—as Greenblatt points out (1980, 175)—that Spenser himself is probably doing the same thing as Greenblatt when he fashions an Artegall, a Mercilla, a Calidore, or a Guyon by threading through those names various topics, scenarios, and discourses relevant to their positions in the text. And both Spenser and Greenblatt, purporting to fashion gentlemen, compose allegories of Tudor England in six parts in which six heroes (or seven, counting twice for Book IV) are to impersonate six virtues, or powers. When Greenblatt asserts that "It is art whose status is questioned in Spenser, not ideology" (192), he displaces his own thesis, in which he somewhat reluctantly makes ideology, not poetry, the centerpiece. And Spenser appears to share this reluctance too, in fact appears, like Greenblatt, to make something like ideology or the poetics of culture conspicuous in Books V and VI so as to open an "internal distantiation" in the text of Tudor myth that Greenblatt does not read in Spenser. "Art is questioned," Greenblatt writes of Spenser, "precisely to spare ideology that internal distantiation it undergoes in the work of Shakespeare or Marlowe" (192). It is this "internal distantiation" that I would like to reconsider now by way of a celebrated writer, whose essay on Spenser bridges old- and new-historical interests.

One can hear Greenblatt's Spenser anticipated in W. B. Yeats's characterization—his allegory of Spenser, I should say—which suspects the poet precisely of institutional bad faith, of displacing authority and responsibility from the conscious fiction of his poem to the nonconscious fictions of Elizabethan polity. This view of the poet also introduces a subtler, more resonant view of Spenserian disillusionment, connecting ordinary personal disappointments with anxiety prompted by a cosmos that has abandoned "the first point of his appointed sourse, / And being once amisse growes daily wourse and wourse" (V proem 1).

> One is persuaded that his morality is official and impersonal—a system of life which it was his duty to support. . . . His processions of deadly sins, and his houses, where the very cornices are arbitrary images of virtue, are an unconscious hypocrisy, an undelighted obedience to the "rugged forehead." . . . He had learned to put the State, which desires all the abundance for itself, in the place of the Church, and he found it possible to be moved by expedient emotions, merely because they were expedient, and to think serviceable thoughts with no self-contempt. . . . Spenser had learned to look at the State not only as the rewarder of virtue but as the maker of right and wrong, and had begun to love and hate as it bid him. . . . When Spenser wrote of Ireland he wrote as an official, and out of thoughts and emotions that had been organized by the State. He was the first of many Englishmen to see nothing but what he was desired to see. (Yeats 1961, 369, 371, 372)

These are representative fragments from Yeats's vilification of the epic element in Spenser's poetry. Drawing the author's life out of the work, Yeats persistently alludes to sentiments voiced in Book V and in Spenser's *View of the Present State of Ireland,* and he accounts for them by developing a notion of "unconscious hypocrisy," the poet's blindness to the error of his ways induced by "the State," "a system of life," something organized, official, impersonal.

Yeats is close to describing in Spenser a form of disenchantment that Max Weber saw as ushering in the modern sensibility. This sense of disenchantment would see the poet in a world where "there are no mysterious incalculable forces that come into play," where "one can, in principle, master all things by calculation. This means that the world is disenchanted. One need no longer have recourse to magical means in order to master or implore spirits, as did the savage, for whom such mysterious powers existed. Technical means and rational calculation perform the service" (Weber 1958, 139). Yeats indicates this by the trade of the sacred, the Church, for the secular, the State. His influential portrait of Spenser also emphasizes the rational calculation, the "intellectualization" (Weber 1958, 139), the "rugged forehead" that empowers both poet laureate and the burly official masters he serves.

However, I invite you to consider Yeats's criticism of the author as a description of the poem. The place of intellect or reason in *The Faerie Queene*'s evolutionary scheme is informed by Weber's view, and it also supports Yeats's view of the poem's disenchantment, culminating in Books V and VI. Bear with me while I briefly reprise this evolutionary scheme. Spenser demarcates an arena of justice in Book V from the romance landscapes of Books III and IV, where he has explored the appetitive human being and the impersonal and transpersonal structures of appetitive behavior. In Book V he offers a discourse of the "rugged forehead" of reason, government, and justice as these express conscience and self-consciousness. Book V's themes are public rather than private, centering on society, law, history, politics, vocation, economics, and official religion and culture.[6] Like the conventions of appetitive behavior and courtship in Books III and IV, practices depicted in Book V are also human-made and institutional, but they are less fixed to the elemental nature of the human and therefore less deterministic, in a way "degendered," or unnatural, by comparison (V proem 2). The allegorical echo of the Temple of Venus is the Temple of Isis and its euhemerized, humanly revised religion. Scudamour's description of the former stresses immediacy, sensation, and behavioral automatism; the poet's description of the latter stresses interpretation and deliberative action, as well as the artifice of the temple's construction and the poetry of its theology. Book V, in the more neutral terms of Weber, thus gives us a "disenchanted" reality that invites the technical means and rational calculation of justicer and poet. On the other hand, in light of Yeats's ethically charged language, this disenchanted reality invites the recourses of bad faith, "unconscious hypocrisy," that would willfully mystify or reenchant the mythology that Spenserian intellectualization has exposed as ideological calculation.

Humanly produced orders that result from purposeful, disenchanted interventions in historical process prove less credible as determinisms than

24

the more natural-appearing orders they would supplement or displace; positive law lacks the bloodlines of natural law. People who unquestioningly follow the dictates of nature more readily question authority when they perceive it issuing not from the eternal light of natural law but from the will of other human beings or, in Radigund's case, from the will of mere men. To guard against such perception, human-made orders more strenuously emulate the orders they displace, fortifying human institutions and legislation with propaganda, ideology, and rationalization. These discourses are quite audible in Book V's rhetoric—for instance, in the hero's debate with the egalitarian giant, in his remonstration with Burbon, or in Britomart's restoration of patriarchy in Radegone. In these episodes we hear a sometimes strident apologetics that Yeats and many others, in characterizing Spenser, describe rather well, seeing it as Spenser's quest of the Virgilian vocation according to Philip Sidney (Yeats 1961, 370-71). But the poem makes more sense, I am arguing, if you imagine an Artegall, a Radigund, or a Mercilla rather than Edmund Spenser as exemplifying the biographical propositions of Yeats, if you see *The Faerie Queene* recording their lives rather than Spenser's.

In a striking example of apologetics and of Weberian disenchantment, Artegall encounters a leveling giant in canto ii of Book V. This giant with balances exemplifies, in an extreme and comical form, rationalizing tendencies already manifest in poet and hero—what Weber describes as "rational calculation"—though the giant is somewhat at a loss, as the knight usually is not, for the technical means to achieve his purposes. Against the giant's disenchantment with the world's status quo, that "each estate quite out of order goth" (V ii 37), Artegall utters many of the old spells of the theocratic cosmos, rich in the enchanting cadences of familiar biblical poetry (V ii 40-42). But the knight is not persuasive; Talus—representing the "technical means" that the giant lacks—suddenly quits the challenger in his brutally efficient way. This whole episode registers the triumph of disenchantment, not of theocracy—in the rhetorical posturing and re-presenting of venerable myths and texts, in its emphasis on instrumentality, and in the expedient poetic justice of its denouement. The disenchanted attitude is rendered more conspicuous by a clear affinity between the giant's suspicions of the worsening world and the poet's similar complaints in Book V's proem, which has likewise displayed the old enchantments—the poetry of the zodiac—jeopardized by too curious a rational calculation of astral change (V proem 5-8).

A variation on the giant's disenchantment occurs with the character of Radigund, who has declared enmity against "All the brave Knights, that hold of Maidenhead" (V iv 39). This is the result of her one disappointment with "*Bellodant* the bold,"

> To whom she bore most fervent love of late,
> And wooed him by all the waies she could:
> But when she saw at last, that he ne would
> For ought or nought be wonne unto her will,
> She turn'd her love to hatred manifold,
> And for his sake vow'd to doe all the ill
> Which she could doe to Knights, which now she doth fulfill. (V iv 30)

One lesson here is that, in Book V's postromance arena, frustrated love is made a federal case, and individuals feel entitled to indict the world for insufficiencies experienced by the self; a personal disappointment becomes a universal disenchantment. Like the giant, Radigund intends to upend an unjust system, and most readers, I think, take some pleasure in seeing her try, especially with neophytes like Sir Terpine, himself another example of disillusionment and despair when his too great expectations founder.[7]

For both Radigund and Terpine disenchantment results in part from their overconfidence in purposive scenarios rooted in poetry and myth and in the power of their practical reason to compass these purposes. If Terpine overestimates chivalry, Radigund is later seen overestimating courtship, and in a way probably meant to reflect on her troubles with Bellodant. Suddenly resolved to win Artegall's love as well as loyalty, Radigund studies how to win the knight's goodwill, then dispatches her maid, in a sense her "technical means," to do this labor in comically unrealistic terms:

> Goe now, *Clarinda*, well thy wits advise,
> And all thy forces gather unto thee;
> Armies of lovely lookes, and speeches wise,
> With which thou canst even *Jove* himselfe to love entise. (V v 34)

Like Terpine, Radigund has apparently read too many romances where such hopes flourish. In her commission to Clarinda, moreover, she has entangled her sentiments in the rhetoric of art and strategy, expecting her maid to apply the requisite formulas and techniques in channeling even irrational powers.

Probably the most grimly celebrated example of Book V's disenchanted elves is the poet who figures so reproachfully at the entrance to Mercilla's court. His tongue is "nayled to a post . . . For that therewith he falsely did revyle, / And foule blaspheme that Queene for forged guyle" (V ix 25).

> Thus there he stood, whylest high over his head,
>   There written was the purport of his sin,

26

In cyphers strange, that few could rightly read,
BON FONT: but *bon* that once had written bin,
Was raced out, and *Mal* was now put in.
So now *Malfont* was plainely to be red. (V ix 26)

This is not just a bad poet: this is a bad poet who was once thought a good poet. The change of names, that is, seems to imply the story of a poet who earned the earlier ascription by espousing the court myth of "joyous peace and quietnesse alway" (V ix 24) that Mercilla so strenuously cultivates but who later lost faith in this myth, saw it for the calculated illusion it is, and thereupon "blasphemed" Mercilla "for forged guyle."[8] What other relevant point could there be for introducing the "BON FONT" in the first place, if not to accent, albeit in law French, a subject's awakening to the theatricality of monarchical power, the artifice of which the poem proceeds to spotlight? This example of disenchantment, in a very brief space, "internally distantiates" its author, marking his difference from two of the more common types that continue to undergird the poet's lives: Spenser as Bon Font, infatuated with the possibility of a Tudor myth; Spenser as Malfont, despairing of such a possibility.

Each of these episodes shows Spenser representing meanings about aspects of disenchanted self and society that too many new and old readers have construed as the "unconscious" presenting of authorial symptoms. Information that might be processed into interpretations of the 1596 *Faerie Queene* is thereby drawn off instead to satisfy the appetite of biographical or historical narratives. The episodes that I have quickly touched upon should, of course, be weighed with other passages that offer varieties of disenchantment as a theme: the flight of Astraea, the portrayal of Mercilla's artificial golden age, the pragmatism of Burbon, the idolatry in Isis's temple as well as in Geryoneo's temple. And much more extensively at stake are the mentalities of Britomart and of Artegall, whose development, or maturation, is allegorized in the Spenserian way through these episodes, which reflect and test the prospects of "enlightenment": "Enlightenment is man's leaving his self-caused immaturity. Immaturity is the incapacity to use one's intelligence without the guidance of another. . . . Statutes and formulas, these mechanical tools of a serviceable use, or rather misuse, of his natural faculties, are the ankle-chains of a continuous immaturity" (Kant 1949, 132, 133).[9]

The passages in Book V to which I have referred show human reason, calculation, and technique laboring, so to speak, in the shadows cast by such an enlightenment. The struggle to revise or supplement received mythologies, or to invoke them cynically or opportunistically, premises both enchantment and enlightenment in self-defeating collaboration, in a kind of "unconscious hypocrisy," or bad faith. Insofar as the poem makes such labor and struggle conspicuous—as I believe it usually does—there is an internal distantiation opened in ideology that invites us to read the accounts of Yeats, Greenblatt, and others as descriptions of the poem's action, of its project, rather than as diagnoses of the author. Such distantiation also opens up when I try to answer the question about Colin Clout, who is not—despite his disingenuous disclaimers—knowing or keeping his authorized place, whose very presence in Book VI testifies to a puzzling mobility that has made this passage an interpretive crux. More generally, the mobility of authorities among Colin, leveling giant, proem poet, Artegall, Mercilla, and others might remind one of an internal distantiation that underlies many problems of tone and voicing that readers (though by no means all or even most readers) have traditionally reported of *The Faerie Queene*. If you look or listen closely—and maybe this is too closely—you detect a basic unsteadiness of voice, an uncertainty about the ethos of speaker, of poet, of inferred or actual authors. This uncertainty prompts critics to report multiple narrators or multiple impersonations or the modulation of heterogeneous discourses. This uncertainty has prompted one biographer to report two Edmund Spensers, one of whom is usually known as Francis Bacon (Harman 1914).

My third set of responses to the who-knows-not-Colin-Clout question would thus include interpretation that, in the general rush to history, hesitates a little longer at the possibility of something more specifically literary, ways of reading that have not wholly abandoned New Critical or new New Critical practices, in part because they are not yet sure just what Spenser's literary text is or what it is capable of doing. For such readers *The Faerie Queene* continues to present a literary opacity that does not readily translate into historical or biographical information, readers for whom old- and new-historical studies are deeply interesting but inadequate as "Spenser interpretation." This more literary focus on the poetic processing of theme tends to see a poet not submerged by discursive resources but continuing to operate in, with, and through them.[10]

Long ago, when commenting on the proem to Book V that shrilly laments the worsening of the wicked world, Donald Cheney perceptively construed the deliberate comic overstatements in this complaint—for example, the cartoonlike buffeting of images in the zodiac (1966, 152-53). Here is one instance of a distinctive Spenserian signature that bends the surface of the narration with archness—a kind of insincerity signaled by diction, juxtaposition, overreaction, disingenuousness, indirect narration, or an impersonation of voices. But Cheney's account of the archness of this proem complaint, which might align it with the myopic rhetoric of moral pastors in *The Shepheardes Calender*, has not even slowed other critics eager to hear in Book V's proem the authentic voice of the author embittered by Ireland, failed ambition, and the dissolution of his laureate hopes. Too often it doesn't matter—though it should—that the proem to Book IV, from which we also often draw an authentic, plaintive Spenserian voice, is quite out of character with Book V's proem, the one a plea for license against the censor, the other the censor's own plea. In fact, the proem to Book IV is also distorted by its archness, for instance in presuming to shelter its license behind the scandalous, anomalous example of Socrates and Critias dallying with *acrasia* in the shade.[11]

The arch manner of the Book V prologue in fact matches and highlights Book V's Ovidian matter; both matter and manner broach the strikingly Ovidian texture of Book V. This may be Spenser's homage to another poet in virtual exile, but it also seems a deliberate distortion—coupling the poem's brute topicality, its historic factuality, with poetry at its most notoriously far-fetched. The motif of metamorphosis is one way the poem foregrounds its process rather than reporting as accomplished fact its transformations of abstract truth or concrete history into current official "versions of the Real." Drawing on an old debate—bruited in Aristotle, renewed in Castelvetro, Sidney, and others—about the specific discursive practice of poetry, Book V seems to foreground its own response to a new-historical manifesto: "a new socio-historical criticism takes as its subject that interplay of culture-specific discursive practices in which versions of the Real are instantiated, deployed, reproduced—and also appropriated, contested, transformed" (Montrose 1986b, 7). Louis Montrose is writing about interpretations of Spenser (and other texts), but like Stephen Greenblatt, he does so in a way that indefinitely overlaps what the text itself is doing. That is, it is not clear that the symptoms the text presents to such a critique are not also meanings it in some sense represents. Though Book V is surely the site of such an "interplay of culture-specific discursive practices," it is uncertain whether that interplay is predominantly pathological or poetic or even critical (in a sociohistorical way), uncertain whether Spenser is patient or poet or something else.

The Ovidian texture of this interplay helps foreground or stage questions of instantiation, reproduction, and transformation, introducing the element of internal distantiation, of self-difference in the unstable, metamorphic Spenserian text. Through such interplay of discursive practices Astraea becomes virgin Justice or Lord Grey becomes Artegall. This interplay is how Britomart becomes Isis or Equity, how Burbon becomes a Catholic, how Elizabeth becomes Mercilla, but also how Munera becomes an example or Bon Font becomes Malfont or Ireland becomes the land of Irena, or Peace—in short, how a person becomes a personification or an event becomes a routine or rule, how history is made or reshaped discursively. And remember that these are persons and events shown resistant to the transformations the poem puts them through. Why raise such expectations, for example, of the merciful figure of Mercilla, then give her the hopeless case of Duessa-as-Mary-of-Scots to adjudicate? Or why against reason insist on chivalric romance and rescue as the measure of a career like Lord Grey de Wilton's?

To portray lives rather than the life in his poetry has Spenser plying a familiar craft, which outwits our hope for biography in the manner of ironists he emulates—in the manner of Plato, of Virgil, of Horace, of Ovid, of Chaucer, of Erasmus, and others. The frustration of biography in Spenser's case, however, might encourage us to read his text more closely and thereby distinguish better between Spenser's biography, for which *The Faerie Queene* is not very helpful, and biographies of Spenser, biography according to Spenser. Here the poet's life-writing of Colin, Malfont, Melibee, Radigund, and the rest anticipates and collaborates with Stephen Greenblatt, Louis Montrose, and others in its feel for a Tudor anthropology. To read the life in *The Faerie Queene* is commonly to embody, to allegorize, this anthropology in a character named Edmund. In this event, we don't need to be asking what we can read of the life in *The Faerie Queene*. As a corrective, and this is my conclusion, we should instead be asking what we need to retrieve and read of *The Faerie Queene* in what has passed for Spenser's life.

Factions and Fictions:
Spenser's Reflections of and on
Elizabethan Politics

VINCENT P. CAREY AND
CLARE L. CARROLL

In the last fifteen years critics have questioned the reliability of Spenser's biography and the applicability of his biography to his poetry. Most narrowly, scholars have been cautioned against making assumptions about Spenser's life based on the scant documentary evidence that remains. We have been urged to make a distinction between the "historical Edmund Spenser" and his "biographical fictions," between "particular facts" and the "golden world of Spenser's fiction" (Cheney 1983, 3; Oram 1983, 45). In other words, our interpretations should not make a one-to-one correspondence between fact and fiction. In response to these interpretive caveats and in an attempt to rethink the relation between the historical and the poetic Spenser, we would do well to remember with Vico that the "true is precisely what is made" (*Verum esse ipsum factum*), meaning that "human truth is what man puts together and makes in the act of knowing it" (ed. 1988, 46). Both history and poetry are made. History fashions its truth as factual fiction; poetry fictionalizes facts as true history, or myth. As Hayden White and Paul Ricoeur have pointed out, while the world does not "present itself to perception in the form of well made stories with central subjects, proper beginnings, middles and ends," it is only through such craft that a historical account "seems to both reader and writer as real, meaningful and/or explanatory" (White 1987, 24; Davis 1987, 3). Conversely, not only does history call for narrative in order to make sense out of documentary and contextual evidence, but when fiction represents the historical world it, too, becomes part of the historical record, a story that shapes history in such a memorable form that it influences the perception of history by future generations. It is through narrative that we establish and interpret the facts of Spenser's biography, and it is through narrative that we interpret the history Spenser has created in his poetry.

The dual tasks that we have set for ourselves are to answer, on the one hand, the historical question of how Spenser was sent to Ireland in 1580 and, on the other hand, the literary question of how Spenser's responses to the events and to the personal and political affiliations formed during 1579 and 1580 are represented and reinterpreted in his poetry. The historical question is also one of narrative: we need to read between the lines of evidence to make narrative sense of events. The literary question is also historical in that Spenser's biographical and historical fictions document the view of history and of his relation to it that he wanted to leave as a monument for posterity. Historical documents and contexts are no less susceptible to conflicting interpretations than biographical and historical fictions; and these fictions are in turn as important historical evidence as Spenser's autograph in the manuscript State Papers, Ireland, in the Public Record Office, London. The history of how court faction brought Spenser to Ireland is a story, or fiction; and the fictional afterlife of his relation to court faction may be traced in his poetry as biographical fact.

The story of how Spenser came to Ireland and the context in which the story needs to be told may be pieced together from documents relating both to him and to others who sought similar positions. The direct evidence concerning Spenser's arrival in Ireland in 1580 is brief: his handwriting first appears in the State Papers, Ireland, in a letter from Lord Deputy Arthur Grey de Wilton to Burghley on 28 November 1580—as Jenkins notes, "virtually conclusive proof of Spenser's presence at Smerwick" (1937, 338-39), where Grey ordered the execution of 600 Italians and Spaniards who had surrendered on condition that their lives be saved (Ellis 1985, 281-82). In addition to the fifty letters written by Spenser and the thirty-six addressed in his hand from 28 November 1580 to 22 January 1589, there is this reference to him in a letter of 27 January 1582 from Lord Grey to Burghley: "the lease of a house in Dublin belonging to Baltinglas for six years to come unto Edmund Spenser, one of the Lord Deputy's secretaries," and "of a custodian of John Eustace's land of the Newland to Edmund Spenser, one of the Lord Deputy's secretaries" (*Cal. S. P., Ire., 1574-85*, 344-45). Even within two short years, Spenser had turned his job in Ireland to his advantage. Because he gained this lease and land, and because he shared service in Ireland with such well-connected young men as Sir William Russell, and Captains Edward Denny and Walter Ralegh, it seems unlikely that the position as one of Grey's secretaries was entirely a punishment.

But how did the poet get the position, and is it possible for us come to any conclusion as to whether this appointment was an advancement or the equivalent of a posting to an English "Siberia" (Greenlaw 1932, 128; Bradbrook 1982, 29)? Given the absence of direct documentary evidence, these questions can be answered only by a reconstruction from the contemporary evidence of the method by which Lord Deputy Grey and his staff were chosen to serve in Ireland in 1580 and by a consideration of the factors that motivated them to embark on this enterprise.

Before this is attempted, however, it should be noted that a lack of documentary evidence for Spenser's appointment is not unusual. His minor position was within the lord deputy's household, and if any documentation did attach to the poet's initial employment it was unlikely to survive in the state archives or in the private collections of the leading government officials of the period. A contemporary and related example best illustrates this point. Of the recorded 200 letters written by Leicester to his followers and servants requesting them to prepare to serve him on his expedition to the Netherlands in 1585, only one survives. This letter to Sir John Wynn of Gwydir requests him (typically, we can only surmise) as one of Leicester's "good friends and servants" to prepare "a good horse and arms to serve your sovereign under me" (Williams 1979, 125-26).

If we can reconstruct from the contemporary evidence how Grey was sent as lord deputy in 1580, and if we weigh this evidence against our knowledge of the complexities of Tudor court politics and its mechanisms of patronage and advancement, we should be able to arrive at a clearer understanding of how Spenser ended up in Ireland by November 1580. If we can explain how and why Grey was chosen, the significance of this choice in terms of the politics of faction at the Elizabethan court, and the factors that attracted Grey, his followers, and a large number of prominent young courtiers to this particular campaign, we can better explain why Spenser went to Ireland and why this move represented an advancement rather than a dashing of hopes.

Most people acquired their posts in the Tudor administration after a competitive struggle up the "winding stair of preferment" (Williams 1979, 89-94). This competition for patronage occurred because the Tudor bureaucracy not only administered the country but, in addition, meted out political rewards through which the regime secured loyalty among the political classes of the kingdom. The main approach to these rewards was through the informal avenues to royal favor which were controlled by the few gatekeepers who had access to the sovereign. Such control of these rewards in turn ensured that important administrative positions became the focus of conflict among the leading courtiers and their dependent and competing factions. Access to such posts was essentially dependent on the ascendancy of particular court factions and the advertising abilities of the factional leaders who were close to the queen.

Appointment to the position of the monarch's personal representative in Ireland, the lord deputyship, was no different. In fact, given the extraordinary powers attached to this important post and the political capital of reward and patronage in the Irish administration, it is not surprising that this position had become an important trophy in sixteenth-century English court politics. Success in this post presented the aspirant with the potential for real advancement and glory, with the additional effect of reflecting favorably on the policies of the particular faction that had championed his candidacy. Between 1560 and the mid-1580s, the post had become a target of the court's two main factional rivals, Robert Dudley, earl of Leicester, and Thomas Radcliffe, earl of Sussex (Brady 1986a, 41-46).

Arthur, Lord Grey de Wilton's appointment to the Irish lord deputyship took place in this environment and as a direct consequence of factional preferment. The documentary evidence leaves no doubt that Lord Deputy Grey owed his appointment to the earl of Leicester. This evidence not only suggests the source of Grey's advancement but also clearly demonstrates the factional mechanism by which others—and almost certainly Edmund Spenser—attached themselves to his administration and cause.

Grey had been considered for the Irish position as early as 1572; however, in that instance, Leicester, who had a direct hand in his candidacy, also had the option of his more prominent and Irish-experienced brother-in-law, Sir Henry Sidney (Grey 1847, 66). Since Sidney's initial service in Ireland as lord deputy in 1566, he had assured Leicester that he "cared for no one" who was the earl's enemy and "that he wished to be a feather in his cap." Sidney's adherence to Leicester was so direct that he always displayed the earl's arms (the bear and ragged staff) with his own, had his servants decked out in Leicester's livery, and advised his son Philip to model himself on his more illustrious mother's side of the family (Canny 1976, 45-47).

Although Sidney's last tour of duty turned out to be a disaster, the straitened circumstances of Ireland in November 1579, with a major rebellion in Munster assisted by a foreign Catholic expedition, forced the queen and her Privy Council once again to turn to a Leicester protégé—despite her recent cooling toward Leicester throughout the Alençon marriage proposal.[1] With Leicester as the head of the anti-Alençon faction and Sussex as the head of the pro-marriage group, the Privy Council and court were bitterly polarized from August to early October 1579. The choice of Grey and Leicester's involvement in his selection suggest that the earl was back in favor by early 1580 (Judson 1945, 56-57; MacCaffrey 1981, 259-66).

The most direct evidence for Leicester's involvement in Grey's selection is their correspondence. Initially Grey was not eager to take up the appointment and begged Leicester to relieve him of the burden. Although he volunteered to go to Ireland and to provide at his own expense a company of thirty of his own household and followers, he claimed he could not afford the expense of the country's chief administrative position.[2] Grey's hesitancy was a negotiation tactic and was primarily based on the level of financial support that the queen was willing to guarantee, for he had clearly learned a lesson from Sir Henry Sidney's recent Irish downfall in a dispute with the Old English over the "cess," or tax levied to support the deputy's household and army (Brady 1985). Grey realized that if he were not adequately supplied with resources from the center, his administration would grind to a halt in Ireland and leave him vulnerable to the machinations of the rival faction at court. In this regard, he asked Leicester, whom he addressed as "he that I most depend on," to plead with the queen to ensure that his demands be met (Grey to Leicester, 7 April 1580).

Their prolonged discussions had begun in the previous winter and involved a ten-week attendance on the queen. Grey's initial unwillingness and his subsequent conditions for serving caused such "dislike" on the part of the monarch toward her prospective deputy that he feared for his political future. Only Leicester's personal intervention (which, as recorded in Grey's letter of 12 May 1580, took place in the queen's privy chamber at Greenwich) smoothed things over and eventually resulted in Grey's appointment and acceptance of the post at the end of June 1580. Leicester's intimate access and renewed influence with the queen had produced the desired results and was a fulfillment of his previous promises of "favours and friendship" to Grey (Grey to Leicester, 12 May 1580).

Between 29 June and 15 July 1580, the elaborate details of Grey's departure, supply, and responsibilities in Ireland were worked out.[3] Included in these deliberations were travel arrangements for Grey's servants and a household or "traine" of thirty. More significant, however, were the negotiations surrounding the supply and command of the large force of over 2,000 men that was to be dispatched at the same time.[4]

Here was a major source of potential employment and advancement for the large number of militarily inclined gentlemen and minor nobles who hung around the court. It was in this area that Leicester, and now Grey, would have the greatest influence. And factionally rewarding it was intended to be. The right of appointment to major offices in Ireland was one of the major issues in the deputy's negotiations with the queen and Burghley. In addition Grey wanted to know what was to happen to the government of Munster as soon as he had suppressed the rebellion there. Much more significantly, he wanted a determination made on the subject of the disposal of the vast lands of the Munster rebels.[5] Potentially, a successful campaign against the Munster rebels would place Grey and his patron Leicester in positions of enormous influence in the disposing of administrative posts and confiscated rebel lands.

Such patronage alone was sufficient to attract those young courtiers and university-educated minor figures who associated themselves with Leicester and who had an interest in the English colonial project. Fulke Greville, a Leicester associate through his intimate friendship with Sir Philip Sidney, was already off the coast of Ireland in the service of Admiral Sir William Winter and reporting back on the spoils to be had in Munster. By 15 July, Edward Denny and Walter Ralegh were appointed as officers to serve under Grey.[6] Both were known friends of the Sidneys, and Denny, in particular, was a close friend of both the young Philip Sidney and Arthur Grey. For those intent on a career in the royal service, the Grey expedition represented an ideal opportunity. So much so, indeed, that Philip Sidney expressed envy at Denny's participation and dissatisfaction at the fact that he was denied foreign service.[7] Philip Sidney, Fulke Greville, Gabriel Harvey, and Edmund Spenser had all shown prior interest in England's imperial mission. Sidney speculated heavily in the Frobisher voyages, and Greville used his time in Ireland in 1579-80 to write glowing reports of the settlement prospects of land in Munster (Wallace 1915).[8] Both Gabriel Harvey and Edmund Spenser had emerged from a milieu in Cambridge where they had debated colonial projects in Ireland and, more generally, England's imperial mission as the new Rome (Jardine 1990). Indeed, there is some evidence to suggest that the Leicester/Sidney group contemplated a major settlement on the confiscated lands of the earl of Desmond as soon as the rebellion was crushed. Geoffrey Fenton certainly thought so, when in a September 1580 letter to Leicester he, in addition to begging the earl to advance his interests with Grey, also detailed a major settlement of Leicester supporters on the earl of Desmond's lands in Munster. Fenton planned for Leicester to acquire a vast estate in Kerry from the possessions of the executed Irish lords and for Sir Philip Sidney to settle beside him with the newly acquired title of baron of Kerry. Fenton promised enormous benefits both in terms of the advancement of English "civility" in Ireland and in terms of personal profit and pleasure.[9]

The major avenue to such potential colonial rewards was the mechanism of court faction. Access to the gatekeepers at court was the means to securing advancement. Grey's appointment set off a series of letters to those prominent at court requesting to be commended to Grey and promising allegiance and service.[10] One of these letters, from Henry Sheffield to Burghley, complains about the process by which a change of governor often brought about a factionally inspired purge of personnel in the Irish administration. In addition, he suggests that his prospects for advancement in Ireland will suffer unless he can be recommended to the new deputy. This letter clearly demonstrates the mechanism by which most of Grey's staff were selected. Sheffield begs Burghley to use his influence on his behalf because, otherwise, faction alone would determine the composition of the deputy's new administration. Indeed, Sheffield's letter suggests that faction was the typical route to advancement in Ireland: "in this land it is better to find favor than [to] deserve well. Every governor seeks to prefer his own men and such gentlemen as doth either come over with him, or otherwise shall bring letters in their commendations." [11] Just as Grey was Leicester's man, so, too, those who accompanied Grey would have been adherents of both.

Against such a background it is not unlikely that a minor poet on the periphery of the Leicester group would want to join these young court aspirants on a potentially enriching colonial expedition. But if this was the background of factional adherence and potential colonial advancement that encouraged men to flock to Ireland in 1580, and if association with the Leicester faction was the means by which one entered Grey's service, how did Spenser meet Grey? Or, since such a meeting would have to be accompanied by formal introduction or a letter of commendation, who wrote in Spenser's favor, or who introduced him to Grey? The three most likely candidates are Sir Henry Sidney, his son Philip, and obviously Robert Dudley, earl of Leicester. Each of these men was interested in the situation in Ireland in 1580. Each was closely connected with Lord Grey. All shared political views that Spenser identified with. And for Philip Sidney and Leicester there is from the period 1579-80 some written and contextual evidence of a connection with Spenser.

Henry Sidney was lord deputy of Ireland on and off from 1565 to 1578, and during 1576 his son Philip served with him there on military campaigns. Contrary to a recent assertion that Philip "never visited that rebellious country" (Heninger 1987, 239), there is evidence of his purchase of horses in Dublin, his combat with the native Irish in Connaught, and his conversation with an Irish clan leader, whom his father described as "a most famous feminine sea captain, called Granny O'Malley" (Osborn 1972, 440-43; Duncan-Jones 1991, 109-12.). Not only did Philip hunt down the native Irish by his father's side, but he also supported his father's policies. Philip's "Discourse on Irish Affairs" of 1577 defends his father's exaction of the "cess," an exorbitant land tax (Sidney ed. 1973). Beyond this, Philip also advocated the military conquest of Ireland, a policy Spenser, too, promoted in *A View*, and by no means the only policy being put forward during the last twenty-five years of Elizabeth's reign (Bradshaw 1988). Further proof of both Sidneys' continued interest in Ireland is in Henry's letter of 17 September 1580, where he writes to Grey, the new lord deputy: "you shall have the beste advice that I shalbe able to geve you; protestinge that if Philip Sidney were in your Place, who most ernestlie and often hath spoken and writen to doe this lovinge Office, he I saie shold have no more of me" (Collins 1746, 1:281-83). He closes the letter with "I comend my self, my Sonne Phillip . . . and the Friendship and Service of us both." Both father and son knew Grey. In the Denny letter of Whitsunday 1580, written at Wilton, Philip counsels his friend on what he should read while in Ireland and seems to intend the advice for Spenser as well: "but good will carries mee on to this impudence to write my councell to him that (to say nothing of yourselfe) hath my Lord Grayes company" (Osborn 1972, 535-40).

It is more likely that Philip rather than Henry Sidney introduced Spenser to Grey, not just because Spenser claimed in October 1579 that Sidney and Sir Edward Dyer held Spenser "in some use of familiarity" but also because of their common Cambridge connection, Gabriel Harvey (*Letters,* in Spenser ed. 1912, 635b). There is some speculation that Spenser might have met the earl of Leicester through Harvey's acquaintance with Sidney at Cambridge in the early 1570s (Duncan-Jones 1991, 118-20). Harvey had a wide circle of powerful friends and acquaintants, one of whom, Sir Thomas Smith, was having discussions with him in the early 1570s about Roman colonies as a model for Smith's own colony in Ulster (Jardine 1990). That through Harvey's powerful connections Spenser might even have been acting as Leicester's messenger to Sidney in Ireland as early as 1577 is an intriguing hypothesis—one with potentially significant influence on both the writing of *The Shepheardes Calender* and Spenser's going to Ireland in 1580 (Jenkins 1933, 331; Welply 1933b, 348). Outside of the suggestion in *A View* that Spenser was an eyewitness to Murrogh O'Brien's execution, however, there is no evidence that he was in Ireland in 1577. Nevertheless, since we know nothing about his activities from 1576 until 1578, we do not have conclusive proof that he was not in Ireland then.

What is suggested by the evidence of Leicester's influence on Grey's appointment, and the evidence of how others acquired positions on the deputy's staff, is that Leicester, whether directly or indirectly, had a large hand in Spenser's going to Ireland in 1580. Indeed, Leicester's influence on Irish appointments was far greater than that of either of the Sidneys. The earl's winning the lord deputyship for his brother-in-law Sir Henry was the crowning achievement of an Irish policy that stretched back to the 1560s, when Leicester and his satellites, which included Kildare, competed for patronage against Norfolk and his followers, Sussex and Ormond (Ellis 1985, 244). Colonial politics were influenced then by court faction and continued to be in the 1570s and 1580s. Leicester's support of Grey for the lord deputyship in 1580 shows his continued influence on colonial political patronage and at the least his indirect influence over Spenser's going to Ireland as part of Grey's household. Leicester's clientage was far-flung; he played a tactical game, in which one client could be pitted against another. One of the ironies in his practice of simultaneously patronizing political rivals was that, even as late as May 1580, he was supporting both Grey and the Old English earl of Kildare at the same time.[12] Months later, at the behest of New English officials, envious of Kildare's support at court, and on the basis of incriminating but inconclusive evidence of treason, Kildare would be imprisoned by none other than Grey.

In the summer of 1579, two events occurred that had major repercussions for colonial policy and court faction and at some level also had direct effect upon Grey's and Spenser's going to Ireland: the outbreak of the Desmond rebellion and the Alençon marriage proposal. James Fitzmaurice Fitzgerald's raising the papal banner at Smerwick and Elizabeth's considering marriage to the French Catholic Alençon both symbolized the Catholic threat to Protestant England and evoked a militant Protestant reaction. In the case of Ireland, the Desmond and Baltinglas revolts of previously loyal Old English lords united around the Catholic cause found their opponent in the militantly Protestant Grey. Similarly, the Alençon marriage proposal caused a hue and cry—not only the attack of Stubbes's *Discovery of a Gaping Gulf* but also the protest of Sidney's "Letter to the queen." Sidney's letter represented the views of his father, Leicester, and Walsingham, all of whom opposed Burghley's and Sussex's plan for a "defensive Anglo-French entente . . . against Spain," in which the Alençon negotiations played a strategic role, and all of whom favored military intervention in the Netherlands (Guy 1988, 282). The main Catholic threat to England during this period, of course, was Spain; from 1576 on there was increasing English involvement in aiding the Low Countries, which culminated with

Leicester's accepting the office of governor general, against Elizabeth's instructions. In 1586, when Leicester needed political allies to defend him against the queen's opposition, he tried to have Arthur, Lord Grey appointed to the Privy Council (Guy 1988, 337). The main proponents of military intervention in the Low Countries were also the main opponents of the Alençon marriage proposal and the main supporters of Grey: the Leicester faction.

The evidence that Spenser aligned himself with the Leicester faction is literary: first of all, he dedicated *The Shepheardes Calender* (1579) to Philip Sidney rather than to Leicester as originally intended (Ringler 1961, 159-61). Why Spenser made this change is uncertain. Whether the dedication was changed to Sidney because of Leicester's suffering the queen's displeasure over his secret marriage, or because of Sidney's greater interest in poetry, or because of Harvey's hope that Sidney would set up a literary circle, or because of Spenser's hope that Philip would intercede with his uncle to patronize the poet, we will never know. Whether Spenser knew these two as well as his correspondence with Harvey would lead us to believe has been questioned (Heninger 1987, 243, 247). But it seems unlikely that he would risk appearing ridiculous and possibly offensive in print to two potential if not actual patrons by claiming to know them when he did not.

What is clear is that politically Sidney and Leicester were in agreement and that the politics of *The Shepheardes Calender* echoes their views: consistent and repeated opposition not only to Alençon but to the threat of Counter-Reformation Catholicism, and a similarly adamant support for the radically Protestant Archbishop Grindal. In the June eclogue, the "trecheree" of Menalcas (a possible partial anagram for Alençon) and his being received "disloyally" (Argument) make this story at least partially a figure for the Alençon marriage suit.[13] Similarly, Elizabeth's mystical marriage to England may be suggested by "Shee is my goddesse plaine, / And I her shepherds swayne" ("April" 97-98). Implicitly, Elizabeth is claimed here as England's lady against any threat of foreign marriage (Spenser ed. 1989, 69). The straightforwardly anti-Catholic content of the poem includes the Fox as a figure for the "false and faithlesse Papistes, to whom is no credit to be given, nor felowshippe to be used" (E. K.'s gloss to "Maye" 174), and the topic of "the abuses . . . and loose living of Popish prelates" (Argument to "September"). References to the outward symbols of Roman Catholic ceremony as "reliques and ragges of popish superstition" (gloss to "Maye" 240), along with the allegory of Elizabeth's punishing Archbishop Grindal for not forbidding "prophesyings" in the story of Algrin[d] ("Julye" 217-32), align Spenser's ideology with the Dudleys' particular support of Grindal and general championing of hard-line Protestantism. Spenser even indirectly alludes to Leicester through the figure of Lobbin in "November" and directly mentions him in "October," where "the most honorable and renowmed the Erle of Leycester" (gloss to "October" 47) is described by Piers as a fit topic for epic poetry:

> And sing of bloody Mars, of wars, of giusts,
> Turne thee to those, that weld the awful crowne,
> To doubted Knights, whose *woundlesse armour rusts*,
> And *helmes unbruzed* wexen dayly browne.

> There may thy Muse display her fluttryng wing,
> And stretch her selfe at large from East to West:
> Whither thou list in fayre Elisa rest,
> Or if thee please in *bigger notes* to sing,
> *Advaunce* the worthy whome shee loveth best,
> *That first the white beare to the stake did bring.* (37-48; emphasis added)

Not only does Piers identify Leicester by the Dudley crest of the bear and the ragged staff under which Henry Sidney had fought in Ireland, but he also exhorts Cuddie to praise the earl in "bigger notes" than he would need to sing of Elisa. There is an interesting juxtaposition here between action and inaction, between the "fluttryng wing" of a Muse that would "sing of bloody Mars, of wars, of giusts" or alternatively "in fayre Elisa rest." That these knights are "doubted" suggests that they are both feared and uncertain. This ambiguity is adumbrated by the description of how their "*woundlesse armour rusts,* / And *helmes unbruzed* wexen dayly browne." It is as though the poet's singing of their deeds will stir these idle knights to action.[14] The "October" eclogue would seem to refer at least in part to the actual inaction and restlessness of the Leicester faction at this juncture. From 1579 to 1586, Leicester promoted a more aggressive military policy in the Low Countries, and both he and his nephew were impatient with the queen's more cautious policy and reluctance to spend money. Similarly, Henry Sidney and later Lord Grey both met with the queen's disapproval of their excessive expenditures on military campaigns in Ireland.

A second major source of literary evidence for Spenser's connection with the politics of the Leicester faction is the *Complaints*, printed in 1591. *The Ruines of Time* bears a dedication to Mary Sidney, in which her brother Philip is referred to as "that most brave Knight" and "Patron of my young Muses" (Spenser ed. 1912, 471a). Half of the poem (lines 176-343) is a panegyric to the Dudley family and perhaps contains parts of the *Stemmata Dudleiana*, mentioned in Spenser's letter to Harvey of April 1580 (ed. 1912, 612b). Here the poet defends Leicester from his enemies (lines 214-17):

41

> And evill men now dead, his deeds upbraid:
> Spite bites the dead, that living never baid.
> He now is gone, the whiles the Foxe is crept
> Into the hole, the which the Badger swept.

To understand just how opposed to Leicester's and Spenser's politics the Fox Burghley was, we should consider his comment that the Dutch had less cause to protest Spanish oppression than the Irish did English tyranny (Read 1960, 8). The traditional identification of Burghley with the Fox here may also inform the portrayal of the Fox in *Mother Hubberds Tale* as aider and abetter of the Ape, an English pun on the name of Alençon's ambassador Simier. While *Mother Hubberds Tale* was also published in the 1591 *Complaints*, Greenlaw speculated that it had been written back in 1579 at the time of the marriage negotiations (1932, 104-32). The recent evidence which Richard Peterson has uncovered in a 1591 letter by the recusant Tresham indicates that the *Complaints* were recalled at least in part because of their criticism of those like Burghley still powerful at court.[15] Whether Spenser or his printer Ponsonby chose to publish the politically controversial *Complaints*, the poems themselves attest to the poet's loyalty to Leicester and his politics.[16] The recall of this text certainly proves the lasting character of court faction; even after the deaths of Sidney, Walsingham, and Leicester, criticism of their enemies could still offend.

In *The Ruines of Time*, Leicester and Sidney are portrayed from an elegiac perspective with their lost hopes and their enemy's spite overcome by the poem itself, which memorializes Spenser's heroes: "And here thou livest, being ever song / Of us, which living loved thee afore" (338-39). This same concept of the poetic monument as a redemption for loss unites *Ruines of Time* with both *Astrophel*, an elegy for Sidney, and *Virgils Gnat*, Spenser's only poem dedicated to Leicester. Greenlaw interpreted the allegory of *Virgils Gnat* as the story of Spenser's warning to Leicester of the Alençon marriage plot and subsequent punishment for this by being sent to Ireland. Another possible reading is that the gnat who saves the shepherd commemorates the Leicester faction's trying to warn Elizabeth of the need for a more militant approach to England's defense—with respect to both Ireland and the Netherlands. The shepherd who inscribes the tomb with verse in honor of the gnat could represent the queen giving her loyal servants their due but could also suggest the figure of the poet—given the poet-shepherds of the *Calender* and *Colin Clout*. It is Spenser who rescues the gnat from oblivion, Spenser whose poetry repeatedly reminds the reader of the aspirations and achievements of Leicester and his faction. If the note of complaint at the outset of *Virgils Gnat* reflects regret, perhaps it is over not having been sent by Leicester to the Continent, since Spenser had written to Harvey in October 1579, "let me be answered, ere I goe . . . I goe thither, as sent by him" (ed. 1912, 638b). We still do not know exactly what Spenser did for Leicester, nor do we know exactly what Leicester promised Spenser in return.

If we consider that Grey was recalled from Ireland in 1582, that Sidney died in 1586 and Leicester in 1588, while Spenser returned to England only in 1589, Spenser's continued loyalty to these men, long after they ceased to be patrons, needs to be explained in relation to his consistent admiration for their politics, as evident in a third major literary source: the 1596 *Faerie Queene*. Grey's military excesses and his ultimate administrative defeat in Ireland are rewritten as Artegall's "having freed Irena from distresse" (V xii 27.8). An example of how political positions on the Alençon marriage and Ireland were connected in Spenser's imagination is in his allegorical account of Grey's massacre of the papal forces at Smerwick, where the title of Stubbes's tract *Discovery of a Gaping Gulf* is used to describe the mouth of the monster Grantorto, which "gaped like a gulfe" (xii 15.8). Leicester's failure to defend and to govern the Dutch states is transformed into Arthur's protecting Belge by destroying both Geryoneo (Philip of Spain) and the Monster (the Roman Catholic church) (xi 20-35). Arthur's chivalrous denial of reward from Belge may be read as an idealized revision of Leicester's "ambitious acceptance of the Governor-Generalship of the Low Countries" (J. Fowler 1982, 154): "Deare Lady, deedes ought not be scand / By th'authors manhood, nor the doers might, / But by their trueth and by the causes right" (xi 17.3-5). Spenser pays literary tribute to what he sees as the justice of the cause rather than its success. And far from a success it was, according to John Guy: "Leicester was incompetent both as soldier and administrator. . . . when Lord Willoughby de Eresby was installed as the new commander of the English forces—with strict orders not to meddle in politics—the myth that Leicester's intervention would redeem the Dutch was exposed for what it was: Protestant chivalric romance" (Guy 1988, 336, 338). The Protestant chivalric romance of *The Faerie Queene* V is an allegorical rewriting of the defeats of the Leicester faction.

Spenser both cautions against and invites such decoding of allegory in his dedication of *Virgils Gnat* (5-12):

> But if that any Oedipus unware
> Shall chaunce, through power of some divining spright,
> To read the secrete of this riddle rare,
> And know the purport of my evill plight,

> Let him rest pleased with his owne insight,
> Ne further seeke to glose upon the text:
> For griefe enough it is to grieved wight
> To feele his fault, and not be further vext.

Whatever the "griefe" Spenser suffered at the hands of Leicester, who is referred to as "causer of my care" (2), it in no way interfered with the poet's loyalty to the earl and his politics. The various connotations of *griefe* (injury, anger, sorrow), *grieved* (oppressed, made angry, troubled), *fault* (neglect, offense, culpability), and *vext* (subjected to physical force, annoyed, distressed) suggest both anger and sorrow (see the *OED*). The last two lines of this passage can be read simultaneously to express the poet's anger at the patron's slight and the poet's sympathy with the patron's plight. It would seem that in the *Complaints* there is an implied analogy between the poet's own "griefe" and that of his aristocratic patrons and cultural heroes, just as in *The Faerie Queene* there is an idealized rewriting of those griefs, a gilded world of politics.

If we include the reader—"Oedipus unware"—as a cause of "griefe" through his "glos[ing] upon the text," then *vext* may even take on the further meaning of "to be subjected to severe or prolonged examination." Spenser may be warning his reader not to bring disaster, or grief, upon himself through overreading, but at the same time he suggests that the meanings and the connections are there to be interpreted. By bringing the poet's and his patron's "griefe" to light, the reader raises the "vext" question of the relation between biographical fiction and court faction, between Spenser's poetry and life, and between poetic and historical myths.

"All his minde on honour fixed": The Preferment of Edmund Spenser

JEAN R. BRINK

Anecdotal evidence and scholarly conjecture have compounded the inconsistencies and overshadowed the importance of the one contemporary statement that offers a concise summary and interpretation of Spenser's life—that of William Camden (1551-1623). Born only a year before Spenser, Camden was the principal contemporary historian of sixteenth-century England, and an authority whom Spenser himself celebrates as "the nourice of antiquitie, / And lanterne unto late succeeding age" (*Ruines of Time* 169-70; in Spenser ed. 1912, 473b). This contemporary witness interprets Spenser's Irish appointment, on which Camden's remarks focus, as a preferment that will assure Spenser's having the time and means to concentrate on his verse:

> by a fate peculiar to Poets, he alwaies strugled with poverty, though he were Secretary to the Lord *Grey*, Lord Deputy of *Ireland*. For scarce had hee there gotten a solitary place and leisure to write, when hee was by the Rebels cast out of his dwelling, despoyled of his goods, and returned into *England* a poore man, where shortly after hee dyed. (Camden ed. 1635, 501)

Camden gives no indication that Spenser's appointment in Ireland was perceived as a punishment imposed as a result of official or unofficial reaction to political allusions in his verse. Nevertheless, the idea that Spenser was shunted off to Ireland by Robert Dudley, earl of Leicester, for writing an impolitic work (*Mother Hubberds Tale* or perhaps *The Shepheardes Calender*) has influenced our perception of his Irish appointment through much of the twentieth century (Greenlaw 1910, 556-57; Oram 1989, 327-29; Lewalski 1990, 534-35).

This negative view of Spenser's employment as Lord Grey de Wilton's secretary is not only opposed to that of Camden but is also unsupported by any other contemporary testimony. Further, the notion that Spenser's employment in Ireland was an enforced rustication orchestrated by the earl of Leicester assumes that he had previously attained significant preferment under Leicester in England (e.g., Rambuss 1993, 8; Waller, 1994, 15). Leicester's secretaries have been identified by Henry Woudhuysen, and there is no documentary evidence that Spenser held a position in his household (Woudhuysen 1981, 47-49). His membership in the Areopagus club, a literary circle supposedly composed of Leicester's nephew Sir Philip Sidney, Sir Edward Dyer, and Fulke Greville, is similarly suspect (Heninger 1987, 245). Even after Eleanor Rosenberg suggested that Spenser's appointment might have been a preferment arranged "through Sir Henry Sidney," Philip's father (1955, 342), no systematic attempt was made to show that the appointment was a preferment or to identify patronage relations that would connect Spenser with Grey. Although we know that the poet John Donne sought unsuccessfully to obtain secretaryships in Ireland and Virginia, forced exile, by default, has continued to be the received view of Spenser's Irish appointment (Bald 1970, 160-62, 304).

Except for Camden's succinct statement, we lack the kinds of specific contemporary sources that would allow us to document the remarkable preferment that an appointment as personal secretary to Grey—a peer of the realm created Knight of the Garter in the same ceremony as William Cecil—represented for Master Edmund Spenser, aspirant to advancement by benefit of education and art. My approach to the complexity of what preferment meant and how it could be achieved by a talented young man such as Spenser, will therefore employ more indirect and circumstantial means: first a reconstruction of Spenser's views of an ideal courtier from his early verse and a related examination of the values of the Sidney circle— a group of courtiers for whom Spenser expresses admiration in his correspondence with Gabriel Harvey; and second, an analysis of the records we do have for Spenser's friend Harvey, whose attempts to gain preferment, and whose failure to do so, are well documented. Although we lack documentary evidence regarding Spenser's access to patronage, the efforts of Harvey, who faced many of the same social obstacles, by analogy shed a historical light on Spenser's situation. Beyond such general illumination, however, the details of these efforts support my hypothesis that ironically it might have been Harvey who provided a crucial link in the chain of connections that led to Spenser's Irish appointment, but not to his own preferment.

That it is even necessary to make a circumstantial case tells us something about Spenser. He was not in his own day as socially privileged a figure as he has since become. It is true that he claimed relationship to the

Spencers of Althorp, but the precise nature of this relationship and the extent of its benefit, if any, to him beyond the unspecified "particular bounties" of Lady Strange (born Alice Spencer), to whom he dedicated his *Teares of the Muses*, and the "so excellent favours" of Lady Carey (born Elizabeth Spencer), dedicatee of *Muiopotmos*, are undocumented, despite the efforts of experienced genealogists and biographers.[1] Although contemporary poets honored Spenser, and Camden elevated him above Chaucer, calling him the "prince of poets," no one who knew him intimately wrote the story of his life or kept the kinds of records we have for Philip Sidney. Spenser himself, moreover, left few records. The recovery of even a few letters to Sidney or Grey would change the shape of his biography. We can chart the aspirations of many of Spenser's contemporaries, such as Harvey, Lodowick Bryskett, Geoffrey Fenton, Walter Ralegh, and George Carew, because their letters requesting favors, offices, or property survive in the State Papers or in the family papers of the Cecils or Sidneys or other influential families, but no personal letters by Spenser, except for some problematical correspondence with Harvey, have survived. As I have already suggested, in order to assess the biographical significance of Spenser's Irish appointment, we must consequently turn to the records that do survive—Spenser's verse and the lives of his relevant contemporaries, particularly as they bear on the desirability of government service and on the means of access to it.

To judge from Spenser's verse, preferment for him meant joining a circle of "brave Courtier[s]," whom he describes as having their "minde[s] on honour fixed" (*Mother Hubberds Tale*, 718, 771). Spenser characterizes the ideal courtier as serving his prince in "Armes and warlike amenaunce," as well as in "wise and civill governaunce" (781-82). Throughout his published works, he repeatedly links the figures of the soldier and the scholar, both in setting forth ideals and in censuring a system that fails to reward men of arms and learning: "learning lies unregarded, / And men of armes doo wander unrewarded" (*The Ruines of Time*, 440-41). To be a soldier involved battling the Spanish in the Netherlands, fortifying Ireland against the Spanish, or subduing Irish rebels. Ambitious men could also win preferment—and make fortunes—by exploring distant lands destined to become part of an empire; feats such as these prompted the queen to knight Francis Drake and Humphrey Gilbert. Learning, particularly in Latin and European languages, might also elevate men such as Thomas Smith and Francis Walsingham to foreign service and ultimately to positions on the Privy Council. But Smith (1513-77), although the son of a sheepfarmer, was born, bred, and well established before Elizabeth's reign, and Walsingham, a scion of the gentry, was the only son of a lawyer and grandson, on his mother's side, to Sir Edward Denny of Cheshunt; he had the resources to live abroad before entering government service, as well as possible access to court through his stepfather, Sir John Carey, and the Hunsdons. Men of humble background, such as Spenser, about whose family the very absence of records speaks suggestively, and Gabriel Harvey, the ambitious but gifted son of a ropemaker, could claim the title of gentleman only by virtue of their education. For them, preferment could be won only by success in the patronage systems that effectually controlled appointments in the university, church, court, and other such institutions.

In still sharper contrast to Spenser and Harvey, Sidney, godson of Philip of Spain, was born a courtier, splendidly educated, schooled in languages, and furnished with European connections by a Grand Tour that lasted nearly three years. Longing to lead a great Protestant crusade, Sidney repeatedly chafed at his lack of government employment (Levy 1972b, 9; Berry 1989, 22), even though at the age of twenty-three he had already been sent as the leader of an embassy to the Holy Roman emperor and to the courts of Protestant princes. Like Spenser's ideal courtier, he wanted to serve his queen and country as a soldier and councilor. Disappointed because the queen had decided not to send a military force to the Netherlands, he wrote impatiently to Hubert Languet on 1 July 1578, complaining about his lack of employment: "For to what purpose should our thoughts be directed to various kinds of knowledge, unless room be afforded for putting it into practice, so that public advantage may be the result, which in a corrupt age we cannot hope for?" (Pears 1845, 143). Since Sidney had just returned from leading an embassy, his complaints about lacking suitable employment illustrate his obsession with proving himself on the battlefield.

It probably did not help matters that other members of Sidney's circle experienced the adventures that Sidney himself craved. His good friend Edward Denny accompanied the first earl of Essex to Ireland in 1573 and in 1578 he sailed to the New World with Sir Humphrey Gilbert. Fulke Greville accompanied Sidney on his embassy, but immediately upon his return to court in the summer of 1578, jeopardized his standing with the queen by rushing off to the Netherlands without her permission (Rebholz 1971, 35). Frustrated by Elizabeth's unwillingness to allow him to prove himself in the Dutch war against Spain, Sidney, accompanied by Greville, escaped from court in 1585 and made his way to Plymouth in order to sail to the West Indies and America with Sir Francis Drake, but by royal command Drake was forbidden to receive Sidney into his fleet (Duncan-Jones

1991, 273; Rebholz 1971, 70-73). Although Elizabeth prevented Sidney from risking his life on Drake's voyage, she relented sufficiently so that he was finally allowed to join the war in the Netherlands, where he met his death, just as she had feared. Sidney, like Greville and Spenser's Lord Grey, embraced an ethic in which military service for queen and country was a duty. While the desire to gain wealth and property enhanced the attraction of military and colonial ventures, it is difficult to overestimate the glamor of military service in France, the Netherlands, or Ireland or the allure of joining an expedition with Drake, Gilbert, or Ralegh. In the New World, plantations were granted to those who undertook to finance colonization; in Ireland, each of the sixteenth-century rebellions resulted in the confiscation of vast tracts of land from the rebel earls, and these lands were frequently awarded to military servitors (MacCarthy-Morrogh 1986, 55-56). Profit was undoubtedly a motive, but mistaken as it would be to idealize these adventurers, it is equally short-sighted to assume that their motivation was exclusively mercenary.

The complicated links between courtly aspiration and military service in a foreign land like Ireland and the relationship of both to scholarship are difficult for us to understand, but they clearly existed in the minds of Elizabethans. Writing to Denny in 1580, shortly before his friend was to leave for Ireland with Grey, Sidney outlines a program of study requiring that Denny take a considerable library with him (Osborn 1972, 537-40). Similarly, when Greville went to Ireland in the sea expedition of 1580, Sir William Winter described his cabin as so well furnished with books that he might be at court (Rebholz 1971, 42). Sidney, Denny, and Greville are typical of Spenser's ideal courtier who wanted not only to "raise / Himselfe to high degre" but also "to winne worthie place; / Through due deserts and comely carriage" (*Mother Hubberds Tale*, 774-77).

Prior to Grey's appointment as lord deputy in 1580, Sir Henry Sidney had let it be known that he would consider resuming the position, if it were agreed that his son Philip could accompany and succeed him as deputy. Sir Henry describes Philip as having "most ernestlie and often . . . spoken and writen to doe this lovinge Office" (Collins 1746, 1:281). Philip reveals his disappointment at not receiving this preferment in the same letter in which he outlines his recommended program of study for Edward Denny: "And very willingly doe I beare the preferringe of the noble *Lord* Gray; since so I preferre him to my selfe, as I will ever be most glad to doe him service with affectionate honor, which truly I am but to very fewe" (Osborn 1972, 537). Philip's interest in an Irish appointment was probably heightened by his trip to Ireland in the summer of 1576. His visit coincided with the death of Walter Devereux, the first earl of Essex and father of Penelope Devereux, Sidney's Stella. Essex, like Sidney's father and Sir Thomas Smith, had been engaged in plans for colonizing Ireland in the early 1570s. The earl had arrived in Dublin on 23 July 1576 and then visited with the Sidneys on 10 August near Dublin (Duncan-Jones 1991, 109). Philip traveled widely in Ireland, from Dublin on the east coast to Galway on the west. His desire for military action was also gratified. Sir Henry, describing guerrilla warfare to the Privy Council, indicates to Burghley that his son can offer more specific details: "I pray your Lordship in the rest of Ireland for this time give credit to Ph. Sidney" (Public Record Office, State Papers, Ireland, 63/ 56/32). Sidney's expedition came to an abrupt conclusion, however, when Essex died suddenly on 22 September. At the time, there were rumors that the earl had been poisoned. Later, scandalmongers charged that Sidney's uncle, the earl of Leicester, had poisoned Essex in order to clear the way for marriage with his wife Lettice (*Leicester's Commonwealth* 1985, 80-84). Conceivably, Sidney accompanied Essex's body back to court to give an account of his death and to counter rumors of intrigue and murder.

We know that Sidney's experiences in Ireland deeply impressed him. They furnished him with anecdotes later reported by foreign dignitaries and even influenced whom he visited during his 1577 embassy. In one of the few instances in which Sidney's table talk has been preserved, Philip Camerarius of Nuremberg vividly recounts Sidney's explanation of why there are no wolves in England and comments that this "discourse of Sydneys" was "accompanied with other memorable speeches touching Ireland, where his father governed."[2] Sidney also met with the English Jesuit Edmund Campion, whose career had overlapped with his own at Oxford in 1568-69. Sir Henry Sidney had cooperated with the Stanyhurst family in 1571 in saving Campion's life, and Campion later dedicated his history of Ireland to Leicester, whose patronage he had received (Rosenberg 1955, 85-88). Herein, a further thickening of Irish connections.

When Sidney returned from his embassy to the emperor in June 1577, he was immediately plunged into political maneuvering over Ireland. While he was abroad, his father's administration had been repeatedly criticized as too costly and too abusive to Irish peers, whose spokesman, the earl of Ormond, was particularly effective in persuading the queen that Sir Henry had been guilty of extravagance and corruption. Sidney's "Discourse on Irish Affairs," aimed at vindicating his father's administration, was completed by the end of September 1577, the same month in which Sidney is reported to have quarreled with Ormond (Collins 1746, 1:228).

It is therefore possible that Sidney was interested in being appointed lord deputy principally to safeguard his father's reputation, but evidence suggests that appointments in Ireland were sought by many of the young men in his immediate circle. In 1580 Fulke Greville and Edward Denny, two of Sidney's intimate friends, went to Ireland. In April 1580 Greville sailed as captain of the *Foresight* to guard the Irish coast against an expected Spanish invasion. Like Ralegh, Denny accompanied the Grey expedition. Writing to Walsingham from Ireland in 1581, he repeatedly mentions his devotion to Sidney (Denny 1904, 251). These courtiers in the Sidney circle shared his glorified view of the soldier-scholar who fixed his mind on honor and "noble fame" (*Mother Hubberds Tale*, 769), values so eloquently praised by Spenser. Spenser himself joined the Grey expedition shortly after publishing his *Shepheardes Calender* with a dedication to Sidney. His acceptance of the position of Grey's personal secretary suggests that he shared the preoccupation of the Sidney circle with Ireland. That he was offered a position with the respected and experienced Grey also indicates that he was recognized as sharing the values of those whom he honors in his early verse.

School and university connections are most likely to have led to Spenser's initial preferment as secretary to John Young, bishop of Rochester, and they are likely to underlie his preferment as secretary to Grey as well. But it is in regard to Spenser's employment by Young that Harvey, whose career was also furthered by Young, becomes relevant. It is therefore to what I might term the Harvey connection that my discussion will turn after attending briefly to a preliminary point that Thomas Nashe's brilliant satires of Harvey in the 1590s make necessary. In order to understand the relationship between Harvey and Spenser, we must differentiate the considerable promise of the young Harvey from the self-importance of the buffoon whom Nashe so brilliantly ridiculed for listing the many important men who had thought well of him (Nashe ed. 1958, 3:35, 107-8). In contrast to Nashe's depiction of Harvey as a pompous and inept court sycophant, Harvey was recognized as a gifted student with unusual linguistic talents when he and Spenser were both at Cambridge University during the 1570s.

We can ascertain a fair amount about Spenser's early career from the sources detailing Harvey's aspirations for promotion and attempts to win favor. Since Harvey's library, correspondence, and publications have survived and have now been thoroughly researched, we can use this information to make inferences concerning Spenser's preferment and to reconstruct his and Harvey's connections with the Sidney circle. Shifts in Harvey's attitudes toward Spenser are also suggestive of Spenser's status with his contemporaries. Harvey appears to have begun by regarding the younger man as a protégé whose career he wished to promote, but he also appears to have become increasingly uncomfortable with Spenser's accomplishments as his own prospects dwindled. Early in their relationship, it seems likely that Harvey made his connections available to Spenser because Harvey's interest in advancing his own career did not prevent him from promoting his relatives and friends, perhaps with an eye to reciprocal help or to mutual advantage. For example, he includes samples of his brother John's versifying in *Letters* (Spenser ed. 1912, 626-27) and in the same work is openly adulatory about Spenser's achievement in authoring *The Shepheardes Calender* (628). Spenser, too, regarded Harvey affectionately, to judge from appreciative references in *The Shepheardes Calender*. The evidence that Spenser had access to Harvey's connections is circumstantial, but its cumulative weight is impressive.

As I suggested in an earlier context, the opportunities available to educated men such as Harvey and Spenser were limited. Neither appears to have wanted a career in the church, and careers in the university were carefully regulated. Pembroke College, for example, limited the number of years that a fellow could maintain his stipend without taking holy orders, and most colleges resisted awarding fellowships to married men. The competition for positions in government service was fierce, and those from privileged backgrounds who had traveled abroad had a definite edge. Foreign émigrés also supplied a pool of talented linguists.

The vast number of books in languages other than English in Harvey's library suggests that he wanted to be part of a European intellectual community. Harvey also seems to have aspired to foreign service, an aspiration that Spenser's life indicates he shared. The Continent, however, was not the only possibility. Harvey had reason to consider Ireland a land of opportunity as well. He received academic patronage from his neighbor Sir Thomas Smith, Elizabeth's principal secretary before Walsingham. Smith, who regarded the English conquest of Ireland as a parallel to the Roman conquest of England, invested heavily in expeditions to colonize Ireland in the early 1570s, ensuring that Harvey would have been familiar with the view that Ireland was a land of opportunity (Quinn 1945, 547; Jardine 1990, 73). Harvey received a fellowship at Pembroke College in 1570 through the sponsorship of Smith, whom he variously describes as his patron, neighbor, and kinsman. He pointedly thanks Smith for his "frendli or rather fatherli taulk" and comments that it is a "singular bennefit and blessing of God" that he has "sutch a patron, or rather a father to resort unto" (Harvey ed. 1884, 168).

Harvey's early involvement with Ireland and with those who served there is a matter of record. In 1568, two years after Harvey had matriculated at Christ's College, Cambridge, and a year before Spenser matriculated at Pembroke, Harvey's marginalia in his folio volume of Livy show that he read the "First Decade" of the Roman history with Smith's illegitimate son Thomas (Stern 1979, 150). The younger Thomas Smith, born in 1547, was recognized by his father as his heir. At the time that he read Livy with Harvey, he had just been discharged with a pension after serving as an officer in Ireland, and he subsequently entered the service of the earl of Leicester (Quinn 1945, 548). An introduction to Leicester House for Harvey may thus have come through the younger Thomas Smith, who could personally testify to Harvey's skillful analysis of Livy, whose political significance was alive for sixteenth-century readers.

Spenser matriculated at Pembroke in 1569, and in the following year Harvey was elected to a fellowship there. Spenser's perception of Ireland as a land where initiative and enterprise would be rewarded is likely to have begun during his early acquaintance with Harvey. By 1573 Harvey would have been well known to Spenser—and to everyone else at Pembroke—because he had become the central figure in a controversy over the power of the fellows to forbid or assent to the conferral of degrees. Harvey could not receive his master of arts degree until the fellows had agreed that his grace be promoted at Regent House, a necessary preliminary step to the official award of an M.A. The fellows, organized by Thomas Neville, refused their consent in order to prevent Harvey from receiving his degree. Harvey charged that "tales [ran] up and down the town" so that all but his "nearist acquaintanc," one of whom was Edmund Spenser, thought "veri il" of him (ed. 1884, 17).

Harvey was probably being treated unfairly; otherwise, he would not have received support from Humphrey Tindall, a senior fellow, and from Dr. John Young, master of Pembroke, later the bishop of Rochester to whom Spenser was secretary. Tindall even volunteered to ride to London to persuade Young to come to Cambridge to assist Harvey. When Young actually came, he saw to it that the degree was awarded and appointed Harvey to a lectureship in Greek, an appointment that Harvey describes as making him infinitely bound to Young, "by caus it was frely offrid of yow, not ambitiusly souht of me" (ed. 1884, 45). More ill will was generated by this appointment, and it was necessary for Young again to intervene. As a student who was to receive his baccalaureate degree in 1573, Spenser would have witnessed these power struggles at first hand and would have been made aware of the seamier side of academic politics.

We do not know whether Spenser left Cambridge in 1574, before he received his master's degree, or in 1576, after it was awarded (Judson 1945, 42-44). Moreover, the biographical tradition from Grosart to Judson has assumed that *The Shepheardes Calender* contains the only evidence of what transpired after Spenser's departure from Cambridge. Grosart postulates a visit to family in "north-east Lancashire," where Spenser falls in love with Rosalind and is spurned (Spenser ed. 1882-84, 1:3-61); other accounts fill in the "lost" years with service in Ireland or France (Jardine 1990, 70), but in no instance has the identification of any of several Mr. Spencers with Edmund Spenser been conclusive.

The one surviving document shedding light on Spenser's whereabouts during this period has been misinterpreted. We know that Spenser had the position of secretary to Bishop Young in 1578 because Harvey carefully lettered a note on the title page of Jerome Turler's *Traveiler* (1575) to the effect that the book had been given to him by Spenser on this date: "ex dono Edmundi Spenserii, Episcopi Roffensis Secretarii, 1578." Examination of the Rosenbach copy of Turler's *Traveiler* confirms that the note concerning Spenser identifies his position at the time that he gave Harvey this book. Later in the same volume Harvey writes "Legi pridie Cal. Decembrus. 1578" and signs his name. In compiling his library, Harvey habitually recorded the dates on which he acquired books as gifts or through purchase. Thus, while his note in *The Traveiler* tells us that Spenser was a secretary in Young's service in December 1578, it does not tell us when or in what capacity his services were first engaged.

Very likely, Spenser joined the London household of John Young right after he left Cambridge. Young's intervention on Harvey's behalf in 1573 demonstrates that he took an interest in the fortunes of Pembroke students. Young himself had profited from the patronage of Archbishop Grindal (variously Algrind and Algrin in *The Shepheardes Calender*), whom he had served as a chaplain. Also a graduate of this college, Grindal served as master of Pembroke and then recommended Young, another graduate, as his successor; then, in 1578, Young passed the mantle to William Fulke, likewise a Pembroke graduate. During the 1560s and 1570s Young held a number of ecclesiastical livings in different parts of London (Long 1916, 718); for example, he held a prebend under Alexander Nowell, dean of St. Paul's, for over fifteen years, not resigning it until a year after he became bishop (Judson 1934, 8). He was installed as prebendary of Westminster on 26 April 1571, a position he retained until his death. Suggestively, one of Spenser's letters to Harvey is addressed from Westminster (Spenser ed. 1912, 612).

Because of the Pembroke College ties, my assumption is that Spenser joined Young's London household immediately upon departing from Cambridge and that he did so in 1574; although Spenser's degree was awarded in 1576, there are no references to him in the Pembroke College accounts after 1574. From the dates that Young is awarded positions and relinquishes them, we can determine further parameters for Spenser's connection with his household. The bishopric of Rochester became vacant in 1577, but it was not until 31 January 1578 that Young was nominated to this position by the queen and not until 1 April that he was installed. He would then probably have left London and taken up residence at Bromley, Kent, only about ten miles from London. In the meantime, however, Young was succeeded as master of Pembroke by William Fulke on 10 May 1578, at least seven months prior to the date of Harvey's note concerning Spenser's employment as Young's secretary. By the end of November 1578 ("pridie Cal. Decembrus"), when Harvey finished reading *The Traveiler*, Spenser's gift to him, Fulke, rather than Young, would have felt responsible for offering patronage to Pembroke graduates, and so it is probable that Spenser had joined Young's household earlier than May 1578 and most plausibly by 1574, if this is indeed the date, as I deem likely, of his departure from Cambridge. He probably remained in Young's service at least until early 1579.

It is more difficult to account for the possibility of Spenser's having achieved access to Leicester House. Various possibilities are suggestive, but none can be documented. Since few Elizabethan bishops seem to have followed the court, a position in the household of the bishop of Rochester would not have ensured that Spenser had access either to the court or to Leicester House (May 1991, 23). University connections deriving from attendance at the same college cannot be dismissed, however. Harvey was a protégé of Humphrey Tindall, who, as a senior fellow, had backed him during the Pembroke power plays over his degree in 1573. Tindall, moreover, had sufficient credit with John Young, when he was located in London, to get him to intervene and prevent the Pembroke fellows from blocking the award of Harvey's degree. Tindall also officiated at the marriage ceremony between Leicester and Lettice Knollys, widow of the earl of Essex, on 21 September 1578; his participation in this secret ceremony shows that he was trusted by the earl of Leicester (Wilson 1981, 227). Thus Tindall, enjoying the confidence of both Young and Leicester, could have given Harvey or Spenser access to Leicester House.

The linguistic and literary promise of Harvey and Spenser could also have secured them an introduction to Leicester House. Certainly there were poets who had been in the service of the earl of Leicester. Of early Elizabethan writers, George Gascoigne was the most successful in realizing a combination of the roles of author and soldier and in developing patronage connections that gave him access to prominent courtiers, such as Leicester and Grey. Before Grey made Spenser his personal secretary, he and his wife had also exhibited an interest in patronizing gifted poets by supporting Gascoigne and George Whetstone. Gascoigne knew Grey when he dedicated *The Steele Glas* and *The Complaynt of Phylomene* to him on 15 April 1576 (Prouty 1942, 91). Though Gascoigne was probably not intimate with either Spenser or Harvey, he furnished them with a model of success. The gloss to the "November" eclogue of *The Shepheardes Calender* praises Gascoigne as "the very chefe of our late rymers" (141). Ralegh, a soldier poet himself, wrote commendatory verses for Gascoigne's *Steele Glas*, indicating that he, too, admired his verse. In his *Letter-Book* Harvey alludes three times to Gascoigne's works, puts him next to Chaucer in a catalogue of writers, and composes epigrams and an epitaph on him (ed. 1884, 69, 85, 100; 134; 55-58, 68-70). Gascoigne also attained some stature as a rhymer who could entertain the court. In 1575, when the queen expressed an interest in seeing the manuscript of Gascoigne's Woodstock entertainment, he enthusiastically produced a polyglot manuscript, advertising his linguistic talents. Harvey imitated Gascoigne's tactics, employing precisely the same strategy during the queen's visit to Cambridge and progress to Audley End in 1578.

Although the means of Harvey's or Spenser's access to Leicester House is uncertain, by late 1576 Harvey had established a connection with Leicester's nephew Sidney (Stern 1979, 150). He specifically mentions discussing Livy with Sidney shortly before the latter left England in February 1577 to lead the embassy to the emperor. Even allowing for some exaggeration of his intimacy with Sidney, Harvey's reference is so precisely dated that the meetings alluded to must have occurred: "The courtier Philip Sidney and I had privately discussed these three books of Livy, scrutinizing them so far as we could from all points of view, applying a political analysis, just before his embassy to the emperor Rudolf" (Jardine and Grafton 1990, 36). The history and current events in Ireland would have been on the minds of those who gathered at Leicester House to use Livy as a springboard for political analysis. Sidney had just returned from a visit to Ireland where he had witnessed the death of the first earl of Essex, who had written a lengthy treatise on the reformation of that troubled land. Edward Denny had served with Essex in Ireland, and Harvey's library contains a presentation copy of

Richard Davies's funeral sermon for Essex, which Harvey annotated with testimonials to the earl's virtue (Stern 1979, 208). Essex's death would also have reminded Harvey of the ugly fate of the younger Thomas Smith, who was poisoned by a neighbor and then boiled and fed to dogs (Churchyard 1579, F3v).

Virginia Stern was the first to point out that a note in Harvey's copy of Joannis de Sacrobosco's *Textus de Sphaera* (1527) derives from an actual conversation or discussion with Sidney (1979, 79, 234). After his signature, Harvey writes the note: "Plus in recessu, quam in fronte. Arte, et virtute. 1580." On sig. aii, he adds, "Elenchus insignium materiarum. Sacrobosco & Valerius, Sir Philip Sidneis two bookes for the Spheare. Bie him specially commended to the earle of Essex, Sir Edward Dennie, & divers gentlemen of the court. To be read with diligent studie, but sportingly, as he termed it." Stern was also the first to connect Harvey's marginalia with a letter that Sidney wrote to Edward Denny on 22 May 1580 before Denny left for Ireland (1979, 79; Jardine and Grafton 1990, 38-39). In the relevant passage, Sidney says, "For the other maters allott your selfe an other howre for Sacroboscus, & Valerius, or any other of Geography, and when you have satisfied your selfe in *that*, take your history of England, & your Ortelius to knowe the places you reed of" (Osborn 1972, 540). Harvey, then, must either have heard Sidney recommend Sacrobosco or have seen or heard about Sidney's letter.[3]

In addition to reading Livy with Sidney, Harvey reports that he was also thanked by Sir Edward Dyer and Sir Edward Denny for having supplied them with information on politics and history (Stern 1979, 151; Jardine and Grafton 1990, 38). Denny, who had participated in the 1573 Essex expedition and later accompanied Grey as a captain in 1580, constitutes an important link between the Sidney circle and Lord Grey. Denny was the fifth but eventually second surviving son of Sir Anthony Denny, chief gentleman of the privy chamber, privy councilor and executor to Henry VIII, and guardian to Edward VI. Sir Anthony Denny and Sir Henry Sidney were very close to Edward VI, who may have died in Sidney's arms. On his mother's side, Sir Edward Denny was a first cousin to Sir Francis Walsingham, who was the son of Sir Anthony Denny's sister. Likewise, Sir Humphrey Gilbert and Sir Walter Ralegh were also his first cousins since they were the sons of his mother's sister. In addition, Denny was closely related by marriage to Lord Grey (Denny 1904, 249). Grey's sister Honora was the wife of Denny's older brother Henry; and her son, another Edward Denny, later became Grey's ward (British Library, Lansdowne MS 22, item 83, fol. 194).

After his preferment as lord deputy of Ireland, Lord Grey asked Sir Henry Sidney's advice on whom to trust and how to proceed (Grey 1847, xiv-xv). Sir Henry recommended a number of people but mentioned neither Spenser nor Lodowick Bryskett, who was a former servitor of Sir Henry's and who had accompanied Philip on his Grand Tour (Grey 1847, 68-74). But the elder Sidney does send affectionate greetings to Edward Denny (Denny 1904, 249). Since we know that Grey consulted the elder Sidney on appointments and that Spenser was not mentioned in their correspondence, Edward Denny becomes another plausible source for the introduction or recommendation of Spenser to Grey via a Harvey connection. Denny had read Latin with Harvey and was intimately acquainted with the Sidney circle; moreover, he had the requisite kinship ties with Grey.

Since no documentary evidence places Spenser at Leicester House, most attempts to date his connection with the Sidney circle derive from Harvey and his published correspondence.[4] Although the evidence is admittedly conjectural rather than documentary, I would like to suggest that we can infer the dates of Spenser's connections with Leicester House from shifts in Harvey's attitudes toward publicizing his relationship with Spenser. In order to make this case, I assume that Harvey began to advertise his relationship with Spenser only after the younger man had established a relationship with the Sidney circle and had achieved sufficient preferment to make Harvey think that it would further his own career if he were publicly known as the intimate of Spenser.

Harvey suffered a series of setbacks in 1577. His principal patron, Sir Thomas Smith, died on 12 August 1577. At the funeral he offended Andrew Perne, Cambridge vice-chancellor, because Perne objected to Smith's widow's having given Harvey some rare manuscript books. To make matters worse, Harvey's position at Cambridge was already delicate. His fellowship at Pembroke would expire in November 1578, and he could not be reelected unless he committed himself to studying divinity or succeeded in obtaining a dispensation. His concern about his future may have led him to publish *Ciceronianus* (June 1577) and *Rhetor* (November 1577). Not unlike Spenser, who sought recognition by publishing *The Shepheardes Calender* in 1579, he hoped that his reputation as a gifted rhetorician might pave the way for a career as a civil servant.

Similarly, Harvey viewed the royal progress of 1578 as crucial to his chances of receiving preferment at court. When Elizabeth stopped at Cambridge on 26 July 1578 on the way to Audley End, he presented himself as a linguistic virtuoso, eligible (and eager) for service abroad as part of an embassy. While he may have aimed at a diplomatic career, at the very least he hoped to secure Leicester's support for extending his fellowship. In addition to participating in a disputation, Harvey presented four manuscripts of Latin verse to the queen. He supplemented the manuscript versions with material reworked from his *Letter-Book* and other sources and presented the queen with a printed text entitled *Gratulationes Valdinenses* on 15 September at Hadham Hall (gloss to the "September" eclogue, line 176, of *The Shepheardes Calender*).

Book I of Harvey's *Gratulationes Valdinenses*, an anthology of Latin poems, is dedicated to Elizabeth, who, Harvey says, let him kiss her hand. In it he reports that, when Leicester was asked whether he intended to send Harvey to France and Italy, he replied affirmatively and that the queen then told him that he already looked Italian (Harvey 1578a, F1-2). Significantly, in Book II Harvey urges Leicester to marry Elizabeth and warns him against Alençon and the French match (Jameson 1941, 647-48). According to Greenlaw (1910), precisely this kind of admonition prompted Leicester to banish Spenser to Ireland. Far from earning Harvey a rebuke, however, his venture into politics seems to have passed unnoticed. Book III is addressed to Burghley, and Book IV contains encomia of Oxford, Hatton, and Sidney. In keeping with the values and philosophy of the Sidney circle, Harvey states that it is more important for a courtier to be a soldier than a scholar and then offers one of the first celebrations of Sidney as the ideal courtier.

Harvey, like Gascoigne in 1575, advertises his fitness for foreign service by showing his knowledge of Latin and his rapport with the international community. In *Gratulationes Valdinenses*, he includes numerous Latin tributes to Leicester written by Continental authors, as well as by English ones. He was able to produce these testimonials on the spur of the moment because many had already appeared in print. Harvey's selection of English authors is carefully focused; every one of them had enjoyed Leicester's patronage (Rosenberg 1955, 325-28). One particular omission may therefore be of importance for Spenser's biography: Harvey prints nothing from Spenser's pen, excluding the "Immerito" who not very many months later will be represented as his intimate friend throughout *The Shepheardes Calender* (1579).

Harvey's work was a bid for Leicester's favor, and had Spenser been in Leicester's service in September 1578, it seems likely that Harvey would have included a poem by Spenser either to promote his protégé or to advertise his own connection with him. Unquestionably, Harvey flaunts his connection with Spenser in *Letters* (1580) and continues to do so in other prose tracts written in the 1590s, beginning with *Foure Letters* (1592). In the 1590s Edmund Spenser becomes Master Spenser to Harvey, but he remains his bosom companion—as Harvey tells the story. On these inferential grounds, I conclude that Spenser had no serious connection with Leicester House in September 1578 but had attained acceptance by the Sidney circle and access to Leicester House prior to 10 April 1579, the date of the Epistle to *The Shepheardes Calender*.

Harvey's own bid for Leicester's favor in 1578 was successful, although not in the way he may have hoped. William Fulke, the new Master of Pembroke, tried to get Harvey a dispensation so that he could keep his fellowship. He wrote to the fellows assuring them of his support for Harvey and telling them that "the earle of Leycester hath made earnest request for the continuance of Mr. Harveyes fellowshipp for one yeare" (Harvey ed. 1884, 88), but Harvey had entirely alienated his peers. The fellows denied the request, and further intervention by the master and senior fellows seemed unlikely to ameliorate the situation. Nevertheless, in December 1578 Harvey was elected to a fellowship at Trinity Hall, where he could study civil law and follow in the footsteps of his former patron Sir Thomas Smith.

We know the events that transpired in December 1578 largely because of the survival of Harvey's library and marginalia. Shortly after learning of his fellowship, Harvey met Spenser in London. He recorded in his copy of Murner's *Howleglas* that he met Spenser on 20 December 1578 and that the book was given him on the condition that he read it plus Skoggin, Skelton, and Lazarillo before 1 January or else forfeit his four volumes of Lucian (Stern 1979, 49, 228). This meeting in London could also have afforded Spenser and Harvey an opportunity to confer on the publication of *The Shepheardes Calender*. S. K. Heninger, Jr., has convincingly argued that Harvey was influential in determining the visual appearance of the text, which imitates the format of the Sansovino edition of Sannazaro's *Arcadia* (1988, 45-51).

That Harvey was involved in preparing E. K.'s commentary seems especially likely because of the specificity with which Harvey's "triumph" at Audley End is described. Spenser, who had joined Young's household at the latest by May 1578, would not have been in Cambridge during the queen's visit. Since Harvey's recognition by the queen occurred in September, E. K. writes in the gloss to the "September" eclogue (line 176):

> Nowe I thinke no man doubteth but by Colin is ever meante the Authour selfe. Whose especiall good freend Hobbinoll sayth he is, or more rightly Mayster Gabriel Harvey: of whose speciall commendation, aswell in Poetrye as Rhctorike and other choyce learning, we have lately had a sufficient tryall

in diverse his workes, but specially in his Musarum Lachrymae, and his late Gratulationum Valdinensium which boke in the progresse at Audley in Essex, he dedicated in writing to her Majestie. Afterward presenting the same in print unto her Highnesse at the worshipfull Maister Capells in Hertfordshire.

Only Harvey would have known the sequence of events that included his first presenting an oration to the queen, then dedicating a written version to her, and then personally presenting a printed copy to her in Hertfordshire.

Since Harvey throughout his career celebrated his relationship with Spenser when it was to his advantage to do so, I assume that we can make inferences from negative evidence. Thus I date Spenser's association with Leicester House as beginning after 15 September 1578, when Harvey omitted Spenser's name from *Gratulationes Valdinenses*, and before 10 April 1579, when the preface to *The Shepheardes Calender* was written. *The Shepheardes Calender* repeatedly calls attention to the Harvey-Spenser relationship, leaving no doubt that Harvey is the "especiall good freend" of Immerito. *The Shepheardes Calender* is also dedicated to Sidney and praises Leicester, "the worthy whome shee loveth best" ("October" 47) as the subject matter for a heroic poem. By the time *The Shepheardes Calender* had progressed to the publication stage, probably by April 1579 when E. K.'s preface was written and certainly well before 5 December 1579 when *The Shepheardes Calender* was entered in the Stationers' Register, Spenser appeared to Harvey to be securely on the road to preferment. Both *The Shepheardes Calender* and *Three Proper, and wittie, familiar Letters* (1580) advertise the relationship between Harvey and Spenser, depicting Harvey as the younger man's mentor and intimate friend.

Spenser's success seems also to have spurred Harvey's aspirations to higher status. On 24 April 1579, two weeks after the date of E. K.'s letter prefacing *The Shepheardes Calender*, Harvey wrote to ask Leicester for preferment to a prebend and to recommend the appointment of Dr. John Still to a bishopric. He told Leicester that he was sure that Still would appoint him as his chancellor but acknowledged that a deputy would be necessary until he could complete his degree (Stern 1979, 49-50). In the same letter he alluded to an epic poem called *Anticosmopolita*. By 30 June 1579 he had entered *Anticosmopolita* in the Stationers' Register. Harvey's poem was never printed and may never have been completed, but he seems to have wanted to hurry it into print before *The Shepheardes Calender*.

It is understandable that Harvey would feel competitive with the younger Spenser, who had achieved the acceptance and recognition that he coveted. His mixed feelings about Spenser's success are revealed in his private *Letter-Book*. In July 1579 he fantasizes situations in which irritation with Spenser would be justified, the most revealing of which is a series of responses to Spenser's having supposedly published Harvey's "Verlayes" without his permission. Stern assumes that Spenser actually published something of Harvey's, but Josephine Waters Bennett correctly treats this event as Harvey's "daydream" (Bennett 1931, 172). Parts of these private letters were reworked and included in *Three familiar Letters* (Harvey and Spenser 1580), suggesting that the latter should be interpreted more as fictional creations of Harvey than as documents authorized by Spenser.

Contemporary accounts of Harvey and of Spenser's connections with the Leicester circle invariably caricature Harvey, and they suggest his uncomfortable reaction to his younger friend's success. The most significant of these occurs long before the publication of *The Faerie Queene* or Harvey's ill-advised exchanges with Thomas Nashe. On 6 February 1581 Harvey was satirized in the Cambridge play *Pedantius* as a schoolmaster whose rhetorical pronouncements are borrowed from Harvey's writings and whose vanity makes him highly vulnerable (*Pedantius* 1963, viii-xi). As G.C. Moore Smith points out, the audience would have identified Spenser as Leonidas, the student whose high favor with a nobleman wins Pedantius preferment (xlv). The nobleman shows some initial interest in Pedantius as a client but later sends him away. Pedantius is left in such a precarious financial position that he may have to sell his fabulous library.

More than a decade after Spenser's preferment, Nashe revived the story of Harvey's discomfiture, mocking him as a "would be" courtier who was found to be unworthy of favor. He pictures Harvey as an overdressed fop with "a paire of moustachies like a black horse tayle tyde vp in a knot, with two tuffts sticking out on each side" and offers details of his rejection: "He that most patronizd him, prying more searchingly into him, and finding that he was more meete to make sport with than anie way deeply to be employd, with faire words shooke him of, and told him he was fitter for the Universitie than for the court or his turne" (Nashe ed. 1958, 3:79). Nashe's ridicule is rendered poignant by Harvey's response in *Foure Letters*. After extensive self-promotion—including claims that Spenser and Bodin have compared him with Homer—Harvey concludes with a sonnet, which he attributes to Spenser, that praises him for never fawning "for favour of the great" and celebrates him as "a great Lord of peerelesse liberty" concerned with "Honours seat" (Harvey ed. 1966, 100-102). Nashe accused Harvey of having written this sonnet himself, a not unlikely possibility, unless we are to imagine that Spenser was blind to the faults of a man whose enormous ego and frustrated ambitions had made him a figure of fun in Cambridge and then an object of ridicule in London.

Although Harvey's connections appear at first to have benefited Spenser, in time Harvey had nothing to equal his younger friend's Irish appointment. Unquestionably a preferment rather than a punishment, Spenser's secretaryship to Lord Grey assured his new or renewed access to a larger circle of courtiers, including Sir Edward Denny, Sir Walter Ralegh, Sir Humphrey Gilbert, and Fulke Greville, all of whom had received or would later receive knighthoods or titles for their service as soldiers or councilors. In a sonnet appended to *The Faerie Queene* (1590), Spenser acknowledges his debt to Lord Grey as the "Patrone of my Muses pupillage" and thanks him for his "large bountie" (ed. 1912, 412a).

Thus the light that Harvey's connections and failures cast on Spenser's successes is finally ambivalent, suggesting at once a relationship of similarity and one of contrast. Primarily, I have pursued the former, but in closing it is the latter that I would reemphasize. Despite a surprising lack of documentary evidence that Spenser actively courted preferment as persistently as did Harvey, Fenton, Bryskett, and numerous others, it has become a biographical article of faith that he was dedicated to self-promotion in his verse and that he was driven by ambition to find an appointment in the house of a courtier prominent at court. In this case, however, a lack of hard evidence should give us a moment's pause. As we are aware, Sidney, who had invested the lot of a soldier with chivalric grandeur, inveighed bitterly against the frivolous life of a courtier, and Spenser—albeit very possibly a Spenser chastened by experience—just as bitterly condemned the lot of a client who has to sue for favor (Nelson 1963, 12-13 15-16):

> Full little knowest thou that hast not tride,
> What hell it is, in suing long to bide:
> To loose good dayes, that might be better spent;
> To wast long nights in pensive discontent;
> . . . .
> To fawne, to crowche, to waite, to ride, to ronne,
> To spend, to give, to want, to be undonne.
> (*Mother Hubberds Tale*, 895-98, 905-6)

Ironically, Spenser's scruples about self-promotion, whether early or late in coming, may have increased the difficulty we have in appreciating just how truly impressive his preferment as Grey's secretary was. While it is conceivable that he was not averse to a system that required him "to fawne" or "to crowche," his conjectured but undocumented efforts to gain favor have been deduced or elaborated from dedications and poetic images that have as much to do with conventions as with personal feeling. An alternative view of Spenser ought now to be considered. He may have been successful in winning preferment precisely because his values were not so very different from those of Sidney, who took seriously the view that a courtier should have "all his minde on honour fixed." That he, like Sidney, died before the end of the Golden Age may have ensured that he remained caught up in an idealism regarding individual dignity that later seemed old-fashioned.

Spenser and Court Humanism

F. J. LEVY

a man endewed with good knowledge in learninge and not
unskillfull or without experience in the service of the warres.
Privy Council recommending Spenser as sheriff of Cork
(Acts of the Privy Council, 1598-99, 205)

Half a dozen years after he settled in Dublin, Spenser addressed a sonnet
to Gabriel Harvey, envying the happiness of his old friend

> that, sitting like a looker-on
> Of this worldes stage, doest note, with critique pen,
> The sharpe dislikes of each condition. (ed. 1912, 603a)

Coming as it did just as Harvey's high hopes for office were suffering their
greatest disappointment, Spenser's lines praising a life spent in contemplative criticism of the *vita activa* have a certain irony, which charity would
make us suppose accidental. Nor is it impossible that the poem more clearly
addresses Spenser's own concerns in trying to combine a career as poet
with one as an official in queen Elizabeth's Irish "civil service." Harvey, we
know, did not view his relegation to the status of an observer with equa-
nimity, let alone happiness; and there is no reason to believe that Spenser,
despite his evident pretensions to a laureate status, would at this date have
looked on enforced retirement any more enthusiastically. The two men,
indeed, had much in common in their education and their ambitions, and
this commonality, which they shared with many others of their generation, will be the subject of my essay.

The danger in this proceeding, I admit, is that of losing Spenser's individuality in a mass of detail relating to his contemporaries and, perhaps
worse, of reducing Spenser's poetry to no more than the product of his
biographical particularity. The countervailing advantage, I would argue, is
that it will permit us to make sense of Spenser's career—and especially its
Irish component—by seeing it in terms of other men similarly placed,

without necessarily putting us in the position of forcing his career into a pattern so predetermined and so consistent that common sense rebels.

Beginning a study of Spenser's career with a look at the peculiarly English version of Italian civic humanism in its late, courtly phase has the advantage of allowing us to examine the underlying ideology of the whole generation of which Spenser was part. That will link Spenser to Philip Sidney and Fulke Greville, Gabriel Harvey and Lodowick Bryskett. But while Spenser and Sidney metaphorically shared the same school bench, they shared little else. It seems to me unwise to assume that Spenser, born of a none-too-wealthy London mercantile family, was in any position to have the same ambitions as his nobly born friend, still less to achieve them. A Sidney or a Greville did not depend on poetry to make a career; more critically, neither man depended on royal patronage for his livelihood, though the queen's favor was, of course, necessary for political and economic advancement. Philip Sidney could take an ideological stand—for example, against the queen's French marriage—with no more serious consequences than a temporary rustication to his sister's house at Wilton; Fulke Greville could seek to fight in the wars in France without permission and be denied access for a time; Francis Bacon and Walter Ralegh transgressed even more seriously and so suffered more heavily still. In all these cases, and others like them, promising careers came to a sudden (if usually temporary) halt. The fact remains, however, that none of these men (not even Ralegh) began at the bottom of the socioeconomic ladder; that is, none depended absolutely on royal or noble patronage. Others, like Harvey and Bryskett, were not so fortunate, and it is their careers we should examine in parallel with Spenser's. For them, assuming an ideological stance, even if it was the same as that of their patrons, could be an expensive luxury, and a single error could end a career abruptly and permanently.[1] In addition, the matter of timing is crucial: the opportunities available to the generation of William Cecil, Thomas Smith, and Thomas Wilson had been closed off for their successors, Sidney, Spenser, and their cohort; at the same time, however, this second generation had not yet despaired so greatly as altogether to have abandoned hope and attacked the system itself, a phenomenon exemplified in the Parnassus plays and the classical satire of the 1590s.[2]

Spenser was born early enough still to have hope set before him. His schoolmaster, Richard Mulcaster, stated that "the common weall is the measur of everie mans being" and from that premise argued that anyone able to serve his country was duty-bound to do so. Indeed, he went so far as to insist that "such as live to themselves either for pleasur in their studie, or to avoid foren truble do turn their learning to a private ease, which is the privat abuse of a publik good."[3] Not every Elizabethan educationalist put matters quite so starkly, but because the statement derives from Cicero's *De Officiis*, perhaps the most commonly read Elizabethan textbook, most of Spenser's contemporaries would have been exposed to the sentiment. Indeed Mulcaster, in his accustomed way, expanded on his text and made much of the duty of rulers to provide right education for their subjects, for from these would come the realm's future magistrates as well as those trained to obey them. Like many Elizabethans, he feared the "aspiring wit, which wilbe still a mounting," and found its opposite in an Aristotelian mediocrity, which he defined as the true end of education. Such a man would "bear with all companies in most varietie of behavior, to yeild himself to them in honestie of delite, contrarying none, contemning none, never bragging of his birth, never vanting of his welth."[4] A gentleman of this sort— for this student plainly had both birth and wealth—would, in the end, be a candidate for public office. Possessed of honest disposition and having been taught moral virtue, the young man would enter "civill societie even for honesties sake, without hope of anie profit" (1582, 17). In addition to these qualities of good birth and good breeding, the future courtier also required a kind of political discernment, proof against pressures internal and external. This point was of such great importance that Mulcaster elaborated upon it, defining his wise councilor as one "whose learning is learned pollicie," not policy defined as political deceit

> but as we terme it in learning and philosophie, the generall skill to judge either of all, or of most thinges rightly, and to marshall them to their places, and strait them by circumstance, as shall best beseeme the present government, with least disturbance, and most contentment to the setled state, of what sorte soever the thinges be, divine or humaine, publike or private, professions of minde, or occupations of hande. (Ed. 1888, 202)

To that end, the student and intending public servant had to understand, and learn to master, the idiosyncrasies of circumstance, that is, the way the world worked—perhaps even in the Ireland of the 1580s and 1590s.

Fortunately, the Ciceronian ideal of the orator on which all this was based was broadly defined and not limited to the arts of rhetoric and a knowledge of the laws. Cicero's orator had to be ready to discuss almost any subject and to do so had to read the poets and historians, indeed study and peruse the masters and authors in every excellent art.[5] Most of all, he had to master moral philosophy. All this carried over to the Elizabethan grammar schools and, to a lesser extent, the universities where, however, logic and theology still dominated formal academic life. Increasingly, however, the universities were filling up with young men who had no intention of becoming theologians and who took all too seriously the potential for government employment latent in the theorizing of men like Mulcaster. It was against these young students that Gabriel Harvey directed his half-serious diatribe, complaining that Aristotle now lay shut away, replaced by Castiglione's *Courtier* and other treatises of courtly behavior, together with books on history and military strategy. "You can not stepp into a schollars studye but (ten to on) you shall litely finde open ether Bodin de Republica or Le Royes Exposition uppon Aristotles Politiques or sum other like Frenche or Italian Politique Discourses."[6] Among them were the works of Machiavelli, now as familiar as the books of logic had once been. The general learning Cicero had considered appropriate for an orator had been transformed into a prerequisite for advancement in the hierarchy of Elizabethan civil society.

What had occurred, then, was that Mulcaster, Ascham, and others of the Elizabethan educators had created and propagated a myth of social mobility, of a career open to talents, with "learning" as the ladder by which the heights might be attained. In effect, the norm they established resolved the old debate of whether the active or the contemplative life were preferable by combining the two, though in such a way as to give the active life priority. According to this paradigm, the exemplification of the model citizen might be found in Sir Thomas Smith, a poor boy who became professor of civil law at Cambridge, then—propelled by an astonishing breadth of learning—moved from the university to the court, ending as ambassador to France and principal secretary. Smith's career began when patrons recognized his promise and sent him to the university; and Smith repaid them by doing something similar for Gabriel Harvey. Harvey, in his turn, seems constantly to have kept the image of Smith's success before him, and there is no reason to doubt that Harvey's own students, including Spenser, did the same.[7] Lodowick Bryskett's *Discourse of Civill Life*, a dialogue ostensibly set in Dublin in the early 1580s, exhibits the same basic cast of mind. Why, Bryskett's friends demanded of him, should a man retire early from an apparently successful career? Such an action made no sense. Instead, they insisted, Bryskett

> should rather seeke to be employed, and to advance himselfe in credit and reputation, then to hide his talent, and withdraw himselfe from action, in which the chiefe commendation of vertue doth consist. . . . A man of your sort, bred and trained . . . in learning, and that hath thereto added the experience and knowledge [of travel], . . . ought rather to seeke to employ his ability and sufficiency in the service of his Prince and country, then apply them to his peculiar benefit or contentment.[8]

Bryskett indeed had the utmost difficulty in providing a satisfactory answer and was reduced at last to defending his retirement first on personal
grounds, then by arguing that he planned to abandon only one of his several posts. Meanwhile, he suggested to the friends visiting him in his con-
tented country quiet that they might continue their version of a Ciceronian
dialogue and discuss the making of a model civil servant, at the center of
whose education was the study of moral philosophy. Their project, he assured them, would be much advanced if they could get Edmund Spenser,
seated among them, to read aloud some parts of his new poem, whose aim
was precisely the exemplification of the appropriate virtues.

Interestingly, the group Bryskett had assembled for his country-house
party included four military men, captains of companies sent to keep order in Ireland. These men were by no means upstarts but were, instead,
scions of the gentry, in some cases with court connection and—like Bryskett
and Spenser—eager to carve out careers and estates for themselves in Ireland. Nor were they necessarily unenlightened bluff hearties, younger sons
sent with inadequate educations to make their way in a rough-and-tumble
world. On the contrary, they were often men of broad reading. This should
occasion no suprise, for the theorists of courtesy, like Castiglione, had insisted that the courtier's primary role was military, and the careers of men
like Sir Walter Ralegh (and, to a lesser extent, George Gascoigne) demon-
strate that the model was followed in England as well as in Italy. Edward
Denny, though not present at Bryskett's putative gathering, nevertheless
supplies a good example of the breed. A friend of Philip Sidney and George
Gascoigne, Denny came to Ireland as a captain and was preferred to lord
Gray at much the same time that Spenser became the lord deputy's secretary; there is some evidence that the two men knew each other.[9] Like Sidney,
Denny lacked employment suitable for his station—his father had been a
Henrician privy councilor, and he was related to Ralegh, Humphrey Gilbert, Sir Francis Walsingham, and (through Walsingham) to Sidney himself—and so had asked his learned friend for advice on activities appropriate for his enforced leisure. Sidney did his best to oblige, keeping in mind
that all knowledge could not be his province and that a reading list for a
serving soldier was very different from one for a schoolboy. Scripture and
moral philosophy (as represented by Cicero's *De Officiis*) obviously led the
way, but most of Sidney's letter consists of a discussion of books appropriate "in the trade of our lives" (Osborn 1972, 539). Machiavelli's *Art of War*
(among others) was essential for the study of the military art, together
with a knowledge of arithmetic; history was necessary to evaluate the re-

sults of military actions, and Sidney provided a long list of classical historians, some Latin writers of the early part of the century, and Holinshed's chronicle, along with Froissart, Comines, and Guicciardini. Whether Denny had the time or the resources to pursue such a course of reading remains unknown; but Gabriel Harvey had taught him how to read such books only a few years before, and his friendship with Sidney surely provided an incentive (Jardine and Grafton 1990, 38). Castiglione's soldier-courtier was thus by no means an impossibility, and Bryskett's inclusion of four such in his dialogue suggests that Ireland provided a fair field for them.

Nevertheless, despite his position with lord Grey, Spenser was not on a plane of equality with men like Denny or Bryskett's four friends. If bearing arms was an integral part of the proper courtier's role, how was the poet to qualify? The potentially very lucrative post of captain was difficult to acquire without a great deal of powerful patronage. The most that Spenser could do in these circumstances was to follow his superiors onto the battlefield, with the result that he was almost certainly present at the Smerwick massacre and a number of lord Grey's other engagements.[10] None of this was quite enough to give Spenser a reputation as a serving soldier, but the demonstration of a knowledge of military matters might act as a supplement.[11] Contemporaries were fond of quoting the example of Lucius Lucullus, the Roman who became a successful soldier through precisely the type of study that Sidney had recommended to Denny; and Spenser's "model," Sir Thomas Smith, also showed his military knowledge in his tracts justifying and advertising his Irish plantation, in details that Spenser ultimately borrowed and put to use in the *View* (on all this, Jardine 1990 and 1993). The sum was enough to justify the Privy Council's recommendation quoted in my epigraph.

Yet, while trailing Denny and other captains of like social status, Spenser did remain firmly attached to the ruling elite. By contrast, Mr. Smith, apothecary of Dublin, who was present at Bryskett's country retreat on the first day to prescribe for his host, disappeared thereafter because his business was so different that he "was not so desirous to spend his time in hearing discourses of that nature, which brought no profit to his shop" (Bryskett 1606, 92). A tradesman excluded himself from discussions of "what maner of life a gentleman is to undertake and propose to himselfe, to attaine that end in this world, which among wisemen hath bene, and is accounted the best" (31). A man of learning, on the other hand, might well be the pivot around which the three days' entertainment revolved, and Spenser's reputation as a learned poet had been trumpeted from the beginning of his career.

Embedded in the notes to the "November" eclogue of *The Shepheardes Calender* is a reference to Spenser's poetic predecessor, George Gascoigne, as one who might have equaled the ancient poets had he not "some partes of learning wanted."[12] The very form of *The Shepheardes Calender* was designed to prove that any such deficiency had been remedied in its author. Fully equipped with a long letter to Gabriel Harvey, an introduction, and erudite (if not altogether accurate) glosses, all by the poet's mysterious friend E. K., the book announced itself as a classic, for such treatment was usually reserved for the works of the ancient poets.[13] Moreover, whether or not E. K.'s rather pedantic commentary had an ironic tinge, it pointed very clearly to the fact that the poet's learning was so great as to need interpretation. Nor did the new poet lack ambition. E. K. noted that his anonymous author, by beginning his poetic career with pastoral, was deliberately following in Virgil's footsteps and thus was setting himself in competition not only with the ancients but with moderns like Petrarch, Mantuanus, Marot, and Sannazaro as well. The comparison with Virgil not only referred to the poetry but also laid claim to Virgil's reputation for great learning. Sir Kenelm Digby, a generation later, stated that Spenser's "knowledge in profound learning both divine and humane appeareth to me without controversie the greatest that any POET before him ever had, Excepting VIRGIL," adding that this knowledge was in no way superficial but involved "a solide and deepe insight in THEOLOGIE, PHILOSOPHY (especially the PLATONIKE) and the MATHEMATICALL sciences." Moreover, Digby continued, in his treatment of moral and political learning, the poet showed that "he had a most excellently composed head to observe and governe mens actions."[14] This goes well beyond the standard topoi of the poet as prophet or as sweet teacher of moral philosophy (though these are by no means excluded) and adds to them Cicero's vision of the orator, able to discourse intelligently on a variety of topics, including "the size of the sun and the contour of the earth; and after undertaking this duty he will not be able to refuse to handle mathematics or the cult of the Muses" (*De Oratore*, ed. 1959, 1:247).

Clearly, the incessant claims to learning so often found in commendatory sonnets, and attached more firmly to Spenser than to any other English poet but Milton, are intended to validate the status of *poet*, as against that of rhymer or versifier.[15] Nevertheless, we may make a further distinction between the ordinary learning attained by the mere poet and the extraordinary learning pertaining to the potential laureate. The point had been demonstrated two centuries earlier by Petrarch, when he insisted on having his election as poet laureate validated by a preliminary examination conducted by King Robert of Naples, himself notable as the most learned monarch in Europe. Poetic learning, however, needed cultivation in order to flourish, and behind Petrarch's drama of laureation lay a tradition of patronage associated with Caesar Augustus and Maecenas, and with their dependents, Virgil and Horace. Spenser had argued that

> the Romish *Tityrus*, I heare,
> Through his *Mecoenas* left his Oaten reede . . .
> And eft did sing of warres and deadly drede,

meaning that Virgil's progress from pastoral poetry to epic had been fueled by his patron's largesse (*Shepheardes Calender,* "October" 55-56, 59). Somewhat later, Spenser added to the patron's functions that he save his client from "the malice of evill mouthes, which are alwaies wide open to carpe at and misconstrue my simple meaning" (*Colin Clouts Come Home Againe,* introductory letter to Ralegh in ed. 1912, 536). But the patron's duties did not end there. Most important, he provided the poet with access to political power. If we may believe Horace's satire, so often quoted by the Elizabethans, the poet was much envied precisely because Maecenas's door was always open to him—as that of Augustus was to Maecenas. Lacking epic, however, Horace never reached the poetic heights, and thus penetrated no farther than the anterooms to power. The inner sanctum was reserved for the ruler—and the laureate. In Ben Jonson's vision of the relationship, Augustus readily ceded part of his glory to the poet, exclaiming as he rose to greet him,

> Welcome to Caesar, Virgil. Caesar, and Virgil
> Shall differ but in sound; to Caesar, Virgil,
> (Of his expressed greatness) shall be made
> A second sur-name, and to Virgil, Caesar.[16]

And at the conclusion of *Poetaster,* emperor and poet together pass judgment on the offenders.

Jonson, then, shared the view of most of his contemporaries when he declared that "the *Poet* is the neerest Borderer upon the Orator, and expresseth all his vertues" (*Timber,* in ed. 1925-52, 8:640), and might well have acceded to Cicero's exaggerated encomium of the power of oratory as that which makes men superior to the animals, strong enough "to gather scattered humanity into one place, or to lead it out of its brutish existence in the wilderness up to our present condition of civilization," then able to give this newly established society the laws, tribunals, and civic rights permitting it to survive (ed. 1959, 1:25). All this, however, is to assume a society of active men, one in which arms and learning march together, each bolstering the other.

Spenser's argument in the "October" eclogue is not far different. Like Jonson, he answers the question of poesy's proper place by declaring "Princes pallace the most fitt" (81), though that leaves the further question of how poesy might enter into its proper room. Such an advancement, however, is hindered by the absence of a suitable subject for epic, and of a poet capable of finding and exploiting it. Cuddie and Piers, the eclogue's two speakers, have given up, leaving the coast clear for Colin. To accomplish his aim, Colin needs an intermediary, a Maecenas indeed, but more than a Maecenas. A patron could open the doors to Elisa's court, and Elisa herself would serve brilliantly as the jewel at the epic's center. What was still needed, however, was a way of setting her in motion, as Virgil had Aeneas. Aeneas, for Virgil, served as a parallel to Augustus, the founding of Rome to the establishment of the Roman Empire. For Spenser, too, the ideal epic celebrated heroic action—in his view, the destruction of the Antichrist. As the queen could not lead the forces herself, she required a surrogate. Leicester, "the worthy whome shee loveth best," might have been able to wield "the stubborne stroke of stronger stounds [blows]" had he been turned free (47-49). Instead, with the deaths of Leicester and Walsingham, the cautious Burghley prevailed, who "now broad spreading like an aged tree, / Lets none shoot up, that nigh him planted bee." The result was that "learning lies unregarded, / And men of armes doo wander unrewarded" (*Ruines of Time*, 452-53, 440-41). In other words, in so arid a climate neither of the two components traditionally making up the perfect courtier could survive.

Let me restate the argument to this point. The education Spenser and others like him received at the grammar schools and universities predisposed them to seek an active life of service to the common weal. In terms of the particular situation of late sixteenth-century England, that meant service to the queen and, most commonly, a post in the queen's service. Unfortunately, by the time Spenser sought public office, such posts were becoming increasingly difficult to find. Those of his contemporaries with standing and wealth could at least choose among a number of options, including the military (if the queen permitted), though Sidney's and Greville's failure to achieve high office suggests that even their relative freedom of choice may have been somewhat illusory. Still, in Richard Helgerson's terms, these men remained "amateurs," resorting to poetry when employment failed and, frequently, as a way to regain employment. In any case, Spenser was born without such advantages. He had no Wilton to which he might retire; still less could he afford to live at court for years without recompense. For Spenser, the only way to break through the barrier of his lowly birth and achieve a place near the sovereign was to flaunt his learning. He did so in good humanist style by turning to the ancients for a model and found him in Virgil, the *doctus poeta* seated at the right hand of the emperor Augustus through the agency of Maecenas. The Virgil of the Renaissance was himself a construct, made up of the ancients' ideas of the poet, moral philosopher, and orator, and owing rather more to Cicero than to Virgil himself, but Petrarch, Spenser, and Jonson all accepted the *idea* of the Virgilian poet, of the man who marked himself as fit for public office by demonstrating his ability to follow Virgil's poetic trajectory and by echoing his learning. Petrarch had parlayed his learning and his laureateship into a post at the court of the Visconti. Spenser was no different; he too might—in Sir Kenelm Digby's words—"have bin eminent in the active part that way, if his owne choice or fortune had given him employment in the common wealth" (*Spenser: The Critical Heritage* 1971, 150).

The particular opportunities sought by Spenser, those near the center of power, never came to him, though he did receive advancement. A brief spell as secretary to the Bishop of Rochester—Gabriel Harvey's old friend, John Young—led to an appointment, again perhaps as a secretary, in the household of the earl of Leicester, where Spenser made the acquaintance of Philip Sidney.[17] The connection with the Leicester-Sidney faction might have opened the door to court employment but, unfortunately, it frequently had precisely the opposite effect. Sidney's opposition to the queen's projected marriage with Alençon had derailed his career, to the extent that it never really recovered. The fact that Spenser shared Sidney's religious views, and followed the Leicester faction in its insistence on England's duty to intervene in favor of fellow Protestants abroad, would merely have raised the queen's suspicions.[18] As both Sidney and Francis Bacon found, Elizabeth punished opposition by refusing promotion or even—in extreme cases—access to the royal person (see Levy 1972b and 1986). What Sidney could not get for himself he was unlikely to get for his adherents, least of all those who had no personal claims on the queen's attention. The rules of Elizabethan factional politics indicated that patronage now had to move down one level, away from the court, to offices in the direct control (or under the influence) of the Leicester group. Ireland, where Sir Henry Sidney had been lord deputy, offered opportunities for such patronage, and it was probably through his influence that Spenser found himself in Dublin in the train of the new lord deputy, Lord Grey de Wilton. Once in Ireland, Spenser was politically largely on his own for, unlike his older colleague,

Lodowick Bryskett, who kept open a personal line of communication with Sir Francis Walsingham, the queen's principal secretary, Spenser had no one on whom he could call directly. So, as he involved himself increasingly in Irish politics—and he had no choice but to do so—his knowledge of the details of English factional politics declined.

Spenser's relations with Ralegh provide a good example. Probably the two men met at Smerwick, with Spenser observing a massacre Ralegh helped conduct; however, as Ralegh began his career within the Leicester grouping, it is at least possible that an earlier meeting occurred in London. Their views on Protestant (that is, anti-Spanish) foreign policy largely coincided. There is then nothing inherently improbable in the story that Ralegh came to visit Spenser at the latter's recently acquired Kilcolman Castle, or even in Spenser's own lightly romanticized story of the two poets exchanging verses. Spenser's observation that Ralegh's poem largely concerned himself adds a touch of verisimilitude to the tale. Nor, again, is there any reason to question the statement that Ralegh persuaded Spenser to leave Ireland and try his luck once more at the English court, this time under Ralegh's patronage. What is striking in all this, however, is the extent to which both men overstated Ralegh's influence at court. As a personal favorite of the queen, Ralegh belonged to no court faction; indeed, he was disliked and distrusted by the faction leaders, who did everything they could to undermine his influence. Ralegh could no doubt get his friend an audience at court and so perhaps helped set up the scene wherein the poet read selections from the first three books of *The Faerie Queene* to his monarch, the aftermath of which was a royal pension. Spenser repaid his friend severalfold, not least through his defense of Ralegh's unfortunate marriage in the Timias episodes of *The Faerie Queene,* but the likely result of that loyalty was for the queen's continuing anger against Ralegh to spill over onto Spenser. At the same time, Spenser was already making overtures to the earl of Essex. Ideology no doubt played a part in this: Essex's great appeal was as the political heir of Leicester and Sidney, and to that extent he shared with Ralegh a strong anti-Spanish, anti-Catholic bent.[19] The two men might well have become allies had not Essex been overcome with a long-standing, personal hatred of Ralegh as an upstart competitor, of which Spenser seems unaware. Moreover, Essex too had difficulty in placing his allies, and Spenser never understood the political system at court well enough to manipulate it—a view confirmed by his constant attacks on lord Burghley, the most effective of all founts of patronage.[20] In short, Spenser imitated Sidney and Greville's ideological stance in his approach to the politics of patronage at Elizabeth's court, though without their resources. To advance further in England, Spenser would—like Greville—have had to learn to compromise, to accept that "it was sufficient for the plant to grow where his sovereign's hand had placed it" (Greville 1986, 89).

Spenser's own experiences go some way toward explaining his dyspeptic view of the English court, a view that persisted from almost the beginning of his poetic career.[21] *The Shepheardes Calender* took full advantage of the possibilities for criticism inherent in the pastoral mode—and, typically, praised Archbishop Grindal and others of the left wing of the English church just as the queen was reining them in most harshly. The anti-court stance of *Mother Hubberds Tale* was still clearer. Though not published until 1591, the poem was probably written at least a decade earlier and may well reflect the disappointment occasioned by the events surrounding the queen's proposed French marriage, as well as the failure of Grindal's efforts to reform the church. The moral center of the poem is a passage of seventy-five lines (717-93) describing the good courtier—who, apart from this description, is singularly absent—in terms with which we are already familiar. Such a paragon is marked by his incessant activity, first banishing idleness by practicing "knightly feates" in tournaments and on the field of battle, then refreshing himself with the Muses, "Delights of life, and ornaments of light," then studying the customs and histories of foreign lands, all to the end of spending his days in the service of his prince,

> Not so much for to gaine, or for to raise
> Himselfe to high degree, as for his grace,
> And in his liking to winne worthie place;
> Through due deserts and comely carriage.

Such a courtier, despite Spenser's insistence on his honesty and lack of guile, nevertheless "is practiz'd well in policie, / And thereto doth his Courting most applie," using his knowledge to interpret the "fine falshood and faire guile" of foreign powers and their English allies. Unlike lesser men, this "brave Courtier" remains steady in his honor, unmoved by "the common winde / Of courts inconstant mutabilitie" (*Mother Hubberds Tale*, 738, 762, 774-77, 783-84, 788, 717, 722-23). Nevertheless, the inability to discern the honest from the false, together with the mutability that inevitably ensues, marks the court of Spenser's poem. While the Lion sleeps, the Fox and the Ape have it all their own way. The ruler, whose duty it is to protect the realm from religious and political fraud, has failed, not least by a refusal to make use of the good courtiers who wish to serve. While the basic point of the poem is clear enough, the meaning of the details remains fuzzy. Did Spenser have particular events in mind? Was there a one-to-one relationship between the beasts of his fable and certain of the courtiers thronging Elizabeth's court? In terms of Spenser's career it hardly matters. Surely it was unwise to publish a poem in which many men would identify the Fox with Burghley, with the consequence that the sleeping Lion had perforce to represent the queen.[22] I suspect that Spenser intended no more than a warning, a prediction of what might happen if the monarch dozed. In any event, the poem was called in, not to reappear until well into the seventeenth century.

If the usual dating for *Mother Hubberds Tale* is accepted, the poem reflects Spenser's growing disillusionment with the court in England, and its publication in 1591 is an indication that he was turning more and more toward Ireland as the chosen field for his endeavors.[23] Bryskett's dialogue suggests that the Englishmen resident in Ireland had gone some way toward generating their own version of the literate culture of the home country. Admittedly, that culture was one of exiles, separate from that of the native Gaelic speakers, and separate as well from the Anglo-Irish, Catholic culture represented by men like Richard Stanyhurst.[24] Moreover, the men represented in Bryskett's book, soldiers, bureaucrats, and churchmen, however literate they might be, were rarely more than transient in Ireland. Whatever we may think of it, the Munster Plantation, with its large grants for those willing to invest their time and money, encouraged permanence. The result was that Spenser's colleagues on the Munster Council for a time included Sir Thomas Norris, who had been one of those present at Bryskett's dialogue, as well as Sir William Herbert and Richard Beacon, men of wide reading, both of whom wrote major books offering their solutions to the Irish crisis, and Hugh Cuffe, who may have been the author of a policy study remaining in manuscript.[25] Sir Edward Denny was also a major landholder and sheriff of Kerry in 1589, though he returned to England soon after. These men constituted a "humanist" circle, in the sense that all were products of the same system of classical education and, beyond that, shared interests in recent history and political theory. And, while there is no evidence that he read *The Faerie Queene* to them, we may nevertheless imagine Spenser and his neighbors talking about colonialism and its effects, for the poet plainly did have some knowledge of their views on how to solve the Irish problem.

English humanist education, with its emphasis on service to the common weal, again provides the key to understanding this community and its thinking. Cicero's orator, the model on whom the system was based, was seen as able to lead mankind "out of its brutish existence in the wilderness up to our present condition of civilization," and though in the context of Cicero's text this was considered to be something of an exaggeration, the idea in its full glory was accepted by Renaissance thinkers, in England and elsewhere. The Romans had seen their mission in terms of civilizing their world as well as conquering it, and this involved stamping out the "barbarism" on its periphery, by the force of Roman arms and the Latin language. In England, Mulcaster, defending his own vernacular, explicitly argued in favor of replacing Latin with English as a language of conquest (1582, 253-54; Moryson 1903, 213, elaborates the idea). More practically, Sir Thomas Smith (whom Gabriel Harvey established as the model of the English court humanist) had proposed a plan for conquering Ireland by way of a system of *coloniae* in the Roman style, by which he meant establishing fortified centers of permanent English settlers, army veterans among them, to hold the Irish countryside and eventually "civilize" it by a combination of force and social pressure.[26] Bryskett had something similar in mind when he told his friends he was about to retire to his holding in Wexford where, protected by a small garrison, he would test if "the lyfe of a borderer in this land be a lyke perillous unto all men, and to see if a just and honest simple lyfe, may not even among the most Barbarous people of the world breede securitie to him that shall live nere them or emong them" (Plomer and Cross 1927, 32). Spenser saw his position in Munster much the same way and shared with Bryskett the view that the native Irish were barbarians needing reform.[27]

The agents of reform were to be the men of arms and the men of learning, Castiglione's courtiers placed in a new setting, and clearly Spenser saw himself in this light. Perched in Kilcolman Castle, with more than 3,000 acres of his own lands spread around him, Spenser was able to project for himself a role in the permanent civilizing of the Irish. He would be an "Orpheus, who with his sweete harpe and wholesome precepts of Poetry laboured to reduce the rude and barbarous people from living in woods, to dwell Civilly in Townes and Cittyes, and from wilde ryott to moral Conversation," replacing (if need be, with the help of armed might) the bards of the wild Irish, whose songs had been used "to allure the hearers, not to the love of religion and Civill manners, but to outrages Robberies living as outlawes, and Contempt of the Magistrates and the kings lawes" (Moryson 1903, 199). *The Faerie Queene,* "the fruit of barren field," was an installment of that humanist debt repaid.

When Ralegh, in 1589, prevailed on Spenser to try his fortune in England once more, he disrupted a way of life with which the poet had apparently come to terms, intellectually and socially. Like so many others, Spenser had interpreted the court humanist ethos to fit his current situation; that is, he could justify his position as an Englishman in Irish society, and as a social *arriviste* suddenly become lord of the manor, by reference to his service to the commonwealth, a service originally defined in terms of his learning. *The Faerie Queene* was a manifestation of such learning, obviously of universal applicability but also of direct use in Ireland, where rhymers preaching licentious and civil disorder had to be replaced by poets of a more classical moral philosophy. Spenser's approach to England was thus by no means unambiguous. When the Shepherd of the Ocean first approached Colin and the two sang and played their pipes for each other, Spenser told the tale of Bregog's love for Mulla, that is, he allegorized and idealized the country around Kilcolman, while Ralegh's song dealt with the loss of Cynthia's favor.[28] In a sense, the terms of the argument were already set. Nevertheless, Ralegh was able to play on Spenser's feelings of exile, of being "quite forgot" at court, and he could dangle tales of the queen's peace and bounty before the poet's eyes. Yet Colin's first view of England is of "Faire goodly fields, then which *Armulla* yields / None fairer," and it is only after a good deal of prodding that Colin praises England as superior (*Colin Clout*, 278-79). Even then, England's advantages are those of safety, for here there is "No griesly famine, nor no raging sweard, / No nightly bodrags, nor no hue and cries" (314-15). The shepherds may rest quietly, singing their songs. Yet, despite the presence of sound religion and good poetry, despite even the glorious Cynthia, Colin finds that men abuse the gifts God gave them. The court is full of guile, of "faire dissembling curtesie," a place where learning has been abandoned, "For arts of schoole have there small countenance, / Counted but toyes to busie ydle braines" (700, 704-5). Even the English shepherds do not love as honestly and as well as their Irish counterparts, and Colin returns to his Rosalind with something like relief.

It will not do to treat *Colin Clouts Come Home Againe* as pure autobiography: Colin is not Spenser, nor Spenser Colin, though the two plainly have much in common. Colin's disenchantment with patronage at court must be balanced by Spenser's receiving a royal pension of fifty pounds—not a large sum, perhaps, but nevertheless more than double his fee as clerk of the Council of Munster or his annual rental for Kilcolman. When Spenser was writing *Colin Clout*, in the early 1590s, before the troubles occasioned by Tyrone's revolt, Ireland may have seemed more promising than England. The poet had done well for himself there—better surely than others of his social position had done at home—and he still had high hopes that reform would bring to Ireland the peace he saw as England's chief advantage. Nevertheless, so much accommodation to the realities of English politics had a price. While Spenser's career might be deemed suc-

cessful by poets such as Daniel or Drayton, nevertheless he had not attained everything called for by the court humanism in which he had been
trained. The locus of his activities had been moved from the queen's court
to Ireland, the Virgilian laureate's role of advisor to princes altered to service in Munster. The air of disillusionment pervading *Colin Clout* should
come as no surprise, most especially as more and more of his younger
contemporaries came to share it.[29] By the late 1590s, the very name of
Castiglione was to become a term of insult.[30] None of this might have
mattered very much had Spenser been allowed to live out his years by the
banks of the Awbeg, his beloved Mulla. His personal tragedy was to be
thrown yet again into the court maelstrom he had so firmly rejected, this
time with Kilcolman Castle burning behind him, the apparently solid
achievements in Ireland dissolved into the smoke of rebellion.

Questionable Evidence in the
Letters of 1580 between Gabriel Harvey
and Edmund Spenser

JON A. QUITSLUND

Scholars interested in the private life of Spenser, in the public career that was the context for his pursuit of fame, and in the friendships and other dealings with people that help us to understand who Spenser was and what he thought at various points in his life, have few documents to work with. Under these circumstances, it is understandable that much has been made of the information contained in the exchange of letters between the poet and his friend Gabriel Harvey that was published in 1580, not long after the appearance of *The Shepheardes Calender*.[1] Like the apparatus enclosing Spenser's poems in the *Calender*, this pamphlet gathering five heterogeneous *Letters* contains several references to unpublished poems and the interests of a literary coterie, to current events and affairs of state, and to well-placed people in public life. The *Letters* testify to the credentials of the "new Poete" and his movement toward the "somewhat greater things" implicitly promised in *The Shepheardes Calender*, and they also show us, in the self-revelatory terms proper to the discourse of intimate friendship, glimpses of Spenser at an important juncture in his life: the end of the beginning of his double career as a poet and a public servant.

As soon as we recognize, however, that the *Letters* are public rather than private documents, we have placed their evidentiary value in doubt. The efforts to fashion a poetic persona that had motivated the *Calender*'s elaborate program are also evident in the *Letters*. Why should we expect these texts to provide trustworthy information about the private person Edmund Spenser, whose life and literary endeavors are only hypothetically related to the textual figures of Immerito and Colin Clout? We tend to think of the pen and its creations as dependent on moves made by a mind and hand enjoying an independent and individual life, but is the shape of that life ascertainable, either as a cause or an effect of writing, as it is represented in this text? In the move from autographic script to a printed text offered for sale, what authenticity is lost, and what other purchase on identity may be gained?

Perhaps the most important fact about Spenser, especially at this liminal stage of his life, is that his biography took shape in the public domain, through deliberate moves in which courtiership and service were combined with publishing in pursuit of an author's status. What he exhibited of his private life should be seen in this light—not in the glare associated with publicity in modern experience but in a twilight that renders authors hard to distinguish from the texts declaring their interests, and texts inseparable from the contexts of writerly conventions and public institutions. Another consideration to be stressed at the outset is that all efforts to separate Spenser's identity or character from Harvey's involve a mistaken view of the *Letters*, the intentions inscribed within them, and the cultural matrix they document for us. So my intention in this essay is not primarily to isolate facts about the Edmund Spenser who wrote certain letters in 1579 and 1580 but to articulate what can be found in and inferred from the *Letters* concerning their writers—chiefly but not entirely the young man who signs himself "Immerito."

The relationship of writer to writing may be compared to the black-and-white portions of the classic figure/ground problem, which can be read two ways: the two components and the images they create are interdependent yet sharply distinguished from one another. The same analogy can be taken further: Spenser and Harvey are similarly interdependent as close friends, correspondents, competitors for favor, collaborators with a jest to execute. To the extent that these *Proper, and wittie, familiar Letters* advanced Spenser's interests as a courtier and an author, he would wish to take credit for the writerly persona exhibited in them; but in his rhetorical culture, that would not mean accepting a literal reading as either proper or witty. When Immerito, "mox in Gallias navigaturi" ("about to set sail for France and Italy"), addresses a valedictory poem to G. H. (see Variorum *Prose Works*, 8 and 256; ed. 1912, 637), the itinerary he imagines describes ambitions—those of a poet and a would-be secretary to the earl of Leicester—rather than actual travel plans. Where expressions of friendship and love are concerned (and they concern Immerito much more than his friend), having seen how important love, courtship, and marriage are in Spenser's poetry, one is inclined to winnow the language of these familiar letters for what they can tell us of Spenser's private life. But anyone who regards the hyperbole, allusions, postures, and badinage of Immerito's intimacies as husks hiding kernels of true feeling or the facts of life will be disappointed; only the written words remain.

The text itself puts a distance between the men who wrote these letters and their textual personae. On the title page, the *Letters* are described as "lately passed betwene two Universitie men," and within them the names and personal identities of the writers are treated as meaningful only to those readers who already know by acquaintance who "Master G. H." and "Immerito" are. Jonathan Goldberg, extending the arguments of David Lee Miller and others, has shown how important anonymity was to the author of the *Calender* (1986, 38-67), as a basis for textual identities tenuously related to flesh-and-blood existence. As we shall see, in the *Letters* Spenser takes some pains to declare Harvey's interests and put his own name in Harvey's mouth; who the "two Universitie men" are eventually gains the status of an open secret. *The Shepheardes Calender* had already presented "the Author selfe" and Harvey as "very speciall and most familiar" friends;[2] here they are even more involved in each other's projects, each declaring ideals and ambitions in relation to the other. As we shall see, Spenser anticipates a breach in the correspondence, if not in the friendship itself, consequent upon his marriage and the career that took him to Ireland not long after the letters were published. Read together, these letters "lately passed betwene" Spenser and Harvey represent neither man individually but offer representations of enigmatic intentions shared and split between them, stretching from a somewhat pretentious but promising present into an imagined future, tenuously related to public life and publishing.

Calling into question the modern tendency to regard private experience as constitutive of individual identity, we ought to recognize that, in the Renaissance at least, to the extent that it was articulated at all privacy was largely a function of publicity. In Elizabethan England, only an interest in one's place in the public eye was apt to motivate someone in Spenser's or Harvey's position to lay claim to a private life, containing—in addition to domestic arrangements, which were treated as insignificant—secrets about which the public might be curious.[3] And even if we could reconstruct a full and circumstantial account of either man's privacy, it would be misleading to locate there the origin of either his authorial or his courtly ambitions. It would be more useful if we could reconstruct the dynamics of their relationship, difficult as that must be in our different world: we are just beginning to see how important "homosociality" was in the Renaissance, especially in the constitution of both intimacy and public culture in and around the universities and Inns of Court, aristocratic households, and the royal court.[4]

Our attention as biographers should be given first to the institutional and discursive matrix in which Spenser found himself. Individuality in the Renaissance was not an originary principle but a process and a product of communal culture and specific institutions, involving both willing and unwitting responses—sometimes typical, sometimes idiosyncratic—to meaning and value constituted outside the self. In *The Shepheardes Calender* and the *Letters*, everything is dialogical and intertextual, and to isolate an individual (to settle the identity of E. K., for example) would be to take a fish out of water.

With regard to privacy and secrecy, which were cultivated intensively and variously in the later years of the sixteenth century, it is no accident that those years, in which literature and other arts took a pronounced inward turn, also witnessed a flowering of courtly intrigue, intelligence, and secret diplomacy, proliferating in ways that still confound historians' attempts to account for events and opinions in and around Elizabeth's court (Archer 1993). What, then, do we know? We know less than earlier generations thought they did, largely because the inferences and conjectures that were meaningful in a more positivistic climate make less sense today. We trust received opinions less than the positivists did, and we are also suspicious of the "factual" evidence that has come down to us, perhaps because we doubt the integrity of those who left it behind them.

Reasons for uncertainty may be sought not only in our historical distance and the fragmentary nature of documentary evidence from the sixteenth century but in the designs and habits governing Elizabethan uses of language. It now appears that, when some public purpose was to be served, words were often used to insinuate, manipulate, or deceive, and not so much to fashion a self as to mask fundamental uncertainties about the speaker's or writer's place in a world full of change and variable opinions. Much is made in the *Letters* of the secrets and private lives that may in time be better understood, but the secrets withheld, the private lives we are invited to imagine beyond the nested fictions and indirections of Spenser's pretentious apprentice work, amount to an indeterminate potential, haunting the blank page where writing starts and the hallways where some patron may open the door to a brilliant career.

This essay explores the extent to which the *Letters* published in 1580 differ from anything we might find in manuscript form in Spenser's hand (or even in Harvey's, for whom margins, flyleaves, and odd sheets of paper were apt to serve as hallway mirrors for a man always preparing to do something other than writing). The *Letters* are valuable to a biographer interested in Spenser's frame of mind in the months immediately preceding his removal from London to Ireland as secretary to Arthur, Lord Grey.[5] They also offer some perspective, I believe, on the Edmounde Spenser whose marriage to Machabyas Chylde was recorded at St. Margaret's, Westminster, on 27 October 1579 (Judson 1945, 63; Mohl 1990, 670). They document the interest both Spenser and Harvey took in the earl of Leicester, Philip Sidney, and several of Sidney's associates. I have my doubts, however, about the factual value of references in the letters to several unpublished works, which are often listed by biographers and bibliographers as "lost."[6]

We should recognize in the design of these *Letters* an element of artifice and a sort of fiction uncontrolled by the idealizing rationale of Sidney's *Defence of Poesie*, with its somewhat forced distinction between "making" and "lying."[7] Both Spenser and Harvey anticipate in this text the "unredeemed rhetoric," the "antiworld . . . associated with worldliness, political manipulation, and sophisticated savoir-faire," which Jonathan Crewe has described in his study of Thomas Nashe's writings a decade later (1982, 22). Far from being "golden" in the sense developed by Sidney and celebrated by C. S. Lewis, the terms of this text are more like promises to pay that the writer has not yet signed. The incidental contents and the sequencing of these *Letters* establish a plot of the kind described by Lorna Hutson in her study of the reading habits assumed in Elizabethan prose fiction (1993): the "imaginative ground plot" in such a text may not be a narrative but some other mode of explanation, such as the display of a proper courtier's fitness for advancement. But if we cannot separate the biographical truth in this text from artful pretense, its unreliability is not without evidentiary value in an account of Spenser and Harvey as writers, eager to exhibit their mastery of writing as a *technē* and their understanding of printing as a powerful technology.[8]

For example, the "Welwiller of the two Authours," who serves readers and the authors as a go-between, tells his "Curteous Buyer" in a prefatory letter that he was fortunate to obtain his copies "at the fourthe or fifte hande." This friend (plausibly identified by Thomas Nashe as Harvey incognito)[9] has heard tell of many other letters by Harvey which he "would very gladly see in Writing, but more gladly in Printe" (*Prose Works*, 447-48; ed. 1912, 610). This bid for attention in the marketplace serves as a reminder that Spenser gained his status as a laureate author by means of printing, apparently with little recourse to the courtly traffic in manuscripts.[10] In general, Spenser's printed texts are fully authorized, free from the stigma attached to a book that is only tenuously related to the author's initiative. His contributions to the *Letters*, however, retain until the end the guise of anonymity that had distinguished Immerito in *The Shepheardes Calender;* their authority is thus derived from the earlier and more consequential book.

The anomalous character of the *Letters*[11] has lent credence to the assumption that Spenser was caught unawares in Harvey's awkward attempt to establish himself as not only an impressively learned man but a wit. Some modern readers have followed Thomas Nashe in doubting that Spenser himself wrote the letters attributed to Immerito, but this does Harvey an injustice and lets Spenser off too easily. Nashe's more agile and less scrupulous wit has cast a long shadow across Harvey's reputation and his friendship with Spenser, even though some scholarship on the Nashe/Harvey quarrel offers considerable sympathy to Harvey (Hibbard 1962, 187-97, 223-25; Crewe 1982, 3-4; Grafton and Jardine 1986, 184-96). The account of Immerito's role in *Strange Newes* (1592) is suggestive but untrustworthy: *"Signior Immerito* (so called, because *he was and is his friend* undeservedly) was counterfeitly brought in to play a part in that his Enterlude of Epistles that was hist at, thinking his very name (as the name of *Ned Allen* on the common stage) was able to make an ill matter good" (quoted in *Prose Works*, 484). The asymmetrical dichotomies Nashe employs to divide the (good) Spenser from the (ill) Harvey can be recognized as sophistry, plausible in 1592 but at odds with their reputations in 1580. Construing the "Enterlude of Epistles" as a more or less symmetrical partnership associates Spenser with a man much better established than Immerito was at that time. The praise and the blame earned by Immerito's part in this overingenious literary experiment should be attached to Spenser: the roleplaying in this text is consistent with his career-long fondness for "masking" his identity, and the anticipations of themes in his later poetry are too subtle to have been contrived by Harvey. In support of this argument for Spenser's involvement, which will be substantiated in what follows, we have the evidence of a copy of the *Letters* containing numerous corrections and alterations in Harvey's hand to his part of the correspondence.[12]

Every text creates a role, if not a repertoire, for its readers, to be assumed or resisted in accordance with their interests. Naive readers of the *Letters* will count themselves among those fortunate to gather intelligence from correspondence never meant for their eyes; the wiser sort will imagine that only the naive are being taken in. Harvey is especially prone to this crude manipulation of the audience that he pretends to exclude. His longest letter carries a "POSTSCRIPTE. This Letter may only be shewed to the two odde Gentlemen you wot of. Marry I would have those two to see it, as sone as you may conveniently" (*Prose Works*, 462; ed. 1912, 622b); the next letter carries a similar proviso (*Prose Works*, 477; ed. 1912, 632b). Appearing in a manuscript, these confidences would mean one thing; in such a text as this they are more devious and destabilizing. Conspicuous moves made to set up a "Curteous Buyer" are bound to provoke a resistant or suspicious reading, either the hostile response that Nashe offers or a more generous respect for the authors' fine inventions.

If the letters only occasionally reward a reading as documents with no strings attached, they may still be useful in a biographical inquiry as registers of the terms in which Harvey and Spenser sought to fashion themselves in print. And we are not, I think, merely settling for what is available in dwelling on the textual Spenser: we are attending to the remaining traces of his subjecthood, and also to the dialogical discourse that constituted, for Elizabethans, the sine qua non of a subjective life.[13] It seems likely that from the start the *Letters* were composed with publication in mind, in order to catch the eyes not only of readers interested in the vernacular literature that was emerging during the 1570s, but also of those in positions of authority who recognized the utility of university-trained eloquence and the value of men who could already claim to be well connected.

Before we take a closer look at some passages in the *Letters*, it will be useful to situate the text in its generic category. Considered singly and in collections, letters constituted a recognized literary genre, cultivated in antiquity and conspicuously revived by both Italian and northern humanists (Trimpi 1962, 60-75; Guillen 1986; Clements and Levant 1976). Whether limited to manuscript circulation or published in printed form, the genre was adapted to many uses, personal, polemical, epideictic, didactic, and satiric. Some manuals on letter writing were restrictive in their advice on decorum in form and style, but Erasmus and others encouraged variety through their examples and precepts (Henderson 1983, 1990). Anyone well trained in rhetoric was prepared and often obliged to work within epistolary conventions, and was also free to play with what could be a cornucopian discourse. (For the common reader or "Curteous Buyer" sought by Spenser and Harvey, letter writing was the art form they were most likely to practice, and the *Letters* offered models for admiration and imitation.) Scholarly opinion allowed for some of the same freedoms within the middle style in verse epistles as in prose, and in his Latin verse letter Spenser was following abundant Neo-Latin precedents, harking back to the *Epistles* of

Horace (Trimpi 1962, 76-91). Against this background our pamphlet is not anomalous, though it remains odd. Large and small collections of letters by humanists are numerous in the sixteenth century, but I can find no exact precedents for the publication of a small collection of private letters, recently written, by two virtually unknown men.

What no single tradition explains, a number of kindred instances may render intelligible. Several uses of the letter form bear comparison to what Spenser and Harvey were up to, and with writers so bookish and style-conscious, it is reasonable to suppose an awareness of various precedents, and of the risks they were taking in their own mingling of effects. The *Letters* are as heterogeneous in style and contents as any postmodern text, including political and literary gossip, satiric sorties against pedantry and superstition, a serious appeal to skeptical principles in natural philosophy, crude anti-feminism, various drab verses and specimens in English quantitative meter, and (from Spenser) a Neo-Latin poem of 114 lines anticipating some of the themes in his *Faerie Queene* and later poetry. Humanists' letter collections offered a form that might be made to accommodate such material.

The most important and immediate English precedents will be found in George Gascoigne's two miscellanies: *The Adventures of Master F. J.* in its epistolary form in *A Hundreth Sundrie Flowres* (1573), and *Certayne Notes of Instruction* (a letter to "Master Edouardo Donati") in *The Posies* (1575). There are many signs of Gascoigne's importance to Harvey in the *Letter-Book* and elsewhere (Stern 1979, 31 n., 33, 215-16), and similarities between *The Shepheardes Calender* and *A Hundreth Sundrie Flowres* have been noted by Alpers (1988, 164-65, 170-71). Another significant generic context is indicated by the curious text often cited as "the Laneham *Letter*," a description by Robert Laneham or Langham, ostensibly for the benefit of a kinsman in London, of festivities sponsored by the earl of Leicester to honor queen Elizabeth when her progress came to Kenilworth in 1575. Roger Kuin, this text's most recent and careful editor, regards the letter as an authentic piece of personal correspondence, an instance of the kind of "'personal newsletter' . . . common in Sidney's circle" (Langham ed. 1983, 15). But publication of such letters was not common; political motives on the part of Leicester or his supporters must have figured in the publication of Langham's *Letter*. Still another precedent, showing how letters might be used to stimulate curiosity and influence opinion, is offered by the *Epistles of Obscure Men*, a learned hoax at the expense of pedants and stupid defenders of the status quo, in support of Johann Reuchlin and the new learning that contributed to the Reformation in Germany. Harvey's copy of this internationally popular book survives, signed and dated 1572 (Stern 1979, 238).

In the *Letters*, as in the *Calender* but less elaborately and seriously, political concerns are hinted at; in keeping with the principle of decorum and the precedents just cited, a political agenda is presented in personal terms. Spenser writes as a member of Leicester's household and alludes to his master's enigmatic stance toward the queen's negotiations with the duke of Alençon and Anjou, paying passing attention to inner-circle gossip and public concern. Little is said; one purpose of letters is to establish the existence of secrets without giving them away (Rambuss 1993, 19, 54). At the beginning of his first letter, just before mentioning the earthquake, he observes, "Little newes is here stirred: but that olde great matter still depending. His Honoure never better" (*Prose Works*, 15; ed. 1912, 611a). Here, and in the publicity given to Sidney's agenda for the reform of poetry, the writers associate themselves with men who recognized that the press could be used to influence opinions within a status-conscious and suggestible reading public. Since Sidney had given offense to Elizabeth by offering unwelcome advice on the French marriage and quarreling with the earl of Oxford (Duncan-Jones 1991, 160-67), it may have suited his interests to have it advertised that he was in London, not at Wilton, concentrating on harmless versifying rather than politics.

It will be worthwhile to consider the order of items in the *Letters*, a literary production that seems casual and even disorderly but still possesses a significant form. In the *Letters* as published in 1580, most of the separate items bear dates, but they appear out of chronological order, and this should alert us to the presence of details and patterns in the textual domain that are independent of events in the writers' lives. Except for the prefatory letter ascribed to "a Welwiller," which is dated "This XIX. of June. 1580" (*Prose Works*, 448; ed. 1912, 610), close in time to the Stationers' Register entry on 30 June, all of the dates may be unreliable. From both writers' passing references, changes of subject, and rushed responses to various surprises and mishaps one gets the sense, appropriate to letters as a genre, that time is of the essence, but temporality as a textual effect does not correspond to real time in these writers' lives.

This can be illustrated in two ways, from the first part (*Three . . . familiar Letters*), which is dominated by Harvey's response to a sensational earthquake, and then from Spenser's most substantial contribution to the correspondence, in the separately titled *Two Other, very commendable Letters, of the same mens writing.* On 6 April 1580, an earthquake was felt in London and elsewhere in southern England. Interpreters were quick to moralize upon the event, seeing the hand of an admonitory God in it, and the earthquake's significance remained a subject for pamphlets and ballads for at least the next three months. Harvey's letter on the subject, ostensibly a response to Immerito's inquiry, bears the date "Aprilis septimo, Vesperi" (*Prose Works*, 462; ed. 1912, 622b), but his two-part display of satiric storytelling and up-to-date learning in natural philosophy could hardly have been planned and completed so soon after the event. In fact, Harvey was less concerned with the earthquake itself (although he gives an elaborate account of the circumstances in which he says he felt it) than with unsophisticated responses to it in the popular press, some appearing only a short time before his "Pleasant and pithy familiar discourse, of the Earthquake in Aprill last" went to press.[14] He labors to create the effects of reportage and off-the-cuff analysis, but the context in which Harvey's opinions are meaningful is a textual circus of interpretation, not the pressure of events in the writer's personal life: these are treated as the "imaginative groundplot" for his colorful rhetoric.

Harvey pretends to have been carried away by his disagreement with "these miserable balde odious three halfepeny fellowes, alas, a company of silly beetleheaded Asses" (*Prose Works,* 459; ed. 1912, 620a); in his learned opinion, natural causes suffice to explain earthquakes, and he doesn't see "howe a man on Earth, should be of so great authoritie, and so familiar acquaintance with God in Heaven, (unlesse haply for the nonce he hath lately intertained some few choice singular ones of his privie Counsell) as to be able . . . to reveale hys incomprehensible mysteries" (*Prose Works,* 455; ed. 1912, 617b). Harvey was eager, of course, to be of service to any and all members of the queen's Privy Council (Jardine and Grafton 1990); his evidence of fitness for such responsibilities includes a swaggering attack on men who have been insufficiently deferential, presuming to rise above the modest limits of their knowledge.[15]

Immerito/Spenser's role is more modest than Harvey's. In the first part of the correspondence, *Three . . . familiar Letters*, it is limited to initiating discussion of the earthquake and touting the literary interests that both men claim to have in common with Philip Sidney and his fellows. Spenser's short letter serves to introduce two long ones from Harvey, the first mostly concerned with the earthquake and a second "with sundry proper examples, and some Precepts of our Englishe reformed Versifying" (*Prose Works*, 463-77; ed. 1912, 623-32). Both men seek to be known—if it can be called knowledge—by writings referred to in passing, as yet seen by only a few.

Among these are the *Dreames* being prepared as a sequel to *The Shepheardes Calender* and some part of the work in progress that both men cite as *The Faerie Queene* (*Prose Works*, 17, 471; ed. 1912, 612b, 628b). Both men also appear interested in showing that their experiments in quantitative versification corroborate Sidney's. In this, as in other things, Immerito is content to give Harvey the leading role, and he ends his "Postscripte" with a Latin maxim defining the terms of their friendly rivalry, to the effect that "Nevertheless I shall follow only you, yet never overtake you" (*Prose Works*, 18; ed. 1912, 612b).

Spenser's persona emerges more clearly in the second part of the collection, *Two Other, very commendable Letters, of the same mens writing: both touching the foresaid Artificiall Versifying, and certain other Particulars*; although dated earlier, these letters are presented by the title page (for a facsimile, see *Prose Works*, 3; ed. 1912, 633) as having been "More lately delivered unto the Printer." The first of them (*Prose Works*, 5-12; ed. 1912, 635-38) is Spenser's most substantive contribution, and it offers a counterpoise to Harvey's predominance in the first part. Immerito repeats the maxim about following yet never overtaking his mentor, but now it is coupled with a taunt: "beware, leaste in time I overtake you" (*Prose Works*, 7; ed. 1912, 636b).

Spenser's letter is in two parts, both bearing dates that place them earlier in time than anything in the *Three . . . familiar Letters*; they also predate the poet's marriage to Machabyas Chylde (27 October) and the entry of *The Shepheardes Calender* on the Stationers' Register (5 December). The first part of the letter carries references to its writing on 15 October, with a continuation the next morning in response to something from Harvey (*Prose Works*, 7; ed. 1912, 636a). The letter ends with pages given a still earlier date, "Leycester House. This .5. of October. 1579" (*Prose Works*, 12; ed. 1912, 638b), and a suspect explanation that the Latin verse-letter included with this "last Farewell" had been "through one mans negligence quite forgotten" (*Prose Works*, 8; ed. 1912, 636a).

These pages ostensibly torn from time and rescued from neglect create perspectives on Spenser's life, not documentary evidence of it. While it is reasonable to suppose that Spenser resided in Leicester House in October of 1579 and that he was in correspondence with Harvey at that time, when they were both involved in preparing for publication of *The Shepheardes Calender*, it would be prudent to regard "5 October 1579" and other dates as only accidents of the epistolary genre, offering nothing like the connections to the writer's life and creative processes that are implied by "July 13, 1798" in the full title of Wordsworth's "Lines . . . above Tintern Abbey."

The unreliability of such signs in Spenser's text, beyond their arbitrary meaning within generic conventions, should warn us not to look for clear correspondences between the writer's life and the significant structures, both diachronic and synchronic, in his writings, but to look instead for attempts to transform the personal and transcend a life line defined by time, mixing together topical and allegorical discourses somewhat as the *Calender* does, and as Spenser also does in *Amoretti and Epithalamion* much later.

The belatedness of the *Two Other . . . Letters* is intelligible thematically, independent of the accidents of chronology, in the light of their valedictory content. In several respects Spenser's last letter and Harvey's reply echo the farewell to the flesh emphasis of the *Calender*, while offering variations on the classicizing sophistication associated with Sidney and his circle. Spenser's "Iambicum Trimetrum" is a lover's complaint and a pathetic bid for recognition, ending "And if I dye, who will saye: *this was, Immerito?*" (*Prose Works*, 7-8; ed. 1912, 636). Harvey in turn, responding to Spenser's praise of him as a Cato for their time, begins by urging his friend "to abandon all other fooleries, and honour Vertue, the onely immortall and surviving Accident amongst so manye mortall, and ever-perishing Substaunces" (*Prose Works*, 442; ed. 1912, 639a); he ends with a cento of Latin verses and English translations, reducible to the last line of Harvey's own version, "Vertue alone eternall is, and shee the Laurell weares" (*Prose Works*, 447; ed. 1912, 643). An alert contemporary reader might have caught, in the overtones carried by these *vales*, *aves* to preferment: for an Elizabethan, *contemptus mundi* was paradoxically a fit preparative for an ambitious life at court or in someone's service abroad.

Spenser's valedictory epistle "Ad Ornatissimum virum . . . G. H." refers expectantly to a Continental journey on behalf of the earl of Leicester (*Prose Works*, 12, and ed. 1912, 638b; cf. Judson 1945, 60, and Rambuss 1993, 17-19). The project came to nothing so far as we know, except that in less than a year the author was in Ireland serving Arthur, Lord Grey. Perhaps this was no less than he had hoped for. It seems that his European itinerary (fantastically represented in poetic locutions, beginning with a trip "in Gallias" and extending as far as Rome and even Greece) was never more than an elaborate way of saying, to Leicester and others, "Have pen— will travel." The literal sense of this "last Farewell" is undercut by the chronologically later letters appearing earlier in the collection, as well as by Harvey's response: he wagers "al the Books and writings in my study . . . that you shall not, I saye, bee gone over Sea" (*Prose Works*, 444; ed. 1912, 641a). However, in its position as an appendix, "Ad Ornatissimum virum" invites an allegorical reading of its *Reise-angst*, as pertaining to the end of a phase in the poet's career and portending an uncertain future for his high hopes. It contains some extraordinary foretastes of *The Faerie Queene:* with the wisdom of hindsight, helped by Harvey's references to what he has seen of "that *Elvish Queene*" (*Prose Works*, 471; ed. 1912, 629b), we can approach the threshold of the epic poet's workshop.[16] Equally important to Spenser's inner life at the moment, his poem alludes to Love as a cause of uncertainty and stretches to the breaking point the elaborate code of friendship that had defined his intimacy with Harvey. Returning to this part of the collection later, I will undertake to interpret the confusion and doubling of roles that Spenser was involved in with Harvey, and the uncertainties attending his breaking away and embarking on a career that would take him considerably farther from his mentor than Leicester House was from Cambridge University.

The *Letters* are of interest primarily for what they tell us about the two writers' friendship and Harvey's importance in Spenser's formation as a poet and a public servant. The next phase of his career involved absence from England, an interval of ten years before the first part of *The Faerie Queene* appeared in print, and either the disappearance or the transumption of other projects that had figured—more or less figuratively—in the new poet's earlier promise. It appears that in these years Spenser's friendship with Harvey endured a breach rather than an expansion. In his Latin valedictory letter, Spenser anticipates and in some sense enacts a break: the map across which the poet moves may be imaginary, but at the level of emotions Spenser already appears far from Harvey. The larger world of the would-be heroic poet will not contain Hobbinol; there will be angels in *The Faerie Queene*, but no Gabriel. Yet in 1580 Harvey was still crucially important to Spenser's sense of himself as a poet, and the nuances of this friendship call for a full and accurate understanding. Of all the relationships enabling and informing Spenser's imagination, this is almost the only one documented, and it provides points of reference for other aspects of the poet's developing personal life.

The scene of writing for Spenser in 1580 can be understood in terms of two moments, one recalled as real in the recent past, the other set in a hypothetical future. A comparison of two passages will help us to understand some of what Spenser was going through in the transition from rustic pastoral verse to the next phase of his career, which coincided with marriage and a move from obscure duties in Leicester's household to a larger place in Ireland.

Introducing the subject of "Englishe Hexameters" in the first of the *Three . . . familiar Letters*, and asking "why a Gods name may not we, as else the Greekes, have the kingdome of oure owne Language," Spenser offers four lines as an example of his own experimentation in "your artificial straightnesse of Verse." He asks, "Seeme they comparable to those two, which I translated you *ex tempore* in bed, the last time we lay togither in Westminster?" (*Prose Works*, 16; ed. 1912, 611b). Over against this moment of intimacy remembered we should place the scene, near the end of the *Letters* and in the last lines of Spenser's valedictory verses, where the poet imagines himself alone and far from England, "in the shadow of Mount Oebalius," involved in mourning "the reticence of sacred Helicon" while his "good Harvey, . . . both angel and Gabriel," is back in England (ed. 1912, 638b).[17] Here the contrasting exotic and domestic scenes are both used as backdrops for mutual longing, with Spenser in solitude and Harvey "surrounded by a crowd of friends." The poem ends with a startling bit of ventriloquism; he imagines that his friend will "miss the one absent, *Immerito*," and will say, "'If only my *Edmund* were here.'" In an imagined absence, the poet names himself not only *Immerito* but—in the voice of another—*Edmundus*. Nowhere else in his poetry does Spenser present himself unclothed in this way:[18] passages in the *Amoretti* are emotionally more direct, but the fortyish poet entering his second marriage leaves his Christian name in his publisher's hands and doesn't identify himself outside of literary conventions.

In the first instance, the poet's letter recalls the improvised translation of a lyrical fragment in his friend's presence, prompting Goldberg's observation that "Spenser slept with Harvey, and it is no secret" (1992, 79). In the second scene, imagined in the future rather than recalled, we have a grand gesture revealing the poet's true identity, invoked in his absence. (Both passages involve absence, of course, as the occasion for writing and its substitution of a text for the writer's speaking presence.) Harvey's interest is fundamental to both scenes, and they both involve erotic overtones.[19]

Spenser's most personal revelations of hopes and fears attending a public career as a serious poet are expressed in these two moments. In the first, concerned with an attempt to domesticate classical quantitative meters, and to show himself worthy of a close association with Sidney and his friends, Spenser expresses a desire for authority in "the kingdome of oure owne Language," involving mastery of poetic technique that "will easily and fairely, yeelde it selfe to our Moother tongue" (*Prose Works*, 16; ed. 1912, 611). The quantitative experiments of Spenser, Harvey, and Sidney have been the subject of extensive and expert scholarship (Prescott 1978,

93-95; Weiner 1982; Attridge 1990; Helgerson 1992, 25-40), to which I can add little. In some respects, this effort on Spenser's part is consistent with what he had undertaken in *The Shepheardes Calender:* E. K. in his letter to Harvey observed that "the new Poete" "hath laboured to restore, as to theyr rightfull heritage such good and naturall English words, as have ben long time out of use and almost cleare disherited," in order to renew in "our Mother tonge" its capacity to produce both prose and verse (ed. 1912, 417). In the language of Immerito and E. K., mastery of form and diction is a masculine effort, a systematic regimen without which the English language would lack legitimate issue.

Harvey's response to Immerito's theory and practice of "artificial" versification is worth noting: he refers not to "our Moother tongue" but to "the [queenes] Englishe" (*Prose Works*, 474; ed. 1912, 630a, with Harvey's emendation from McKitterick 1981, 352-53); "we are licenced and authorized by the ordinarie use, and custome, and proprietie, and Idiome, and, as it were, Majestie of our speach." Where Spenser wishes to rule, Harvey would happily serve; in his view, Prosody is "the vulgare, and naturall Mother" who rules in the customs observed in speech, not by precepts derived from Greek or Latin rules (*Prose Works*, 475-76; ed. 1912, 631). In his emphasis on custom rather than rules Harvey was the odd man out within the Areopagus (Attridge 1990, 576), and he opposed Spenser's potentially absolutist overreaching with principles rooted in "a Gothic, common-law tradition" (Helgerson 1992, 27-28).

The scene imagined at the end of Spenser's contributions to the *Letters* presents the poet in a different relation to Harvey. "I beseeche you by all your Curtesies, and Graces, let me be answered, ere I goe: which will be, (I hope, I feare, I thinke) the next weeke, if I can be dispatched of my Lorde. I goe thither, as sent by him, and maintained most what of him: and there am to employ my time, my body, my minde, to his Honours service" (*Prose Works*, 12; ed. 1912, 638b). What sounds in these sentences like a diplomatic mission is also projected in "Ad Ornatissimum virum" as an open-ended journey into the realms of romance and classical antiquity. Exercises in "artificiall Verses" had been one proof of learned aspiration. The Latin language provides a medium for instruction ostensibly addressed to Harvey, employing the Horatian epistolary mode Harvey had used in poems addressed to Sidney in his *Gratulationes Valdinenses* (1578). Spenser no less than Harvey must have hoped to reach Sidney with proof of his promise as a *doctus poeta*. The formal strictures of Latin verse enable him to voice, before a limited audience, a desire for independence and broader horizons than the English kingdom and its language had so far offered; they also provide a vehicle for personal feelings of vulnerability and ambivalence that had been expressed more crudely in the *Calender*.

By various means in the course of his valedictory verse-letter, Spenser puts an exaggerated distance between himself and Harvey, giving us reason to believe that their intimacy has been jeopardized, yet Harvey's interest continues to provide a motive for writing and a confirmation of Immerito's identity, which is a function, equally, of Gabriel's love for Edmund and the poet's distance from home. Spenser's image of himself in solitude and voluntary exile enacts independence as an internalization of interdependence.

As Jonathan Goldberg remarks in his account of Spenser's friendship with Harvey, both the *Calender* and the *Letters* represent the two men in many mirrors, and "[w]ithin this mirror relation, Harvey/Hobbinol functions as an alter ego" (1992, 76-77). This is nowhere more true or more complicated than in Spenser's verse-letter. Some of the positions he takes are appropriated from Harvey, as when he argues that "whoever studies how to please great men / Studies how to play the fool, for the awkward man attracts favor" (ed. 1912, 637b): a large part of the poem, devoted to advice on getting ahead in the world, is based on one of Horace's *Epistles* (1.17), which Harvey himself had imitated in his "Castilio, sive Aulicus," a poem addressed to Philip Sidney in *Gratulationum Valdinensium Libri Quatuor* (1578a, K4v-L1v).[20] Throughout these letters, of course, while Spenser is consistently sage and serious, Harvey has played the fool in several voices, noting at one point that "*David, Ulysses,* and *Solon,* fayned themselves fooles and madmen" (*Prose Works*, 461; ed. 1912, 621b). But Spenser too is playful, in a fashion consistent with his masquerade as Immerito. The Latin verse letter is tinged with irony, especially in its more lavish praises of "G. H." and a corresponding self-deprecation. At the outset, he complains that while everything is set for his departure, Love has rendered him "foolish" (*ineptus*), and he needs help: "Untie these knots, and you will be my stalwart Apollo" (*Hos nodos exsolue, et eris mihi magnus Apollo*). His praise is not unqualified, however; the *Magnificentia* attributed to his friend in an elaborate tribute (ed. 1912, 637) resembles Arthur's self-assurance before his dream of Gloriana, and the limited capacity for virtuous action that Stoic counsels underwrite in the Legend of Temperance. In spite of the complaint with which it begins, much of the poem is devoted to justifying love, reconciling virtue to pleasure. In this, if Harvey serves as an alter ego, he occupies a lofty and self-satisfied position from which the poet distances himself.

The poem's knots, like those imposed by Cupid in the opening lines, invite interpretation in the light of Spenser's marriage. According to

Goldberg, "The love of women does not interrupt" the love between Colin and Hobbinol (1992, 78). It is true that Spenser had (earlier in the text, later chronologically) asked for signs of goodwill toward his *Corculum* and Harvey responded—in Latin, more for the husband's than his sweetheart's benefit—with a copious show of love, concluding, "O mea Domina Immerito, mea bellissima Collina Clouta, multo plus plurimum salve, atque vale" (*Prose Works*, 17, 476; ed. 1912, 612b, 632a). It is easier to construe Harvey's compliments in the context of his pervasive antifeminist rhetoric than it is to appreciate the predicament described at length in Immerito's valedictory verse letter. Love is a problem for him—or perhaps it is two problems. Although the woman Spenser married in the months between his two exchanges of letters has been cloaked in pseudonyms, she is as real in the implied social world around Immerito as Sidney, Dyer, and Daniel Rogers. The triangular desire represented in the *Calender* continues, but Rosalind, or another like her, has been won, and presumably the poet's marriage accounts for his move from Leicester House to the lodgings in Westminster mentioned in his letter after the earthquake. Harvey's response to all that is said about love and marriage in "Ad Ornatissimum virum" is to chide his friend as a "magne muliercularum amator"; he is resolved to "rid you quite of this yonkerly, and [woomanish] humor" (*Prose Works*, 444; ed. 1912, 640b-641a, emended from McKitterick 1981, 353). Harvey's advice is worthy of Musidorus when he discovers Pyrocles in love; and if Sidney read the *Letters* with any care, as a bachelor entering the awkward age of young manhood he must have appreciated the issues left unresolved in these exchanges.

In "Ad Ornatissimum virum," Ulysses figures prominently as a hero motivated by love for his wife, and in his fantasy of Continental travel, the poet sees himself engaged in "endless wandering" (*inexhaustis . . . erroribus*), a companion of Ulysses; he also imagines accompanying the "grieving goddess" (*Deam . . . aegram*) Ceres, in a quest suggestive of Orlando's search for Angelica.[21] So the inescapable quests and idealized feminine figures that appear in so many heroic poems of the Renaissance are already taking shape in Spenser's imagination, uneasily linked with the morality of rational self-control. But these are not the only images of desire that are concentrated together in the last lines of the poem. Immerito's impulse to travel arises from a fear of shame, such as may inhibit a bridegroom; the terms in which he describes a stay-at-home life are suggestive. "For one feels ashamed at heart, at home in shameful obscurity [*Namque sinu pudet in patrio, tenebrisque pudendis*], / An unhappy youth not without talents, / To be wasting the green years in unworthy duties." The poet has not yet had opportunities in the public world worthy of his talents, so he has not yet earned the pleasures of privacy. If marriage is the setting for a mature man's happiness, as earlier passages in the poem imply, some fear or guilt may still attend its bliss.

But intimacy between men also presents dangers: in his last lines the poet comes to rest in what I have already discussed as his imaginary scene of writing, finding his muse mourning "in the shadow of Mount Oebalius" (*sub Oebalii . . . cacumine montis*). Seen in relation to Edmund's separation from Gabriel, who had been praised as "my stalwart Apollo," what can this mean? This out-of-the-way mountain in Sparta has only one literary association, as far as I know: Ovid tells of Apollo's love for Hyacinthus (Oebalides), whom he killed accidentally when the wind caught a discus they were tossing (*Metamorphoses* 10.162-219). The connections between art and life, the author's words and the man's emotions, are no more than dotted lines where Spenser is concerned, but I would suggest that this poem encodes, like so much of Elizabethan literature,[22] the emotional difficulties attending intimacy and desire between men at the point where they come into conflict with marriage, which was both the foundation of patriarchal culture and the matrix for individual identity as the early modern cultural order had begun to define it.

Spenser's Retrography: Two Episodes in Post-Petrarchan Bibliography

JOSEPH LOEWENSTEIN

An eye of looking back, were well.
Jonson, *Pleasure Reconciled to Virtue*

Howdoes the reproduction of texts figure in the biography of poets? As a contribution to the intersecting historiographies of authorial subjectivity and of the institutions of print, this essay concerns itself with Spenser's experience of publication. This is a biographical essay in that it specifies Spenser's engagement in the early 1590s with the printed texts of his own work as an event, the sort of quantum of experience that puts the poet's intellectual and social being, characteristically and determinatively, in play. But since it treats of Spenser's printed *sonnets*, this is also an essay in literary history. The sonnet is traditionally a locus of biographical significance because sonneteering is traditionally an autobiographical event; my purpose is to suggest how the autobiographical valence of Spenser's sonnets is shaped by print. What follows, then, is an account of two episodes in the material history of autobiography, these taken from the era of typography.

I shall be giving an account of minutiae: word choice in translation, the arrangement of poems on a page. I shall be accounting for traces: the failure to print a publicized volume, evidence of assiduous proofreading, the signs of saved compositorial labor in a printed book. I am attempting a bibliographical cultural poetics that accepts the traditional associations of the term "poetics"—its orientation to nuance and drift, to choices that are not, in and of themselves, epochal, but that may refer and conduce to the epochal, to both mindful craft and inadvertent habit. I take it that this is the scale at which the individual ideological laborer—your poet, say—operates, lives.

I should say at the outset that Spenser is an unlikely representative of Typographical Man. Like most Elizabethan writers, he has little to say about printing; Greene, Nashe, and Harvey have more to say, but they are the exceptions. Most commonly, the gift economy of patronage is voluble in the pages of printed books, while the momentously inventive economy of the book trade barely murmurs there. In the most ingenious of the commendatory verses to the 1590 *Faerie Queene*, the unidentified W. L. describes Sidney's discovery of Spenser and compares it to Ulysses' discovery of Achilles masked in lowly *women's* weeds; according to W. L., Immerito/Colin/Achilles could not disguise the epic manliness of his voice. W. L. thus figures a patron-like Astrophulyssides as Spenser's publisher; we must look to the title page to learn of the stationer, William Ponsonby, who brought the poem to the book stalls. W. L.'s poem is indifferent to the impression that print makes, and Spenser himself usually seems diffident. Despite the brilliance with which he had exploited the novelties of both humanist and populist printing in *The Shepheardes Calender*, in the 1590 *Faerie Queene* he displays no comparable engagement with medium or with disseminative conditions. Indeed, Spenser seems to have carried a manuscriptive disposition right into the printshop.

For at least two of its principal producers, the 1590 *Faerie Queene* was momentous, though the moment had different meanings for Ponsonby and for Spenser. Ponsonby's career was utterly transformed in 1590, though the transformation may in fact be traced to late 1586, when he introduced himself to Fulke Greville.[1] On that occasion, Ponsonby informed Greville that one of the several manuscripts of Sidney's *Arcadia* then in circulation had been submitted for licensing by some unnamed stationer. Ponsonby had good intelligence, for he knew of Greville's interest in the manuscript, may even have known that Greville had control of a revised version of the *Arcadia*; at any rate, he explained just how Greville—or Walsingham, to whom Greville wrote immediately of the encounter—could put a stop to the publication by a direct intervention with the licensers.[2] It was a successful power play—in 1588, Ponsonby entered the Greville manuscript to his copy in the Stationers' Register.

By thus coordinating the apparatus of ideological control, licensing, with the apparatus of internal guild regulation, stationer's copyright, Ponsonby and Greville become the Sidney industry: Greville secured to himself some of the powers of a modern literary executor, and Ponsonby became unofficial stationer to the Sidney circle. This constitutes an important moment in English print culture. Although Greville expressed disdain for the "common errors of mercenary printing" in his letter to Walsingham, he was plainly impressed with the stationer's power to stabilize texts and regulate their circulation (Robertson, in Sidney ed. 1973a, xl). Ponsonby was effectively offering Greville the control of Sidney's literary reputation and, thereby, a unique means of preserving the favor and patronage of the Herberts (Brennan 1988, 56). For his part, Greville, supported by Walsingham, enabled Ponsonby to wrest rights in a valuable copy from another stationer.

There is no reason to suppose that Walsingham invoked principle when he stopped the publication of a 1586 *Arcadia*—in 1586 he was at his most formidable. Nor is it clear that such control of publication could have been made a simple matter of principle: since no convention had yet been established to enable authors to restrain publication during their lives, their friends or heirs could hardly hope to restrain posthumous publication. But just such restraints began to hedge the work of the Sidney circle. In 1592, for example, the Herberts managed to curb the unauthorized publication of *Astrophel and Stella*. What has come to be called copyright had originated as a means of regulating competition within the Stationers Company, but the interest of people as powerful as the Herberts, and the aura in which they managed to enshrine Sidney's texts, helped Ponsonby imagine a copyright detached from its industrial origins and reconceived as a piece of heritable intellectual property. Thus, when several stationers infringed Ponsonby's rights in the *Arcadia*, he began an action in Star Chamber rather than an appeal to the stationers' internal Court of Assistants.[3]

It is worth attending to the chronology here. Ponsonby began this court action a decade after his first edition of the *Arcadia*, the edition of 1590; only after a decade of a very particular sort of publishing, only after a decade of richly reciprocal patronage, could the stationer to the Herberts have conceived of the piracy of the *Arcadia* as *thus* actionable. In that decade, Ponsonby registered Sidney's translations from du Bartas as well as *Astrophel and Stella*, he published translations by the countess of Pembroke, *The countess of Pembroke's Ivychurch* by Fraunce, Fraunce's *Emmanuel*, three editions of the *Arcadia* (one as part of a particularly expensive collected edition of Sidney's works), and, with the exception of *The Shepheardes Calender*, every shred of Spenser's verse. He began with the first three books of *The Faerie Queene*.

This is not the usual way of putting it. Biographers and bibliographers usually speak of Spenser's having applied to, or having offered his manuscript to, Ponsonby, but such descriptions are unsupported by evidence; we are at best in a realm of probabilities.[4] Certainly Ponsonby describes himself as the more avid agent of publication in the prefatory epistle to the 1591 *Complaints*, his second Spenser issue: "Since my late setting foorth of the *Faerie Queene*, finding that it hath found a favourable passage amongst you; I have sithence endevoured by all good meanes . . . to get into my handes such smale Poemes of the same Authors; as I heard were disperst abroad in sundrie hands, and not easie to bee come by" (ed. 1912, 470a). That Ponsonby sought to make himself "Spenser's" and "Sidney's" publisher (as well as stationer to the Sidney circle) was a fairly unusual practice within the book trade, an evolutionary adaptation of topic monopolies— like the law patent or the patent in almanacs—toward author monopolies.[5]

Ponsonby's innovation took effect only slowly. His brother-in-law, Simon Waterson, became "Daniel's" printer even before he inherited Ponsonby's line in Sidney and Spenser; his apprentice, Edward Blount, went on to assist in the compilation of the first Shakespeare folio. Ponsonby's procedures rendered the relation of authors to the book trade stable and continuous and so conduced to the slow development of *authorial* property, that crucial adaptation of *regulations* originally designed to promote industrial stability as *rights* ostensibly natural and prior to the exigencies of market production. So the 1590 *Faerie Queene*, like the 1590 *Arcadia*, makes a small contribution to the economic history of authorship.

John Wolfe, the printer of the 1590 *Faerie Queene*, was a rather more important figure in that history and in the history of English monopolistic competition in general: it is worth remembering that the revolt he led in the early eighties against the best-established members of the Stationers Company had been framed as a progressive assault on monopolistic printing patents—Wolfe had styled it a "reformation." In the period between, say, 1582, when Wolfe was imprisoned for pirating the primer, the core of John Day's lucrative printing patent, and 1586, when the Star Chamber intervened to prop up the jurisdictional authority of the company wardens, property relations within the book trade must have seemed remarkably unstable. Still, the period of general disorder passed fairly quickly; in terms of organizational structure, the Stationers Company was a remarkably conservative guild, and the main effect of Wolfe's "reformation" was that the most highly capitalized members of the company consolidated their position. Wolfe had no trouble adapting to the atmosphere of regulatory stringency consequent on the Star Chamber decree of 1586; indeed, in the following year, he got himself made beadle of the company, charged with *policing* the trade, and moved his shop to Stationers' Hall. He continued to engage in duplicitous production, but he confined his shadier dealings to international marketing. Thus in 1584 he began printing a series of more or less scandalous Italian books, works by Aretino, Machiavelli, and others, most of them with false Italian imprints; in 1588 he published, at Burghley's behest, several works of foreign-language propaganda, again with false imprints but also with made-up authors, designed for surreptitious distribution abroad. Wolfe's output is distinguished by its internationalism—his bi- and trilingual editions, his sponsorship of publications from the Italian émigré populations, his cultivation of an audience for French newsbooks.

We know almost as little about the norms of interaction between publishers and printers as we do about the norms of interaction between authors and stationers, so it is difficult to establish why Ponsonby, who had never before used Wolfe, decided to give him the job of printing *The Faerie Queene*. Wolfe *had* printed the most recent edition of *The Shepheardes Calender*, but with no conspicuous excellence. Ponsonby may have thought that the text of a poet who "writ no language" might benefit from Wolfe's experience with foreign-language printing. The famous St. George block used to print the reverse of the last page of Book I of *The Faerie Queene* may have belonged to Wolfe—he had used it before—and it's possible that Ponsonby hired Wolfe on simply for the sake of the block. The best explanation for Wolfe's employ is that if Spenser was to read proof the poem had to be produced quite quickly, for he was due back in Ireland within only a few months of his arrival in London. Wolfe was perfect for such circumstances: ever the progressive capitalist, he had been flouting company norms since the early eighties in pursuit of economies of scale. With four or five presses, his was probably one of the two most efficient shops in London.

Regardless of its length or its lexical and orthographic peculiarities, printing the 1590 *Faerie Queene* did not require unusual expertise, for stanzaic verse can be cast off and set with extraordinary speed.[6] We may begin to assess the place of this industrial event within Spenser's imagination by considering the shock of this productive speed. Spenser had been working slowly on this poem for about a decade, and the sudden pace of its conversion from manuscript to print and the sheer physical energy of presswork must have been startling. Startling, but not altogether unimagined: Wolfe's shop at Stationers' Hall would have occasioned a degree of recognition. If it was not so overtly diabolical as Error's vomiting maw, it surely partook of the uncanny industry of Merlin's cave if not of the infernal energies of Mammon's. And here, at the moment of presswork, we can find Spenser implicated in its industry: in what turns out to be a characteristic gesture, Spenser responds to the industrial energy of presswork with more writing, with a writing that challenges the apparently terminal character of print.

The front matter of the 1590 *Faerie Queene* is, notoriously, almost all at the back.[7] Nashe, his mind always in the printshop, remarked on the format, which suggests that it was a mild curiosity; it was imitated on later occasions, most notably in Chapman's Homer, but there is no reason to suppose the arrangement to have been deeply deliberate.[8] Here is the first sign of Spenser's unsettled relation to the pace of production. Apparently, he was slow to figure out what he wanted to do about dedications and commendatory verses—or at least too slow to accommodate Wolfe's and Ponsonby's schedule—so Wolfe began the text of Book I on the second leaf of signature A, reserving only the title page verso for framing authorial gestures.[9] The dedication to Elizabeth inevitably claimed this proud place, but even so, it staked its claim late, for several copies were printed without it. This disarray would hardly be worth remarking of another poet's book, but we are dealing with perhaps the most ingenious practitioner of the art of disposition in English—certainly the most ingenious between Chaucer and Joyce. An artist of deliberate sequence was being rushed.

He came up with a full gathering (Pp1r-Pp8v), sixteen pages, of terminal preliminaries. It is difficult to ascertain just when Spenser learned that the front matter was to be displaced, difficult to determine whether the presswork itself inspired the themes of belatedness and disarray that permeate the gathering. Displacement begins with the "Letter to Raleigh," centrally concerned with disrupted sequence: in it, Spenser prefaces an account of the poem's conceptual and narrative etiology with a justification of the narrative practice of beginning *in medias res*. With this prefatory account of mediation thus situated in the last gathering of the book, the poem swamps its medium. The rhythm of belated recognition, that rhythm which, together with the ensuings of its stanza, constitutes this poem's fundamental rhythm (and which constitutes, not so incidentally, Spenser's chief legacy to Milton), is thus unfolded out beyond the structure of the poem and into the structure of the book. The letter is followed by six commendatory poems and then a series of ten dedicatory sonnets.

Several of these sonnets mark their terminal and Spenserian character by themselves concluding with a hexameter.[10]

The second of the dedicatory sonnets, addressed to Essex, figures dedication not only as afterword, but as somehow denigrated afterword, Perhaps because Ralegh and Essex were at odds, perhaps because Essex had achieved eminence only after the poem was well underway, Spenser had not yet made a place for him in the epic proper, and he apologizes in the sonnet for the shame of afterwording: "Yet doe not sdeigne, to let thy name be writt / In this base Poeme, for thee far unfitt" (the sonnet as belated version of the "far unfitter" epic). He promises Essex better treatment when he proceeds to "the last praises of this Faery Queene." On the next page, in both the beautifully sinuous sonnet to Oxford and a less distinguished one to Northumberland, the key concept is succession, the earls represented above all as heirs, and poetry and patronage assimilated as defensive embodiments of predecessors. The evocation of modern eminence is drenched in nostalgia: Northumberland is among "the noble Progeny" of earlier heroes, "which them succeed in fame and worth." Nothing novel here—the art of memory and the science of evaluation were indistinguishable for most members of the humanist intelligentsia. The couplet to this poem, however, is something more than commonplace: "To thee therefore right noble Lord I send / This present of my paines, it to defend." This gift—the sonnet, the epic, the material book—this present offers to preserve an intimate culture of patronage, a culture that printing was beginning to thwart. There is, of course, a pun in "this present": like Northumberland, the successor to a heroic past, the gift makes a presence of the past. Both poet and patron, defenders of what has gone before, are located in an aftermath of afterwords.

The defensiveness of this rhetoric—specifically, defense by accumulation—is variously sustained to the end of the book; the gathering concludes, as does each book of the poem, with an attempted recollection of all errata. Yet the gathering was apparently itself egregiously errant. Spenser had begun with a dedicatory sonnet to the Lord High Chancellor, followed by the sonnet to Essex, then Oxford, and so forth. But he had left out Burghley.

Perhaps Ralegh, perhaps Ponsonby, perhaps Wolfe, Burghley's partner in propaganda, someone convinced Spenser that the omission had to be remedied (or that Burghley's inclusion could be hazarded), though not before several copies had been sewn in their original form.[11] The solution devised was the cancelation of the two leaves containing the first eight dedicatory sonnets and the substitution of a single quarto sheet, to be slipped in place of the canceled leaves, just before the last leaf (Fig. 1).

Pp1r-Pp3r "Letter to Ralegh"
Pp3v-Pp5v Commendatory Poems

First State
Pp6r Hatton, Essex
Pp6v Oxford, Northumberland
Pp7r Ormond/Ossory, Howard
Pp7v Grey, Ralegh

Second State
Qq1r Hatton, Burleigh
Qq1v Oxford, Northumberland
Qq2r Cumberland, Essex
Qq2v Ormond/Ossory, Howard
Qq3r Hunsdon, Grey
Qq3v Buckhurst, Walsingham
Qq4r Norris, Ralegh
Qq4v Countess of Pembroke

Pp8r Lady Carew, Ladies
Pp8v Errata

This arrangement was not so complicated that *some* of the extant copies could not preserve just this collation, but it was complicated enough that many copies have the arrangement variously botched—the new sheet (Qq) bound in after the errata sheet or at the front of the volume, or the new sheet included somewhere but without the cancelations having been made.[12] The copy text for the 1596 edition may have been one of several in which the errata page was mistakenly canceled along with the preceding two leaves, so that in a momentary triumph of Spenserian cultural atavism the traditional pursuit of patronage kept print from its modern function of stabilizing a corrected text. The desire volubly to please all and offend none corrupts Spenser's text, giving us one more bibliographical referent for the increasingly logocentric demons of the epic's next installment. In this second edition of an incomplete epic, the longing for closure intensifies; the closure may be specified as the roundup of all Faults Escaped, a closure at once narrative and editorial.

I have been considering the first state of this final gathering as a sober meditation on the belatedness of dedicatory and prefatory gestures, have been considering that what provokes these afterthoughts was the bibliographic fact that the "Letter" and the dedicatory sonnets had been physically displaced. Of course, since we cannot fix the moment at which this material was written, the term "meditation" may be too strong. Since Spenser may have written this material before he learned that it would not be used as front matter, the mutual convenience of form and theme may well be merely serendipitous. However, we probably can date the dedicatory sonnets of the second state, which were almost certainly written during the last stages of Wolfe's print run. If the deft insertion of dedicatory sonnets to Burghley and others was a careful response to social exigencies, it was also an artisanal response to the exigencies of material production and, thus, an occasion for the quickening of Spenser's bibliographical imagination.

The new sonnets were written to fit. They are variations on those already composed, interpolated in ways that strengthen the groupings in this collection of sonnets. Inwardly propagated, this collection becomes, in this version, a sonnet *sequence*, a unit now shaped by the material form of the book. The first sequence occasionally pairs its poems to make coherent pages, but the new sequence is organized by opening. The initial poem to Hatton, figuring him as the pillar of a neo-Roman empire, is now paired and isolated on a recto page (Qq1) with the poem to Burghley, which figures him as Atlas. The poem to Burghley speaks generally of the deeper sense concealed by the veil of allegory; the poem to Oxford on its verso is more personal: "th'antique glory of thine auncestry / Under a shady vele is therein writ." Indeed, as one turns the page to encounter a new opening (Qq1v-Qq2)—the sonnets to Oxford, and Northumberland, to Cumberland (a new poem), and the sonnet to Essex (now newly displaced)—the theme switches from cultural maintenance to the personal maintenance of family prestige: three poems on the sinking weight of predecession, what Spenser calls "high descent," proceeding to the sonnet to Essex, that eminent addendum. Essex is self-constructed, awaiting further poetic construction, and with this poem of belatedness Spenser arrests the thematics of family inheritance, so that we turn the page to confront an opening concerned with heroic isolation (Fig. 2).

This opening (Qq2v-Qq3) recalls the boundary anxieties that had intensified at the conclusions of Books II and III and anticipates the labors of civilization that will darken the second half of the poem. The dedicatees are a lord general of Munster; a lord high admiral victorious against the Armada; the queen's bodyguard and hero of a battle for control of the northern border, the battle of the Gelt; and the queen's lord deputy in Ireland—the earl of Ormond, and the lords Howard, Hunsdon, and Grey, a border patrol folded into the center of the new quarto sheet. (Fig. 3) From this rigorous opening, one turns to a chiastic construction (Qq3v-Qq4) that interrogates the relation between martial and poetic prowess, with sonnets to courtier poets—Sackville and Ralegh—framing sonnets to Walsingham and Norris, both poems concerned with the relation between the arts of war and the arts of peace (Fig. 4). The sonnet to Ralegh takes an entirely pastoral turn and so prepares for the final opening (Qq4v-Pp8), a

To looke vpon a worke of rare deuise
The which a workman setteth out to view,
And not to yield it the deserued prise,
That vnto such a workmanship is dew,
  Doth either proue the iudgement to be naught
  Or els doth shew a mind with enuy fraught.

To labour to commend a peece of worke,
Which no man goes about to discommend,
Would raise a iealous doubt that there did lurke,
Some secret doubt, whereto the prayse did tend.
  For when men know the goodnes of the wyne,
  'T is needlesse for the hoast to haue a signe.

Thus then to shew my iudgements to be such
As can discerne of colours blacke, and white,
As also to free my minde from enuies tuch,
That never giues to any man his right,
  I here pronounce this workmanship is such,
  As that no pen can set forth too much.

And thus I hang a garland at the dore,
Not for to shew the goodnes of the ware:
But such hath beene the custome heretofore,
And customes very hardly broken are.
  And as when your taste shall tell you this is trew,
  Then looke you giue your hoast his vtmost dew.

                    Ignoto.

To the right honourable Sir Christopher Hatton,
  Lord high Chauncelor of England. &c.

THose prudent heads, that with theire counsels wise
  Whylom the Pillours of th'earth did sustaine,
  And taught ambitious Rome to tyrannise,
  And in the neck of all the world to rayne,
Oft from those graue affaires were wont abstaine,
  With th'sweet Lady Muses for to play:
  So Ennius the elder Africane,
  So Maro oft did Cæsars cares allay.
So you great Lord, that with your counsell sway
  The burdeine of this kingdom mightily,
  With like delightes sometimes may eke delay,
  The rugged brow of carefull Policy;
And to these ydle rymes lend litle space,
Which for their titles sake may find more grace.

To the right honourable the Lo. Burleigh Lo. high
  Threasurer of England.

TO you right noble Lord, whose carefull brest
  To menage of most graue affaires is bent,
  And on whose mightie shoulders most doth rest
  The burdein of this kingdomes gouernement,
As the wide compasse of the firmament,
  On Atlas mighty shoulders is vpstayd;
  Vnsitly I these ydle rimes present,
  The labor of lost time, and wit vnstayd:
Yet if their deeper sence be inly wayd,
  And the dim vele, with which from comune vew
  Their fairer parts are hid, aside be layd,
  Perhaps not vaine they may appeare to you.
Such as they be, vouchsafe them to receaue,
And wipe their faults out of your censure graue.

                              E. S.

Figure 1. Spenser's dedicatory sonnets to Hatton and Burghley from the 1590 *Faerie Queene*, second state (Qq1r). *By permission of the Folger Shakespeare Library.*

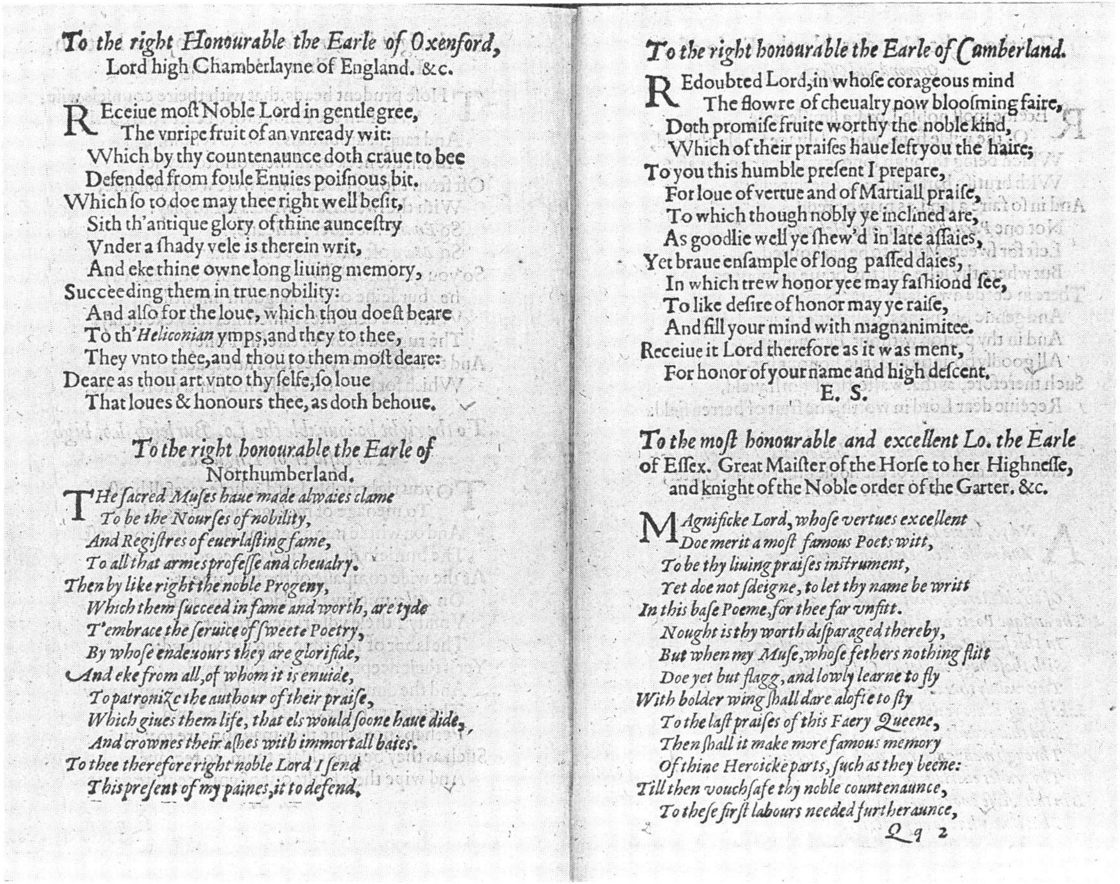

To the right Honourable the Earle of Oxenford,
Lord high Chamberlayne of England. &c.

R Eceiue moſt Noble Lord in gentle gree,
The vnripe fruit of an vnready wit:
Which by thy countenaunce doth craue to bee
Defended from foule Enuies poiſnous bit.
Which ſo to doe may thee right well beſit,
Sith th'antique glory of thine aunceſtry
Vnder a ſhady vele is therein writ,
And eke thine owne long liuing memory,
Succeeding them in true nobility:
And alſo for the loue, which thou doeſt beare
To th'*Heliconian* ymps, and they to thee,
They vnto thee, and thou to them moſt deare:
Deare as thou art vnto thy ſelfe, ſo loue
That loues & honours thee, as doth behoue.

To the right honourable the Earle of
Northumberland.

THe ſacred Muſes haue made alwaies clame
To be the Nourſes of nobility,
And Regiſtres of euerlaſting fame,
To all that armes profeſſe and cheualry.
Then by like right the noble Progeny,
Which them ſucceed in fame and worth, are tyde
T'embrace the ſeruice of ſweete Poetry,
By whoſe endeuours they are glorifide,
And eke from all, of whom it is enuide,
To patronize the authour of their praiſe,
Which giues them life, that els would ſoone haue dide,
And crownes their aſhes with immortall baies.
To thee therefore right noble Lord I ſend
This preſent of my paines, it to defend.

To the right honourable the Earle of Cumberland.

R Edoubted Lord, in whoſe corageous mind
The flowre of cheualry now bloosming faire,
Doth promiſe fruite worthy the noble kind,
Which of their praiſes haue left you the haire;
To you this humble preſent I prepare,
For loue of vertue and of Martiall praiſe,
To which though nobly ye inclined are,
As goodlie well ye ſhew'd in late aſſaies,
Yet braue enſample of long paſſed daies,
In which trew honor yee may faſhiond ſee,
To like deſire of honor may ye raiſe,
And fill your mind with magnanimitee.
Receiue it Lord therefore as it was ment,
For honor of your name and high deſcent.
E. S.

To the moſt honourable and excellent Lo. the Earle
of Eſſex. Great Maiſter of the Horſe to her Highneſſe,
and knight of the Noble order of the Garter. &c.

MAgnificke Lord, whoſe vertues excellent
Doe merit a moſt famous Poets witt,
To be thy liuing praiſes inſtrument,
Yet doe not ſdeigne, to let thy name be writt
In this baſe Poeme, for thee far vnfitt.
Nought is thy worth diſparaged thereby,
But when my Muſe, whoſe fethers nothing flitt
Doe yet but flagg, and lowly learne to fly
With bolder wing ſhall dare alofte to ſty
To the laſt praiſes of this Faery Queene,
Then ſhall it make more famous memory
Of thine Heroicke parts, ſuch as they beene:
Till then vouchſafe thy noble countenaunce,
To theſe firſt labours needed furtheraunce,
Qq 2

Figure 2. Dedicatory sonnets to Oxford and Northumberland (Qq1v), Cumberland and Essex (Qq2r). *By permission of the Folger Shakespeare Library.*

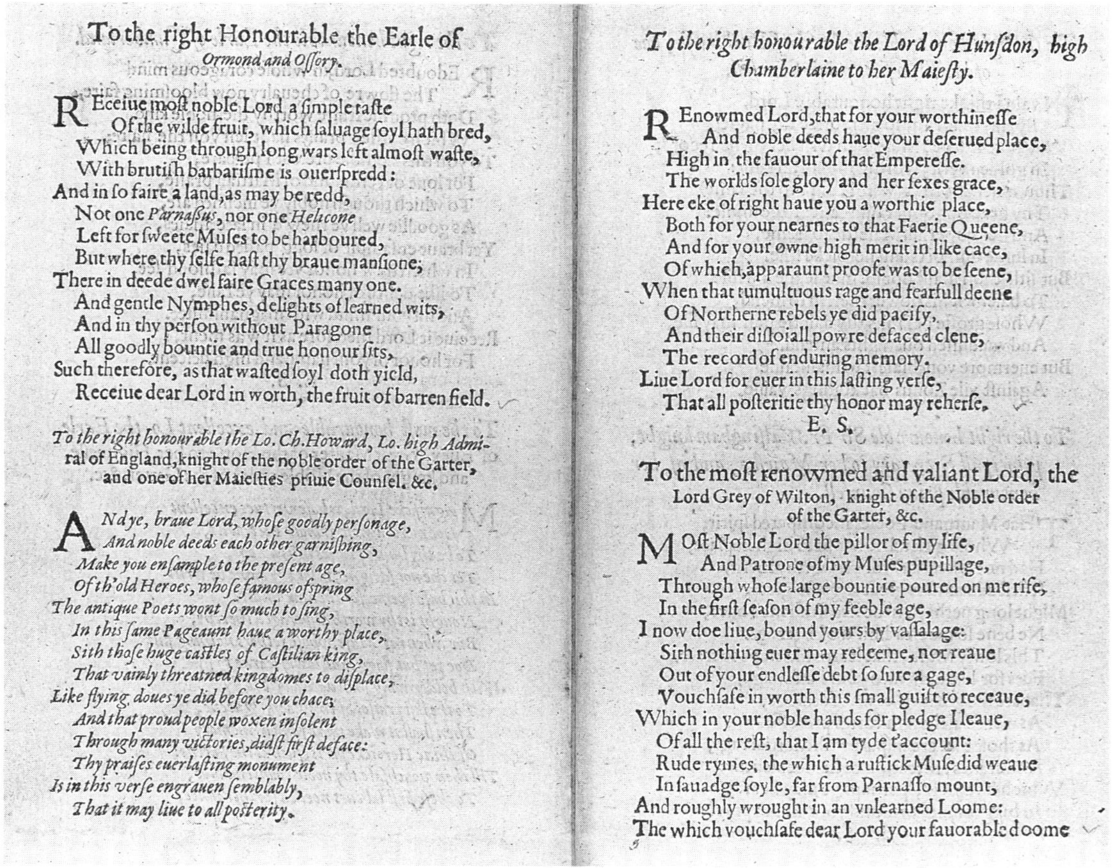

To the right Honourable, the Earle of
Ormond and Ossory.

REceiue most noble Lord, a simple taste
  Of the wilde fruit, which saluage soyl hath bred,
Which being through long wars left almost waste,
  With brutish barbarisme is ouerspredd:
And in so faire a land, as may be redd,
  Not one *Parnasse,* nor one *Helicone*
Left for sweete Muses to be harboured;
  But where thy selfe hast thy braue mansione;
There in deede dwell faire Graces many one.
  And gentle Nymphes, delights of learned wits,
And in thy person without Paragone
  All goodly bountie and true honour sits,
Such therefore, as that wasted soyl doth yield,
Receiue dear Lord in worth, the fruit of barren field.

To the right honourable the Lo. Ch. Howard, Lo. high Admiral of England, knight of the noble order of the Garter, and one other Maiesties priuie Counsell, &c.

ANd ye, braue Lord, whose goodly personage,
  And noble deeds each other garnishing,
Make you ensample to the present age,
  Of th'old Heroes, who se famous ofspring
The antique Poets wont so much to sing,
  In this same Pageaunt haue a worthy place,
Sith those huge castles of Castilian king,
  That vainly threatned kingdomes to displace,
Like flying doues ye did before you chace;
  And that proud people woxen insolent
Through many victories, didst first deface:
  Thy praises euerlasting monument
Is in this verse engrauen semblably,
That it may liue to all posterity.

To the right honourable the Lord of Hunsdon, *high Chamberlaine to her Maiesty.*

REnowmed Lord, that for your worthinesse
  And noble deeds haue your deserued place,
High in the fauour of that Emperesse,
  The worlds sole glory and her sexes grace,
Here eke of right haue you a worthie place,
  Both for your nearnes to that Faerie Queene,
And for your owne high merit in like cace,
  Of which, apparaunt proofe was to be seene,
When that tumultuous rage and fearfull deene
  Of Northerne rebels ye did pacify,
And their dissoiall powre defaced clene,
  The record of enduring memory.
Liue Lord for euer in this lasting verse,
That all posteritie thy honor may reherse.
                 E. S.

To the most renowmed and valiant Lord, the Lord Grey of Wilton, knight of the Noble order of the Garter, &c.

MOst Noble Lord the pillor of my life,
  And Patrone of my Muses pupillage,
Through whose large bountie poured on me rife,
  In the first season of my feeble age,
I now doe liue, bound yours by vassalage:
  Sith nothing euer may redeeme, nor reaue
Out of your endlesse debt so sure a gage,
  Vouchsafe in worth this small guift to receaue,
Which in your noble hands for pledge I leaue,
  Of all the rest, that I am tyde t'account:
Rude rymes, the which a rustick Muse did weaue
  In sauadge soyle, far from Parnasso mount,
And roughly wrought in an vnlearned Loome:
The which vouchsafe dear Lord your fauorable doome.

Figure 3. Dedicatory sonnets to Ormond/Ossory and Howard (Qq2v), Hunsdon and Grey (Qq3r). *By per-mission of the Folger Shakespeare Library.*

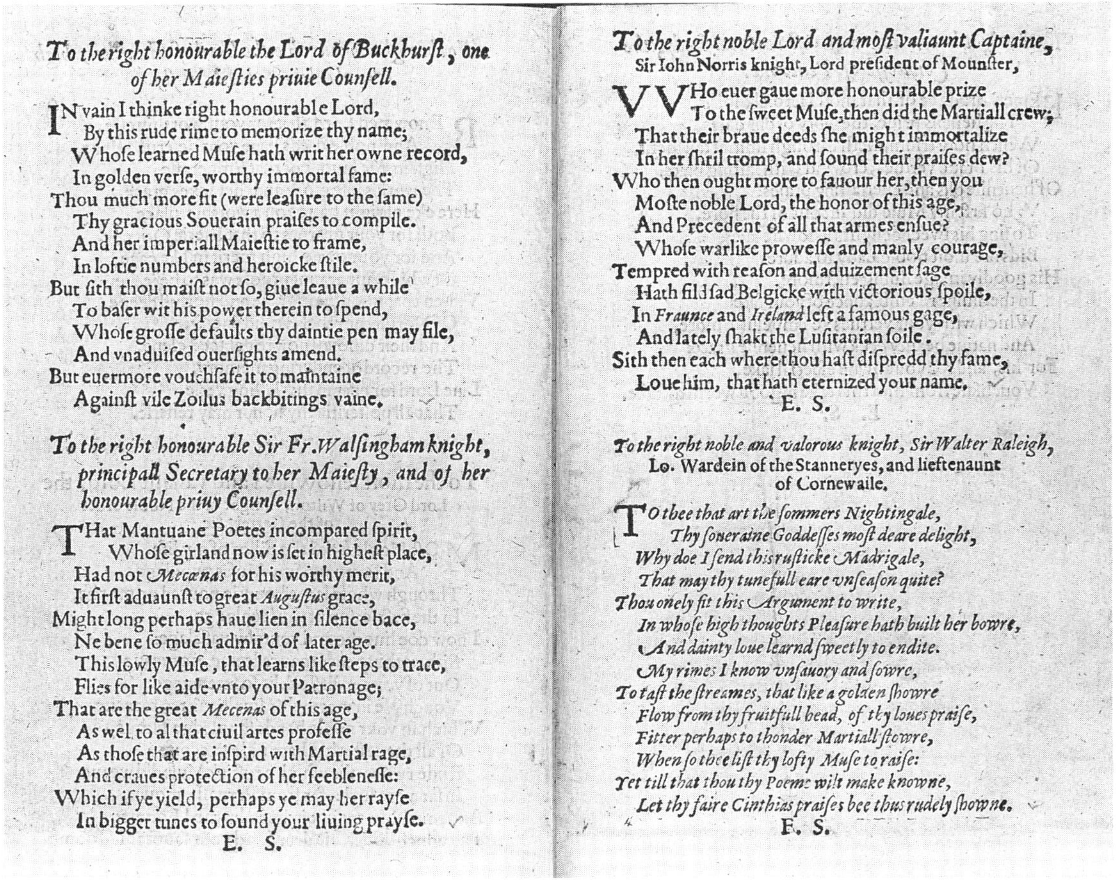

To the right honorable the Lord of Buckhurst, one
of her Maiesties priuie Counsell.

IN vaine I thinke right honourable Lord,
By this rude rime to memorize thy name;
Whose learned Muse hath writ her owne record,
In golden verse, worthy immortal fame:
Thou much more fit (were leasure to the same)
Thy gracious Soueran praises to compile.
And her imperiall Maiestie to frame,
In loftie numbers and heroicke stile.
But sith thou maist not so, giue leaue a while
To baser wit his power therein to spend,
Whose grosse defaults thy daintie pen may file,
And vnaduised ouersights amend.
But euermore vouchsafe it to maintaine
Against vile Zoilus backbitings vaine.
                                        E. S.

To the right honourable Sir Fr. Walsingham knight,
principall Secretary to her Maiesty, and of her
honourable priuy Counsell.

THat Mantuane Poetes incomparde spirit,
Whose girland now is set in highest place,
Had not Mecænas for his worthy merit,
It first aduaunst to great Augustus grace,
Might long perhaps haue lien in silence bace,
Ne bene so much admir'd of later age.
This lowly Muse, that learns like steps to trace,
Flies for like aide vnto your Patronage;
That are the great Mecænas of this age,
As wel to al that ciuil artes professe
As those that are inspird with Martial rage,
And craues protection of her feeblenesse:
Which if ye yield, perhaps ye may her rayse
In bigger tunes to sound your liuing prayse.
                                        E. S.

To the right noble Lord and most valiaunt Captaine,
Sir Iohn Norris knight, Lord president of Mounster.

VVHo euer gaue more honourable prize
To the sweet Muse, then did the Martiall crew?
That their braue deeds she might immortalize
In her shrill tromp, and found their praise dew?
Who then ought more to fauour her, then you
Most noble Lord, the honor of this age,
And Precedent of all that armes ensue?
Whose warlike prowesse and manly courage,
Tempred with reason and aduizement sage,
Hath fild sad Belgicke with victorious spoile,
In Fraunce and Ireland left a famous gage,
And lately shakt the Lusitanian soile.
Sith then each where thou hast dispredd thy fame,
Loue him, that hath eternized your name.
                                        E. S.

To the right noble and valorous knight, Sir Walter Ralegh,
Lo. Wardein of the Stanneryes, and lieftenaunt
of Cornewaile.

TO bee that art the sommers Nightingale,
Thy soueraine Goddesse most deare delight,
Why doe I send this rustike Madrigale,
That may thy tunefull eare vnseason quite?
Thou onely fit this Argument to write,
In whose high thoughts Pleasure hath built her bowre,
And dainty loue learnd sweetly to endite.
My rimes I know vnsauory and sowre,
To taste the streames, that like a golden showre
Flow from thy fruitfull head, of thy loues praise,
Fitter perhaps to thonder Martiall stowre,
When so the list thy lofty Muse to rayse:
Yet till that thou thy Poem wilt make knowne,
Let thy faire Cinthias praises bee thus rudely showne.
                                        E. S.

Figure 4. Dedicatory sonnets to Buckhurst and Walsingham (Qq3v), Norris and Ralegh (Qq4r). *By permission of the Folger Shakespeare Library.*

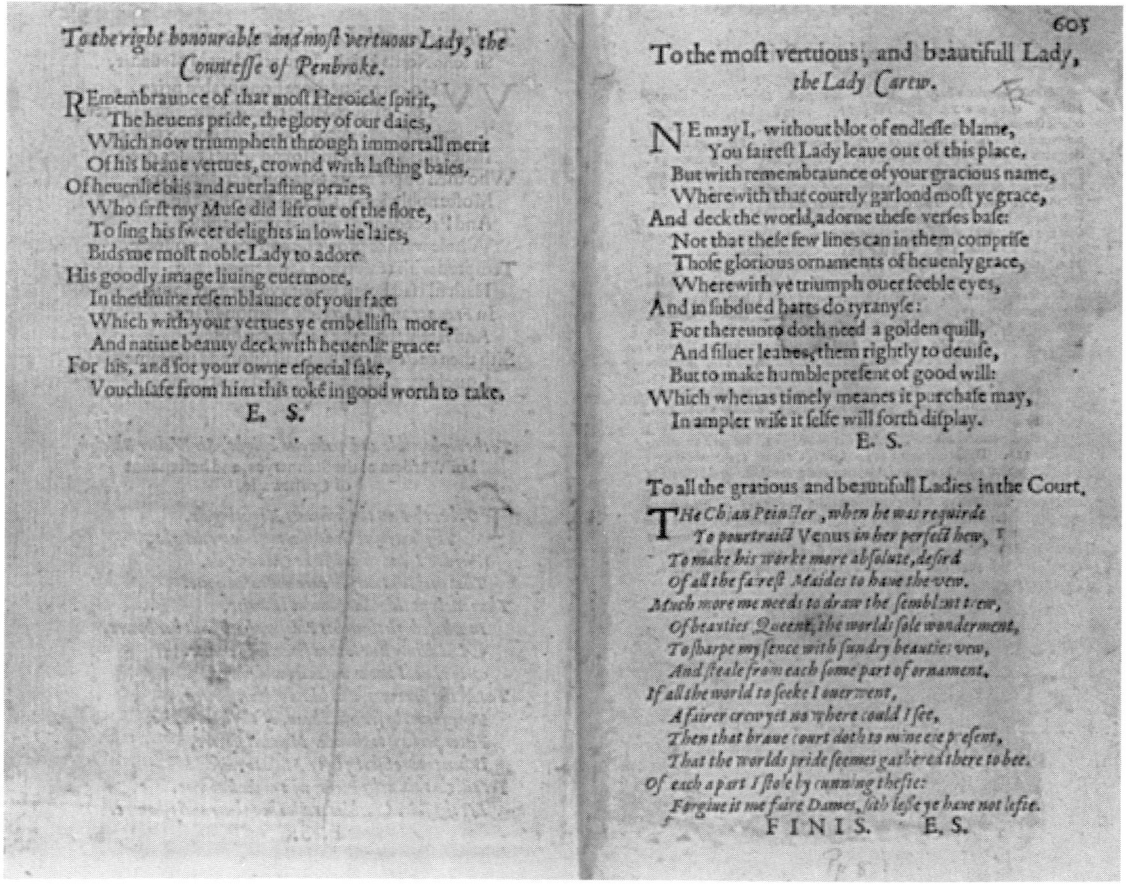

To the right honourable and most vertuous Lady, the
Countesse of Pembroke.

REmembrance of that most Heroicke spirit,
  The heauens pride, the glory of our daies,
Which now triumpheth through immortall merit
Of his braue vertues, crown'd with lasting Baies,
Of heuenfieldis and euerlasting grace,
Who first my Muse did lift out of the flore,
To sing his sweet delights in lowlie laies,
Bidsme most noble Lady to adore,
His goodly image liuing euermore,
In the diuine resemblance of your face,
Which with your vertues ye embellish more,
And make beauty deck with heuenlie grace:
For his, and for your owne especiall sake,
Vouchsafe from him this token in good worth to take,
                                                E. S.

To the most vertuous, and beautifull Lady,
the Lady Carew.

NE my I, without blot of endlesse blame,
  You fairest Lady leaue out of this place,
But with remembrance of your gracious name,
Wherewith that courtly garland most ye grace,
And deck the world, adorne these vertues bale:
Not that their few lines can in them comprise
Those glorious ornaments of heuenly grace,
Wherewith ye triumph ouer feeble eyes,
And in subdued parts do tyranyse:
For there vnto doth need a golden quill,
And siluer leaues, them rightly to deuise,
But to make humble present of good will:
Which when as timely meanes it purchase may,
In ampler wise it selfe will forth display.
                                                E. S.

To all the gratious and beautifull Ladies in the Court,

THe Chian Peincter, when he was requirde
  To pourtraict Venus in her perfect hew,
To make his worke more absolute, desird
Of all the fairest Maides to haue the vew.
Much more me needs to draw the semblant trew,
Of beauties Queene, the worlds sole wonderment,
To sharpe my sence with sundry beauties vew,
And steale from each some part of ornament,
If all the world to seeke I ouerwent,
A fairer crew yet no where could I see,
Then that braue court doth to mine eye present,
That the worlds pride seemes gathered there to bee.
Of each a part I stole by cunning thefte:
Forgiue it me faire Dames, sith lesse ye haue not lefte.
                                FINIS.   E. S.

Figure 5. Dedicatory sonnets to the Countess of Pembroke (Qq4v), Lady Carew and the "Ladies in the Court" (Pp8r). *By permission of the Folger Shakespeare Library.*

112

cadenza in sonnets to the countess of Pembroke, to Lady Cary, and to "all the gratious and beautifull Ladies in the Court" (Fig. 5).

The organization of these dedicatory poems into a sequence resists the disorder first imposed by the pace of printing. The claims of the author had been subordinated to those of the printer when the front matter had been displaced, but the new dedicatory work subordinates compositor to reader, rhetoricizes book design. According to Johnson's bibliographical reconstruction (1933), type for the original sequence had not been distributed when the revision began: individual pages could have been preserved intact and simply reimposed, but in fact composition proceeded quite differently. Instead, type for several individual poems was carefully lifted and moved to new positions as the new galley was arranged, presumably in the interests of sequence and to promote the semantic coherence of the opening. The new poems are written by hand, but the new sequence is "written" in the chase.

In the 1590 *Faerie Queene* writing is quite frequently an affliction. Amoret is *penned* by Busyrane: "with living bloud he those characters wrate" (III xii 31.3). At its best, writing is bitter. The lessons to be learned from unspeakable grief are written upon the heart with iron pen; that most distinctive attribute of Una, Praise-desire, Scudamour, and Britomart is a deep patience called *pen*siveness. But as often as not, writing does more harm than good: even the most well-intentioned writing of women's epic history "does all their deeds deface and dims their glories all" (III ii 1.9). This is not the only such instance: as a result of Busyrane's vicious penmanship, Amoret "had deathes owne image figurd in her face" (III xii 19.6). And when the affliction of writing is not itself a defacing, it can be managed only by a defacing. In Book I, Una rallies Red Crosse:

> Why shouldst thou then despeire, that chosen art?
> Where justice growes, there grows eke greater grace,
> The which doth quench the brond of hellish smart,
> And that accurst hand-writing doth deface. (I ix 53.5-8)

Writing and defacing are thus deeply fused in Spenser's imagination: to write is to deface; to redeem the written, one must deface the written. As Spenser moves towards the stanzas he will cancel, we see this doublet begin to whirl around itself. When Britomart startles Busyrane from his sadistic, disfiguring inscriptions—"His wicked bookes in hast he overthrew / Not caring his long labours to deface"—this defacing is, simply, a turn from figurative to physical violence; it's worth noting that poesis and praxis are firmly distinguished here:

113

> And fiercely running to that Lady trew
> A murdrous knife out of his pocket drew,
> The which he thought, for villeinous despight,
> In her tormented bodie to embrew. (III xii 32.2-7)

Britomart seizes his hand, but Busyrane twists away, and, at this moment, trenchant inscription gives way to trenchant impression:

> And turning to her selfe his fell intent,
> Unwares it strooke into her snowie chest,
> That little drops empurpled her faire brest.
> Exceeding wroth therewith the virgin grew,
> Albe the wound was nothing deepe imprest. (III xii 33.3-7)

From pen to press, darkly. The epic is grimly excited by some horror about writing, but as the first installment concludes, Spenser minutely adjusts the representation of this horror to the impending conditions of publication. The doublet of writing and defacing is on the verge of admitting a third term here—which is to say that we are precisely at that brink at which imagination, the object of criticism, anticipates event, the object of biography. In this case, the event is, simply, the occasion of publication.

The press takes the place of the pen in one of the interpolated dedicatory sonnets, the new sonnet to Hunsdon, which is closely modeled on its predecessor, to Howard. Hunsdon is told, "Here eke of right have you a worthie place," which place is that perpetually unstable locus of the dedicatory page—here in the array of similarly honorable dedicatees, here in the poet's esteem, here in the locus of the heroic poem. He is so honored "Both for your nearnes to that Faerie Queene, / And for your owne high merit in like cace." "In like cace" is also unstable of reference: it means both "in any case" (Hunsdon would be honorable even without the ennobling proximity of Elizabeth) and "in situations resembling those in which the Knights of Maidenhead find themselves." These are strong lines, difficult to construe. It bears noting that another meaning of "in like cace" surfaces, as the jargon of the printshop begins to obtrude:

> . . . for your owne high merit in like cace,
> Of which apparaunt proofe was to be seene,
> When that tumultuous rage and fearfull deene
> Of Northerne rebels ye did pacify
> And their disloiall powre defaced clene,
> The record of enduring memory.

The exercise of imperial power is at once a defacing of rebellion and the imprinting of a permanent record. Here in one of the poems "written" in the chase, the press occupies an imaginative space once occupied by writing.

After Dante and Petrarch, the truly ambitious poet declares his ambitions by constructing—or by inviting the discovery of—an autobiograpical narrative within the sequence of his writings. It is a commonplace of the dominant strain of Spenser criticism that Spenser reaches back past these poets to the more celebrated narrative model of the *cursus virgilianus*. Richard Rambuss (1993) has recently pressed to the forefront of those critical of the Virgilian grid as a means of measuring Spenser's life work. For Rambuss, the internal coherence of this model poetic career, its apparent sufficiency and closure, distracts us from attending to the coherence of Spenser's professional, nonliterary career. Rambuss makes the case that Spenser's career as a secretary was imbued with very particular intellectual and affective regularities, habits of mind and manner that not only shaped his public actions but in turn shaped his literary work. There are other briefs to be filed against the critical insistence on Spenser's Virgilianism, and I wish to linger over two of the least complex. The first is simply that many of his works cannot be plotted along the Virgilian cursus. Spenser's various engagements with the sonnet, that most Petrarchan instrument of literary autobiography, interrupt and even resist the press of his Virgilian self-identification. The second objection to a fixation on the Virgilian cursus is that it is easy for such "career criticism" to represent each stage of the cursus as inevitable, each poem as a function of the career system. Even the most exclusively literary biography ought to steer clear of any account that misses the uncertainties of composition, the mystery of the next thing. In Spenser's case the passage between works is high-strung, nervous, full of backward glances, anything but inevitable. At the brink of publication, he recoils from presswork with new handwriting, new sonnets, and these dedicatory sonnets betray a fundamentally recursive turn.[13]

It might be more useful to speak of this career, then, not as Virgilian but as distinctively post-Petrarchan. For Spenser, as for many of his contemporaries, the sonnet is one of the crucial instruments of literary self-identification, a means of shaping a Life within his Work, but the Spenserian sonnet articulates the Spenserian career quite idiosyncratically. Writing sonnets in the chase, he teases his career out of a dialogue between manuscription and printing, inscribes his career upon a publication history. I take it as a fundamental fact of Spenser's biography that the poet experienced himself bibliographically.

Let me develop this proposition by instancing another way in which the critical insistence on Spenser's Virgilianism is a misrepresentation, albeit a misrepresentation of Spenser's own making. That misrepresentation is inscribed in the first four lines of *The Faerie Queene*, after all, which paraphrase the lines interpolated, prefixed, onto the opening of the *Aeneid* sometime in the second century.

> Ille ego, qui quondam gracili modulatus avena
> carmen, et egressus silvis vicina coegi
> ut quamvis avido parerent arva colono
> gratum opus agricolis; at nunc horrentia (Virgil ed. 1934, 1:241)

At the opening of *The Faerie Queene* we are reminded that Spenser also begins with pastoral and ends with epic. We seldom remark that he leaves out the middle term in the Virgilian sequence, that his lines might remind us that he wrote no *gratum opus agricolis*, and we go about our critical business satisfied that his career is Virgilian *enough*, since he began with pastoral and ended with epic.[14]

Of course, Spenser did not begin with pastoral.

If editors since Todd (1805) are to be trusted (I will take up this problem shortly), when Spenser's pastorals were first published in 1579 his first published verse had been in print for exactly ten years. That the twenty-two sonnets in *The Theatre for Voluptuous Worldlings* are not identified in print as Spenser's should not set them securely outside the circle that includes the poems made canonical by Virgilianist criticism, since *The Shepheardes Calender* is similarly anonymous.[15] The anonymity of Spenser's early sonnets was banal in 1569, but the anonymity of his eclogues is made to shimmer in 1579. There are sidelong suggestions in the *Calender* to promote their attribution and suggestions in the *Letters* of 1580 that are intensified to the point at which attribution is all but secured. All but: the maturation of Spenserian authorship is incomplete until signature Pp3r of the 1590 *Faerie Queene*, where "A Letter of the Authors expounding his whole intention in the course of this worke" (Pp1r) is, finally, attributed—*Ed. Spenser*—although what that maturation entails is by no means a matter of fact. The material, bibliographic continuity that reaches back from this signature, through the letter, through the nearly adjacent poem (there is a blank page [Oo8v] between the "Letter to Ralegh" and the end of Book III), to the announcement, "Lo I the man, whose Muse whilome did maske, / As time her taught in lowly Shepheards weeds," is not extensible further, back to *The Shepheardes Calender;* the ideological extension of that bibliographic continuity is another matter. The reach of this late imprinted signature back into the past, the recursive history of the interpellation of "Spenser," ought to be guided, not constrained, by the exquisitely inexplicit deictic of "Lo. . . ." Actually, the lines do not attribute other poems to the poet; instead they inform us that, whilom, the poet was disguised.

The regress from the signature not only disarticulates poet and poem but also disturbs the very identity of the poet. To put it less gnomically, there is a pattern in the slow emergence of Spenser's identity as poet, as the possible subject of authorial attributions. No evidence deriving from midcentury literary culture connects a young Edmund Spenser to the *Theatre* sonnets; authorial identity is occulted, but not unimaginable, in the bibliographic culture that surrounds *The Shepheardes Calender*, for the 1580 *Letters* reflect quite obscurely on the man in lowly shepherd's weeds; authorial identity is less shadowy in the bibliographic culture of the 1590 *Faerie Queene*, for the name on signature Pp3r shines strongly backward on a sequence of materially contiguous pages. Two volumes published in 1591 bear the phrase, "By Ed. Sp." on their title pages; a title page of 1595 reads "Amoretti / And / Epithalamion. / Written not long since / by Edmunde / Spenser."

I have elsewhere described how the wedding volume of 1595 "interrupts" the *cursus virgilianus* by its pointed address to the suspension of the epic (Loewenstein 1987). Ponsonby's publication of *Complaints* is perhaps an equally serious interruption to a specifically Virgilian cursus since it is the first publication to cast any attributive light whatsoever on the very un-Virgilian poems of van der Noot's *Theatre*. It is a very dim light: the diffidently recursive heading to the last collection of poems in the volume reads simply "The Visions of Petrarch / formerly translated." It is characteristic of the attributive problems raised by the sonnets of *Complaints* that even "formerly translated" is ambiguous. We usually take it to mean that these seven sonnets are revised versions of poems that Spenser translated in his youth for inclusion in van der Noot's *Theatre*. The earlier collection, headed "Epigrams," consists of four douzaines, two sonnets in the Surreyan form, and a four-line envoy; it is followed by fifteen "Sonets," eleven of which appear in revised form, sometimes barely altered, in *Complaints* under the heading "Visions of Bellay," but without designation as "formerly translated." There is another sense in which the poems of the "Visions of Petrarch" may be considered as having been formerly translated, a sense inapplicable to the "Visions of Bellay," for a French translation, Marot's, stands between Spenser's poems and Petrarch's "Canzone of Visions" (*Canz.* 323). That "formerly translated" may refer to Marot's labor and not to Spenser's own prior work registers the insecure tenure that the poems in van der Noot's collection have within the larger canon of Spenser's works.[16] But to concentrate on the awkward mechanics of attribution will be to ignore Spenser's "emergencies" within Elizabethan book culture. The publication of poems formerly translated may interrupt the *cursus virgilianus*, but it assists in shaping a larger bibliographic career of what we might call a steadily increasing onymity.[17] Instead of asking whether Spenser did the translations for the *Theatre*, we may as usefully treat the *Theatre* as a source text for the poet's developing corpus and ask how, in the slow work of "owning" the poems of *Complaints*, Spenser has responded to his source.[18]

The *Complaints* volume both alters the source texts and supplements them with related work. Thus the *Visions of Petrarch* and *Bellay* are complemented by the *Visions of the Worlds Vanitie* and the *Ruines of Rome*, at once formal and modal imitations of the "core" series. This is not the first public "Spenserian" engagement with this mode. If the Spenser-Harvey correspondence is to be relied upon—and whether or not the biographer trusts those letters, they do significantly articulate the "Spenser" of print—a collection of Immerito's *Dreames* was nearly ready for publication as early as 1580, and the description of this volume strikingly suggests a genetic middle term between van der Noot's *Theatre* and Spenser's *Complaints*. The first letter in the correspondence (in ed. 1912, 611-12; Letter 3 in the Variorum *Prose Works*) implies that the anticipated volume was to have been framed along the lines of the *Calender*: Spenser promises illustrations and a running paraphrase by E. K. Indeed, E. K. mentions the *Dreames* in a letter to Harvey prefaced to the *Calender* and, in the gloss to the "November" eclogue, refers the reader to his own "Commentarye upon the dreames of the same Authour."[19] All of these references may be red herrings—certainly Harvey's, Spenser's, and E. K.'s letters all contain references to poems that are difficult to identify and may never have been written—but it is not difficult to credit the plan for a volume of dream-visions. The *Theatre* contains poems accompanied by illustrations and a running paraphrase, which is to say that van der Noot's volume may be described in terms not very different from those that Spenser uses to describe the anticipated volume; certainly it would have cost very little labor to recast the *Theatre* as a volume closely resembling the *Calender*. It thus seems quite plausible that the volume anticipated in 1580 was to have been an expansive revision and adaptation of van der Noot, a proto-*Complaints*.[20]

I am suggesting that Spenser was preparing to make a formal and modal claim on the *Theatre*, if not a proprietary one, at least as early as 1580. One may ask what became of this project *during* the eighties, and here again, the Spenser-Harvey correspondence proves informative. Interesting as these letters may be as an adumbration of the *Complaints*, they are rather more important as a published attempt to associate new poetic concerns with the author of the *Calender*. The letters debate how the pastoralist is to be refashioned, perhaps as an epic poet—more after the manner of Ariosto, in fact, than that of Virgil—and perhaps as a visionary poet—after the manner of, say, the Petrarch of van der Noot's *Theatre*. Harvey's second printed letter, while somewhat disparaging the achievement of the draft *Faerie Queene*, praises the visionary idiom of the soon-to-be-published *Dreames*:

> I like your *Dreames* passing well: and the rather, bicause they favour of that singular extraordinarie veine and invention, whiche I ever fancied moste, and in a manner admired onelye in *Lucian, Petrarche, Aretine, Pasquill*, and all the most delicate, and fine conceited Grecians and Italians. . . . As well for the singularitie of the manner, as the Divinitie of the matter, I hearde once a Divine, preferre *Sainte Johns Revelation* before al the veriest *Mætaphysicall Visions*, and jollyest conceited *Dreames* or *Extasies*, that ever were devised by one or other, howe admirable, or superexcellent soever they seemed otherwise to the worlde. And truely I am so confirmed in this opinion, that when I bethinke me of the verie notablest, and moste wonderful Propheticall, or Poeticall Vision, that ever I read, or hearde, me seemeth the proportion is so unequall, that there hardly appeareth anye semblaunce of Comparison: no more in a manner (specially for Poets) than doth betweene the incomprehensible Wisedome of God, and the sensible Wit of Man.[21]

The closer to apocalypse, the better—hence Harvey's preference of the *Dreames* to the "Elvish Queene." But although Spenser was on the verge of publishing the visionary poems, he seems to have devoted his literary energy in the early eighties to epic. Harvey urges a choice; Spenser adopts a middle course. In order to achieve that hybrid which was to be the *Protestant* romance epic, Spenser strove to accommodate epic and apocalyptic vision each to the other. According to Bennett (1942), Spenser soon began work on his Book of Revelation, the Legend of Holiness, proceeding thence to his critique of vision, of scopophilia, the Legend of Temperance. Thus the project of owning the idiom of the *Theatre* was absorbed into the epic project; it was only reasserted as an autonomous effort a decade later when, in *Complaints*, the work of the *Theatre* is owned and elaborated.

I have already spoken of the way in which the *Visions of the Worlds Vanitie* and the *Ruines of Rome* complement the "core" series. Of course, the *Ruines of Rome* complement the *Visions of Bellay* in another way: the *Visions of Bellay* revise translations of du Bellay's *Songe*; the *Ruines of Rome* translate du Bellay's *Antiquitez de Rome*. Although a long-standing involvement with the visionary emerges unalloyed in *Complaints*, that involvement is further specified by Spenser's particular and sustained engagement with du Bellay. Du Bellay's sonnets of vision break with a Petrarchan tradition of erotic theme and intensely private, intensely psychological attention. His "I"— and thence Spenser's—is little more than an organ of vision, perhaps, too,

119

a small vessel of grief. "I saw," writes van der Noot's translator, and the balance of his poems are pitched toward the object of sight.

Bellayan vision becomes a habit with Spenser. Its full idiosyncrasy may be gauged by comparing his sonneteering manner with that of his most eminent contemporary. Shakespeare's characteristic opening, besides a gasping "O," is a declaration of circumstance, "When"—"When I consider," "When my love swears," "When to the sessions of sweet silent thought." It locates him in a web of external constraint or in a nest of self-conscious meditation. Spenser likes to begin with an ostensive "the," pointing outward, effacing himself; or he will inititate a simile—"Like as a culver," "Like as a ship," "Like as a huntsman"—deferring self-reference for four lines or so and sometimes deferring it indefinitely. His is a world of perception, Shakespeare's a world of experience; his is an epistemological art, Shakespeare's a psychoanalytic one.

The opposition can be overstated, though it provides useful poles for the analysis of the revisions for *Complaints*. As has already been remarked, most of the revisions involve minor prosodic adjustments, and sometimes these adjustments are entirely generic. Again, one senses an impulse toward inconspicuousness. The tendency is actually easiest to trace in the revised *Visions of Petrarch*, where a number of douzaines from the *Theatre* are transformed into sonnets. The revisions often dispense with the schematic calibration of the early renderings and rely on personal response as the extrasyntactic guarantors of shape and coherence, relying, that is, on an entirely generic disposition. The transformation of the fifth poem, a douzaine, into a sonnet tells the tale. In the *Theatre*, the concluding line is perfunctory and nearly formulaic: "For pitie and love my heart yet burnes in paine." In the later version, it becomes

> That yet my heart burnes in exceeding paine,
> For ruth and pitie of so haples plight.
> O let mine eyes no more see such a sight.

"Love" has been expunged as irrelevant (we could attribute this to du Bellay's influence); Spenser will tolerate the dull and redundant "ruth and pitie" in order to secure the excision. It would be perverse to speak of either version of the poem as impersonal and extroverted, but the revision uses privacy to pad out the poem, as a kind of convenience. The last line is more interesting, of course, for it transforms a poem about a vision into a poem about vision, specifically into a poem about the regulation of the visionary. Such specification need not have come late in Spenser's career and may be plausibly traced to the early eighties: the revisions for *Complaints* suggest affinities with the "January" or "Julye" eclogue, as well as with the Legends of Holiness, Temperance, or Courtesy, texts in which the dispositions to vision are as momentous as the sights they render. Those affinities are perhaps most strongly registered in the *Visions of Bellay* when the "monstroit" of du Bellay's French—"did shew" in the *Theatre* (4.9)—is rendered as "seem'd" in the revision (4.9; and see also 13.1, which has no precursor in the *Theatre*), semblance being, for readers of *The Faerie Queene*, the site of deepest excitation, the locus at which the phenomenological and the ethical are locked in most vibrant embrace.

Only rarely are the translations from du Bellay for *Complaints* so distinctive, tendentious. Indeed, they are often surprisingly faithful to their originals: Spenser is clearly checking his French source as he goes about the work of rhyming his blank verse *English* one. In sonnet 2, the description of a crystal edifice is revised more precisely to render its source; thus du Bellay:

> Elancoit mille rayz de son ventre profond
> Sur cent degrez dorez du plus fin or d'Afrique.

The *Theatre* version:

> Out of deepe vaute threw forth a thousand rayes
> Upon an hundred steps of purest golde.

And the revision:

> Out of her womb a thousand rayons threw
> On hundred steps of *Afrike* golds enchase

The recovery of the specifying "Afrike" and "womb" are obvious rectifications.[22] Spenser's rectifications operate at a larger scale as well. Four sonnets of *Songe* had been omitted in the *Theatre*, leaving a sequence shaped to serve van der Noot's reformist purposes. Van der Noot's Protestantism is fierce, and his Rome is very different from that of the (admittedly critical) Catholic du Bellay. Sometimes, to what would have been van der Noot's inconvenience, du Bellay's somewhat aloof historical allegory takes on a possibly topical cast, as for example when the cruel but maternal Roman wolf is slain by a thousand huntsmen descending from the mountains. The fall of the antique Empire is the primary plot here, but other barbarians had more recently threatened from the north. Van der Noot did not print a translation of this sonnet nor of those in which the city is toppled by a storm from the north or in which a rich ship is sunk by a north wind. Indeed, he suppressed anything that might be taken as a swipe, however oblique, at the spirit of northern reform. At best, one can say that he has simplified the sequence by a selection that obscures historical specificities.

Spenser's rectifications, then, manifest more than mere philological con-scientiousness. Restoring the missing poems to *Songe* restored some of the complexity to that sequence, some of the irony that binds the sequence to the longer, far more disenchanted *Antiquitez de Rome*.

The restorations also give us a sequence that flouts the tenor, the tone, and the prestige of Petrarchan sonneteering. The sinking ship is presented as the site of genial literary competition—"Much richer then that vessell seem'd to bee, / Which did to that sad Florentine appeare" (for which, see the "Canzone of Visions" or *Visions of Petrarch*, 2). This sort of relaxed competition with Petrarch was not admitted to the *Theatre*, but it was an early feature of the public representation of Spenser, and it obviously grew in importance, culminating in the fully agonistic wedding volume of 1595. At the outset, it constituted merely a mild detour from the *cursus virgilianus*. Harvey first advanced it in 1580 in the course of praising Spenser's vision-ary poetry at the expense of his sketchy epic: "I dare saye you wyll holde your selfe reasonably wel satisfied, if youre *Dreames* be but as well esteemed of in Englande, as *Petrarches Visions* be in Italy: whiche I assure you, is the very worst I wish you" (ed. 1912, 628b; Variorum *Prose Works*, 471). This competition is reopened at the beginning of the displaced front matter of the 1590 *Faerie Queene*, in W. R.'s commendatory sonnet, itself a vision-ary poem:

> Methought I saw the grave, where Laura lay,
> Within that Temple, where the vestall flame
> Was wont to burne. . . .
> All suddenly I saw the Faery Queene:
> At whose approch the soule of Petrarcke wept. (lines 1-3, 6-7)

So the rectification of the *Visions of Bellay* enacts a reappropriation of the sonnet not only contra van der Noot but also contra Petrarch. Spenser is enacting a preference. Restoring to the latter half of this sequence, for ex-ample, du Bellay's vision of the ship "plus riche assez que ne se monstroit celle / Qui apparut au triste Florentin" demonstrates the deeper resilience in du Bellay's darker imagination:

> I saw both ship and mariners each one,
> And all that treasure drowned in the maine:
> But I the ship saw after raisd' againe.

This restoration, an act of quasi-editorial fidelity, is also an instrument of Spenserian self-assertion. Du Bellay's last line suggests that this ship has some intrinsic resilience—"Puis vy la Nef se ressourdre sur l'onde"—whereas Spenser, in an uncharacteristic gesture of translator's self-assertion, restores the (non-Petrarchan) first-person agent of vision to stressed position and employs a construction—I saw it raised—that hints that the restoration may be a function of the poet's vision itself, the work of a seeing I who presents himself only in English. Spenser at sonnets is the most revisionary of literary autobiographers.

In what sense is Spenser's minute gesture of self-congratulation warranted? Certainly there is reason to regard the publication of this poem—its restoration to the Bellayan sequence of visions, its emphasis on the novelty and strength of a post-Petrarchan sonneteering, its assertion of some special, competitive Spenserian agency in the maintenance and polemical transformation of genre—as having been long delayed; there is reason, that is, to regard the agonistic address to the visionary to which Harvey commended his friend in 1580 as a struggle deferred. To assess why *Dreames* never appeared might enable us to construe the degree and configuration of the grave pleasure conveyed in the announcement that "I the ship saw after raisd' againe."

Many reasons for the *suppression* of a volume more or less ready for publication in 1580 have been offered or might be. The simplest is that something in the volume, something that cannot be located in the translations of either Petrarch or du Bellay—perhaps an early version of *Mother Hubberds Tale*—resumed and intensified the criticism of Burghley or the attack on the Alençon match in the *Calender*. Scrupulous conviction is also a plausible motive: the visionary translations may have seemed too deferential to the French (and particularly to the French Catholic du Bellay) at a moment when Spenser and those associated with Leicester might have wished to distance themselves from France. But this was less a moment for ideological assertion than for caution: Spenser and Harvey were writing in the aftermath of Sidney's rustication and of the revelation of Leicester's clandestine marriage, a moment for lying low. Given the awkward status of the Leicester group in late 1579, the *Calender*, with its dedication to Sidney, had been perhaps too bold. There is good reason to suppose that Singleton, the printer, did not realize how incautious are some of its eclogues when he registered and published it. He had published *The Gaping Gulf* a few months earlier and had barely escaped lurid punishment: his transfer of printing rights in the *Calender* in October of 1580 suggests a slightly tardy recognition that he could regard no Leicesterian poetry as innocuous.[23]

Spenser himself may have absorbed some of Singleton's prudence. The vatic coloring of the poems adapted from the *Theatre*, however pale, could have flashed with dangerous fierceness, particularly if Spenser had chosen to sustain the apocalypticism of the four final poems in van der Noot's volume, visions based on the Book of Revelation, the only poems in van der Noot's book that in no form found their way into *Complaints*. Spenser associates Colin with Piers the Plowman in the envoy to the *Calender* and had so declared a Puritan sympathy that a vatic or, worse, apocalyptic posture would have corroborated—and at precisely the moment at which the queen was dealing most sternly with the religious left. Defense of prophesyings, local convocations for scriptural disputation, which stirred up a grass-roots fundamentalism and threatened episcopacy, had cost Archbishop Grindal his eminence and authority, and a vatic poetry might have seemed too risky for a known supporter of Grindal.[24]

So there were obstacles aplenty, in 1580, to the publication of Immerito's *Dreames*, and many good reasons for Spenser to look back on 1579/80 as a missed occasion. To think of *Dreames* as having been uprooted from its occasion is to revisit, differently, a question that Jonathan Crewe shrewdly posed with respect to another of the poems in *Complaints*, *Mother Hubberds Tale*: "while the poem has mainly been taken as an index of Spenser's *early* career and position *vis-à-vis* the Burghley and Leicester factions, few discussions have fully taken up the question of the poem's 'late' reappearance in the 1591 *Complaints*" (1986, 55). Spenser's critics represent the eighties as an intermission in his literary career, and it bears remarking that this is not only a point of biographical fact but part of the structure of meaning that Spenser writes into his poems. "Lo I the man, whose Muse whilome did maske": virtually the first question that a beginning student asks about Spenser—"What does "whilome" mean?"—turns out to be a question about the eighties. The first lines of the epic recount not only a generic transition from pastoral to epic but also a temporal transition that entails personal discomfort, from whilom to now, from a masking at once celebratory, obfuscatory, and protective to a laborious, indecorous exposure. The poet is being elaborately modest, of course, but he is also elaborately specifying that the eighties entail a critical change in the (always in some sense dissociated) relation of poet to poem.

What does "whilome" mean in *Complaints*? The ruination of time is more than the dominant theme of the poems in the volume. By its constant reference to the decline of the Dudleys, the volume specifies the eighties as a period of cultural dislocation, in which the tasks of poetry become "unfitter." Throughout the volume Spenser finds himself faced with the task not of relocating himself in contemporary Elizabethan culture but of feigning a restoration of his earlier location within a lapsed Leicesterian culture. Thus, in the letter dedicatory to the *Ruines of Time,* he writes of Sidney's death,

> since God hath disdeigned the world of that most noble Spirit, which was the hope of all learned men, and the Patron of my young *Muses;* togeather with him both their hope of anie further fruit was cut off: and also the tender delight of those their first blossoms nipped and quite dead. Yet sithens my late cumming into *England,* some frends of mine (which might much prevaile with me, and indeede commaund me) knowing with howe straight bandes of duetie I was tied to him: as also bound unto that noble house, (of which the chiefe hope then rested in him) have sought to revive them by upbraiding me.

The volume, then, is deeply commemorative: the headlines to *Virgils Gnat* present the poem as "Long since dedicated / *To the most noble and excellent Lord,* / the earle of Leicester, late / deceased"; *Mother Hubberds Tale* is announced as having been "long sithens composed in the raw conceipt of my youth"; the *Visions of Petrarch* are "formerly translated." The opening pair of poems lays out the essential project of the volume: *The Ruines of Time* associates the fate of an anglicized Rome (as represented in Verulamium) with the personal fate of Leicester and goes on to celebrate his lost eminence; *The Teares of the Muses* celebrates the lost security and integrity of English art. In both instances, nostalgia is focused on an "antiquity" characterized by Spenser's intimate proximity to Sidney and Leicester, an antiquity the date of which can be fixed between early 1579 and the middle of 1580.

Fidelity to du Bellay carries the charge of fidelity to Leicester:

> I saw both ship and mariners each one,
> And all that treasure drowned in the maine:
> But I the ship saw after raisd' againe.

The deft assertion of the first person, unfaithful to its "source," marks the dislocation of publication from its proper cultural moment, a hiatus in Leicesterian order that must have seemed, in retrospect (in revisionary retrograph), the beginning of the end. The post-Petrarchan ship has sunk; when it is raised, the mariners are nowhere to be seen.

A similar gesture of conjoined rectification and melancholy self-assertion may be found at the opening of the sequence. After the introductory sonnet which calls the seeing I to attention—"loe now beholde"—du Bellay describes the grand, if vulnerable, crystalline "Fabrique" and the "hundred steps of *Afrike* gold" leading up to it. I have already drawn attention to the minute rectification of the lines from the *Theatre* version of sonnet 2—

> Out of deepe vaute threw forth a thousand rayes
> Upon an hundred steps of purest golde.

—revised as

> Out of her womb a thousand rayons threw
> On hundred steps of *Afrike* golds enchase. (7-8)

This is obviously a happy adjustment: the head of line 8 has been tightened, the merely syllabic clutter of "Upon an hundred" reduced on behalf of a line made now more decoratively, if still densely wrought.[25] But line 8 does more than rectify, for "enchase" is, after all, an innovation, and extremely revealing. It is a complex term, of centrifugal tendency: one enchases a relic by securing it in a reliquary, a stone by setting it in metal; one enchases metal by setting it with stones, or by inlaying it or overlaying it with other metals, or by engraving it. The very flutter in the term indicates how ornamentation compromises the distinction of figure and ground. Spenser usually treats such compromise as insidious, which is what makes his use of the term "enchase" so extraordinary. When Una appears for her betrothal, Spenser will profess that

> My ragged rimes are all too rude and bace
> Her heavenly lineaments for to enchace. (I xii 23.4-5)

The unnamed lady to whom Colin pipes upon Mount Acidale stands in the midst of the Graces "as a precious gemme, / Amidst a ring most richly well enchaced" (VI x 12.8-9); characteristically, the term does not settle the question of where preeminent luster might lie—ring and gem shimmer in conjunction. The term has such privileged honorific force that when the main entrance to Alma's castle is described as "enchaced with a wanton yvie twine" (II ix 24-5) it redeems the otherwise casually pejorative "wanton," making this one of the few instances in which Spenser allows the aesthetic to trump the ethical. Later, in Book VI, "to enchase" will be to blur the distinction not only between figure and ground, but between the aesthetic and the ethical, becoming the term used to describe the courteous, civil education of the bear-baby (VI iv 35.5). Spenser uses the term in *The Faerie Queene* to describe the burnished and shining goodness of craftwork, artisanal labor as the leading metaphor for the fashioning of a "person in vertuous and gentle discipline."

What does "enchase" mean in a poem outside the Virgilian canon? Here in the *Visions of Bellay* the term is employed as a substantive—the only such appearance of the term in the work of Immerito or Spenser, perhaps the only such appearance in English—and its syntax throws its antithetical semantic force into relief. Why import uncertainties about the very object of gaze, the configuration of competing surfaces, the locus of gleaming value? How does this craft-term apply here, if not as a mature reflection on translation, on the relation between intricate attention and diffuse effect in the visionary mode? Spenser enchases du Bellay in a line that confounds answerable rectification and onymous assertion. The term refers here to the intricate artisanry of revision, Spenser's contribution to a brilliance that is irreducibly collaborative. In this instance, moreover, the term refers to that rectification which is the long-awaited, the onymous, commission of the visionary poems to the press, an achievement irreducibly collaborative. Print enshrines an old authorial intention and occasion: in 1591 the manuscript sonnets of the lost Leicesterian setting were finally set in type and locked in the chase. The artisan's excitement, the desire to assist in the mechanical production of the book, may perhaps be gauged from the evidence of press correction.

> The table of variant readings for *Complaints* shows very clearly that the text underwent very careful proof-reading and revision while it was going through the press. In many of the formes a number of important corrections and the nature of many of these is such that it seems highly improbable that they could be the work of any person other than Spenser. If Spenser did not carefully oversee the printing of this volume, our only alternative is to conclude that the printed sheets were subjected to a most painstaking and accurate collation with this original manuscript. (Johnson 1933, 27)

Johnson may perhaps be overstating his case, since it is extremely difficult securely to identify the source of press corrections.[26] Nonetheless, several surviving sheets of *Complaints* were twice corrected—which might suggest unusual meticulousness—and the inner forme of sheet Y, on which most of the *Visions of Bellay* was printed, was corrected thrice—which almost certainly indicates unwonted fastidiousness.[27] From the *Theatre* to *Complaints*, du Bellay remains the object of artisanal enchase.

A few months earlier, Spenser's decade of isolated manuscription had come to an end when, in a complex collaboration between authorial and compositorial artisanry, the sequence dedicatory to *The Faerie Queene* was recomposed in the printer's chase. The immoderate (and unprecedented) proliferation of dedications—to the queen, sixteen named noblemen and noblewomen, and "all the gratious and beautifull Ladies in the Court"—betrays a curiously strained effort, an effort not so much to solicit or document patronage as to enchase, by means of print, the image of a culture of patronage. Yet the dedicatory poems are somewhat more commemorative than celebratory: the community projected in the dedicatory sequence is the residue of a lost culture of patronage, a Museum erected in "This present of my paines."

Of course, the nostalgia of Spenserian sonneteering has many sources—it is only reinforced by the experience of delayed publication. Spenser absorbed a version of his nostalgia from du Bellay, who had given Petrarch's laments over evanescence a social temporality: for Petrarch, lovely things fade from moment to moment; for du Bellay, cultures deteriorate in history. Du Bellay's influence, his use of the sonnet to express cultural nostalgia, can be felt in the dedicatory Museum of *The Faerie Queene* as well as in the rectified translations of *Complaints*. I suspect that Spenser's sonneteering is always a resumption of his relation to du Bellay, which means that it is also always a resumption of his career, a displaced front matter.

Placed as they are, the dedicatory sonnets mark the disruption of the narrative of *The Faerie Queene*, its incompletion. But the narrative progress of *The Faerie Queene* is forever being arrested; attention is constantly being diverted to edifice, pageant, or bower, toward some source of imaginative fixity, a center. The volume culminates in sonnets that not only reenact this antinarrative bent, but also mark its biographical origins in sonneteering. Antinarrative originates, for Spenser, in the sonnets of the *Theatre*, poems that anticipate Spenser's mature interest in the *spectacular* origins of knowledge. If the traditional sonnet returns to the experiences of frustration and incompletion, du Bellay's sonnets render arrested *historical* development, the experience of a balked cultural narrative. They not only lament the circumscription of Roman glory, but by their gnomic manner, which hobbles reference and disables narrative, they act as icons of that circumscription.[28] Later, in *Complaints*, where Spenser finally attaches his name to the translations of the *Theatre*, he also acknowledges his debt to du Bellay, from whom he learned to use the sonnet as an icon of narrative inhibition. The fragmentive sonnet reassembles Spenser's career as Leicesterian client, even as it disrupts his career as an Elizabethan narrator.

I began by remarking how unlikely Spenser is as a representative of Typographical Man; nowhere is his relation to the industry of print more complex than when he is at sonnets. While Ponsonby and Wolfe were making way for new forms of literary property, their presswork enabled Spenser to reconstitute the traditional autobiographical force of the (handwritten) sonnet. Print would eventually bring specifically aristocratic patronage to an end, but Ponsonby had put his press in the service of Leicesterian renown, and he was typical: most late sixteenth-century English stationers and authors regarded the press as a means of confirming traditional structures of clientage, not eroding them. Spenser's use of the printed sonnet to record the passage of Leicesterian patronage (in *Complaints*) and to attempt its impossible reinstatement (in *The Faerie Queene*) is a prescient accident, a message about the medium. The nostalgia of his sonnets is visionary, for the dislocation of the poet from the structures of clientage that these poems signal was only just impending.

Although sonnets brought Spenser to his fullest engagement with the mechanics of publication, they also perform their traditional Petrarchan function as symbols of privacy. I earlier pointed out that the 1590 *Faerie Queene* concludes with fantasies about writing as a defacing of prior inscriptions. If the belatedly composed sonnets dedicatory to *The Faerie Queene* extend this fantasy, by underscoring the incompletions of its narrative and iconography, Spenser's last word on the epic defaces publication itself, restoring the most intimate possible coterie of writing and reading, recovering the epic from John Wolfe's press.

He does so with an inscription on the title page of one of the few surviving large paper copies of the poem. Two words are written there in Greek: *Pros auton*. Shortly before he died, Sir Richard Jebb examined the hand and pronounced it "the Greek of a poet and dreamer of the Renaissance," and if the formulation is reactionary enough to seem quaint, to seem merely sweetly eccentric, Jebb is anticipated by the maker self.[29] A strange dream— the large format customarily pulled for presentation copies, the Greek inscription commending the text *pros auton*, to him. Or rather, *toward* him, for the phrase conspicuously implies a verb of commendation or commission. It seems to have been Spenser's own copy. Go, little book: inscription claims the printed book for manuscript culture, the commodity for gift exchange, but this particular copy is snatched so forcibly from the publicity of the market that it recoils to a privacy near solipsism, a parcel from the author to himself.

This may not be the only authorial commendation to the copy. On the leaf facing the Letter to Ralegh—on the first page, that is, of Spenser's appended front matter, is a draft of the first of the *Amoretti*, commending this book to "those lilly Hands . . . those lamping eies . . . that angells looke": yet another sonnet, a commendation even more belated than the afterwords that Wolfe printed. In this intensely private sonnet "A sa mistresse [sic]," the printed book is replaced by "harts close bleedinge book"; recovered from all spurious publicity, this ascripted sonnet defaces even the culture of patronage: "Leaves, lines & rymes seeke her to please alone / Whome if you please I care for other none." Gollancz regards the sonnet as autograph; Judson disputes the claim: as with the poems of the *Theatre*, the privacy of this sonnet is anonymous.[30] This sonnet is apparently a version of the first poem in a volume of sonnets that will recur to the crisis of erotic culture narrated in the Legend of Chastity, resuming its concerns and displacing its solutions. Whether this manuscript poem was written by its author, by a forger, or by a collector, it performs the characteristic work of the Spenserian sonnet, scribbling over narrative, marking its limitations, managing its publicity. Ponsonby is wresting intellectual property from stationer's copyright; Wolfe is wresting a latent efficiency from the monopolistic traditions of guild organization; the writing hand here wrests a fiction of privacy from the facts of book culture.

Spenser (Re)Reading du Bellay:
Chronology and Literary Response

ANNE LAKE PRESCOTT

Although in recent years it has become fashionable to see in Spenser's work a narrative proliferation that refuses closure, many of us still like stories of his career that have narrative thrust (toward a final discouragement or a turn inward, for instance) or generic tidiness (from pastoral to epic to pastoral, say). To the extent that we can know it, the chronology of Spenser's reading might help clarify the outlines of such tales. After all, there must have been some point in time at which Spenser first opened a volume of Ariosto or Virgil.

In this essay I would like, as a case study in how thinking about Spenser's reading might illuminate his intellectual biography, to look at some hints as to when and whether he read certain texts by du Bellay. Such hints, however, render more problematic the merely forward motion of any intellectual biography. It is not just that much of Spenser's poetry escapes a Virgilian career path or that much of his thought must have been engaged by administrative and familial practicalities. The problem lies with storytime linearity as such. Even mentally organized people can move more like pre-Copernican planets than Pilgrim on his progress, can think and feel in epicycles—in intelligently disorganized scribble.

It is wise to concede how much we cannot know about the directions of Spenser's thinking and to resist an impulse to make our narratives about him, whatever they might be, too neat. Not only do we lack records of Spenser's library, letterbooks, marginalia, and drafts; the very nature and dynamics of reading and reception have in recent decades come to be treated more historically and to seem more problematic. It seems likely, for example, that Spenser would often have read even lyrics more instrumentally than would many later readers; that he would have thought texts legitimately divisible into decontextualized fragments ready for reuse; and that he would have understood the provenance of what he read in ways subtly alien to any culture beguiled by notions of individual genius and authorship.[1]

Also relevant to *how* Spenser read is the fact that we read diachronically: absorbing a text's meaning literally takes time. Yet the time line coils or wavers, even during a first reading, and more intricately as we interpret, reread, reinterpret, or remember in another mood and with knowledge of other more recently read texts. "Reading," it has been said, "is a historically evolving process in that readers as a group change over time, and each reader changes over small periods of time, from day to day, hour to hour."[2] To be sure, the same can be said of writing: in a famous story, Jorge Luis Borges speculates that although an exact modern replica of *Don Quixote* would not differ from the original it would have a new and richer meaning. Yet one need not wait centuries—du Bellay's sonnets on ancient Rome's ruination by inner division and external assault, published in 1558 as *Les antiquitez de Rome*, must have looked different after the French civil wars, domestic plots against Elizabeth I, and the Armada.

In this essay I will set several passages in Spenser's poetry against some of du Bellay's so as to see what emerges that might indicate, imprecisely, something about the shape or pace of his activity. My evidence is Spenser's own writings, for despite the temporal ambiguities inherent in efforts to date a given text, how he responded to du Bellay has chronological and hence biographical implications.[3] I will largely ignore the strictly psychological and literary dynamics of such intertextual moments because they would introduce more variables than I can deal with here. What we make of Spenser's allusions to Chaucer, for example, depends on what we make of Chaucer. Thus, although one critic reads Spenser as a servile apologist for power and Chaucer as Boethian and detached, all we need do to change the equation is to make Chaucer more politically implicated or Spenser more ironic, an easy enough task.[4] Similarly, reading Spenser reading du Bellay reading Rome is a dizzying exercise in multiple uncertainties. When relating older writers to each other it is tempting to grant one text its full measure of slippery ambiguity but to solidify the ground from which to comment on it by stabilizing the intertext. William Sherman is probably right to call reading "adversarial" and to imagine a text as "the site of an active and biased appropriate of the author's material" (1995, 65). But the precise moves in the intellectual struggle are difficult to trace when both the reader and the read are tonally complex and subject themselves to widely divergent—adversarial?—modern readings. Was Spenser subtly critical of the Catholic du Bellay's secular-minded nostalgia for Rome? Perhaps. To argue the point, though, requires either thinking that du Bellay was Catholic, secular-minded, and nostalgic, which oversimplifies him, or thinking that at least Spenser found him too Catholic, secular-minded, and nostalgic, which is impossible to prove.[5]

Even Spenser's explicit compliment to him can be read variously: at the end of his *Ruines of Rome* a sonnet first praises du Bellay as France's first "garland of free Poësie" and then compliments du Bartas for his "heavenly Muse" (an allusion with significance for a history of Spenser's literary responses).[6] Is praising the Huguenot author of scriptural verse a rebuke to the secular Catholic writer of ancient Rome's obituary, a predecessor whom Spenser has imitated but must shove aside? Or is the compliment a way to recapture the turn that du Bellay had effected by appending his more religious *Songe?*[7] It seems likely that Spenser was captivated by du Bellay's melancholia and the frequently emblematic nature of his imagery. I think, too, that he could notice du Bellay's poetic patterns and find his satirical vein attractive. Whether he was influenced by du Bellay, though, or whether he was, rather, drawn to what he already loved is harder to say. Here, then, I will limit myself to three less indeterminate matters, hoping to show something of Spenser's mind at work: the period by which we can know he had begun adapting du Bellay's *Antiquitez de Rome* and the syncretic methods by which he put his reading to work; the probability that he had read du Bellay's love poetry well before getting *Amoretti* into shape, at some point noting not just individual poems but a structure; and the continuing role in his imagination of diction taken from his early translations, phrasing now so much his own that we cannot say if he is recalling du Bellay or himself.

Almost certainly Spenser read du Bellay's *Songe* when he was still in his teens: his anonymous translation appears in the 1569 *Theatre for Worldlings* put together by the Protestant expatriate Jan van der Noot. Although it is true that Spenser's later reading is much harder to track chronologically, because we so seldom know the dates at which he composed or revised, an aged oak in the "Februarie" eclogue of *The Shepheardes Calender* (1579) seems to indicate that he had by now read the *Antiquitez* and was preparing the English version published in 1591 as *The Ruines of Rome*. This is hardly in itself surprising, for much in the *Calender* shows the intricate part that notions of the translation of empire from Babylon to Rome and beyond already played in Spenser's mind. As an index of how and what Spenser was reading, though, it is not only du Bellay's presence in the eclogue that I wish to emphasize but the compacted nature of the *Calender's* imitation here.[8] Venerable but suspiciously Catholic, aristocratic but wormy, taking up space but also protective, the oak is an ambiguous patriarch of a tree:

> There grewe an aged Tree on the greene,
> A goodly Oake sometime had it bene,
> With armes full strong and largely displayd,
> But of their leaves they were disarayde:
> The bodie bigge, and mightely pight,
> Throughly rooted, and of wonderous hight:
> Whilome had bene the King of the field,
> And mochell mast to the husband did yielde,
> And with his nuts larded many swine.
> But now the gray mosse marred his rine,
> His bared boughs were beaten with stormes,
> His toppe was bald, and wasted with wormes,
> His honor decayed, his braunches sere. (102-14)

According to the resentful brier growing beneath it, this tyrannical and "faded Oake, / Whose bodie is sere, whose braunches broke," casts no useful shade, and its "naked Armes stretch" to the fire. But once, says old Thenot, who recounts the story, "it had bene an ancient tree, / Sacred with many a mysteree, / And often crost with the priestes crewe, / And often halowed with holy water dewe."

As the Variorum editors note, this tree descends from one in Lucan's *Civil War* 1.136-43.[9] Lucan, it will be remembered, compares Caesar's father-in-law Pompey to an aged oak; the simile serves the poetry's exploration of generational and civil strife, so understandably Spenser wanted it for "Februarie," probably hoping readers would admire the transplantation. Lucan's oak bears the ancient trophies of a people and the sacred gifts of victors. Towering ("sublimis") but with weak roots, it stands fixed by its own weight, casting forth into the air its nude branches ("nudos . . . ramos") and making shade only with its trunk. Although it totters ("nutet") and will fall to the first wind, and although around it is wood ("sylvae") with firm timber, it alone is revered ("colitur"). Clearly, Spenser knew this passage.

What has gone largely unstressed is specifically verbal evidence that Spenser has also by now read *Antiquitez* 28, itself a paraphrase of Lucan; apparently, by 1579 he had bothered to locate du Bellay's original works, not contenting himself with the selections from *Songe* in van der Noot's *Theatre*.[10] Du Bellay's oak is Rome, not Pompey, but he doubtless meant to recall Lucan and Rome's civil rage; Spenser, living later, would have thought as well of the murderous religious strife in France and, perhaps, of the dangers to England of such dissension. True, du Bellay plays past against present, not old against young, but this theme too is not entirely missing from "Februarie" in view of its oak's worrisome relation to pre-Reformation religion. The *Antiquitez*'s desiccated oak bears a trophy as an ornament and lifts to the sky its old dead head (Lucan mentions no head). Not well "fiché" in the earth, it leans over the field and shows naked arms ("bras," not branches) and a twisted root. Supported only by its own weight, its knotty trunk in a hundred places "esbranché," it owes its "ruine" to the first wind; and although many young ones around it have firm roots, it alone receives popular devotion. Let him who sees it remember how, of the many cities that once flourished, this old dusty honor is most venerated.[11]

The translation in *Rome* follows this closely, but touches hint that Spenser has rechecked du Bellay's Roman model, and some details are his own: the trophies are again plural, if surviving only as "reliques" of themselves, and the oak, like any Latin *quercus*, is once more female (befitting "Roma," Spenser may have thought). Like du Bellay's, the half-disemboweled tree shows naked arms and wreathed roots, but her rotten trunk is "meate of wormes," an affliction Lucan and du Bellay spare her. Sprouts grow from her rind, not just "around" or nearby, perhaps because Spenser also recalls the felled and groaning trophy-bearing oak in *Songe* 5, from whose stump new ecclesiastical and imperial growth begins. Finally, whereas du Bellay asks us to "imagine," Spenser invites us to "record," to activate a memory in the heart and possibly to set it down in writing.[12]

Spenser's February oak is unlike these others in some respects—well rooted, mossy, already storm-beaten, and with a lot to say. The young brier that despises it is presented in language Spenser usually saves for arrogant giants, rulers, and cities: proudly thrusting into the air, it "seemed to threat the Firmament," no mean feat for a bragging underbush, and after its brief victory becomes "Puffed up with pryde." The heaven-threatening or sky-piercing vocabulary has a close parallel in language like "le ciel menassoit" in the *Antiquitez* (cf. *Rome* 4, 11 ["Puft up with pride"], and 12, although du Bellay in turn echoes phrases like "caput extulit" in Ovid's *Fasti* 1:209-10), while the oak itself owes something to *Rome* and its French original. By the time Spenser wrote "Februarie," in other words, he seems to have at least begun translating the *Antiquitez*. Some details, like the way the oak's arms "stretch," recall only Lucan ("per aera . . . effundens"), but the naked arms themselves, like the head (whether dead, hoary, or bald) and honor, are in du Bellay and *Rome*. The oak's "rine" and worm trouble are also Spenser's translation, while its "braunches broke" have a parallel only in the French poem's "esbranché." The *Calender*'s oak will fall, groaning, to

135

Figure 6. Nebuchadnezzar's falling dream tree, from The Bishops' Bible (1568). Spenserians will also note the expiring dragon. *By permission of the Yale University Library.*

the axe of misguided envy and injudicious haste, not—or not only—to the winds of history or providence, but the scene is not without similarities to the moment in Spenser's *Visions of Bellay* 5 when a "clownish" troop cuts down the "faire *Dodonian* tree" that groans as it feels the axe.

Spenser's mixture and dispersal of his models, the way he tangles the roots of his oak's family tree, indicate either a very keen verbal memory for minute details or a process in which, wanting an oak for the fable he was telling, he pulled down not one but several volumes and maybe a rough draft of a translation. Perhaps to these he added the Bible with its fallen dream-tree that Daniel interprets for Nebuchadnezzar as a warning to tyrants (Daniel 4; see Fig. 6): unlike Lucan's or the *Antiquitez*'s, if like that in *Songe* and Spenser's *Rome*, it retains the capacity for new growth. As the object of God's wrath against a pagan tyrant, this item in Spenser's mental collection of big trees would add an antipapal resonance possibly already there in du Bellay but not, needless to say, in Lucan.[13] Perhaps Spenser even had some method like the contraption, a sort of book-holding ferris wheel which can be turned to deliver any one of a chosen set of texts, that

Jardine and Grafton think Gabriel Harvey might have used as a paid "reader" for the great (1990, 47; see Fig. 7). It could not have been only professional readers and annotators who found multivolume methods useful for a primarily instrumental reading, a kind of reading facilitated by annotated editions like the 1571 *Emblemata* of Alciati (the emblem on "quercus" quotes several authors, including Lucan) or handbooks like Thomas Farnaby's *Index poeticus* (1634), which mentions du Bellay under "p" for *patriae desiderium*. Even if Spenser lacked a bookwheel, the mentality implied by his method of growing his oak suggests either a section of table (or floor) on which to pile books or a very impressive inner filing system.

There is, then, a strong probability that Spenser was thinking about the ruined glory of Rome, not only in the apocalyptic terms of van der Noot's *Theatre* but also in the more secular terms of the *Antiquitez*, while or before he was thinking about Cleopolis and Troynovant; and even at the lexical level he was doing so in syncretic ways that imply not so much a debt to individual and discretely remembered "sources" as a close recent reading of several texts near at hand.[14] What he read of du Bellay's Roman verse stayed with him, furthermore, for the stylistic and lexical force field of *Rome* affects many stanzas of *The Faerie Queene*, and not just the one passage the Variorum editors note (IV xi 28, describing Cybele).[15] Two examples: Britomart's lament in III iv may glance at Petrarch, but the language of stanza 13 in which the restless knight expresses her inner flux is very close to that of *Rome* 20, and IV ii 33-34 disconcertingly describes and addresses Chaucer, subject of Time's wear and Spenserian resuscitation, in words strikingly evocative of *Rome* 19, 27, 32, and 33. My suggestion is that this fascination with such phrasing and vocabulary came to Spenser near the time of his epic's inception and that reading the *Antiquitez*, as well as translating the visionary *Songe*, joined with his knowledge of Ariosto, Chaucer, and Virgil to help form his imagination. Sometime during the 1570s, in sum, he began absorbing both a set of topics (mutability, the translation of empire) or pictures (a wailing female city, a moribund tree) and a complex of words and phrases that helped structure his literary thought, making a grid through which he would often feel or perceive.

What else did Spenser read by du Bellay? Aside from the obvious impact of *The Vision of Bellay* on *The Ruines of Time* and other poems in the 1591 *Complaints*, source hunting as recorded in the Variorum edition has turned up traces in Spenser's *Epithalamion* of du Bellay's wedding poem for Henri II's sister Marguerite, echoes of *Les regrets* and "La musagnoeomachie" in *Teares of the Muses*, of "Du premier jour de l'an" and the amatory sonnet sequence *Olive* in *Amoretti*, and his anticourt verses in *Mother Hubberds*

Figure 7. A perhaps imaginary book-holding device that can be turned to deliver any one of a chosen set of texts. Augustino Ramelli, *Le diverse et artificiose machine* (Paris, 1588). *By permission of the Yale University Library.*

Tale. I would add that Spenser's bitter injunction to his own poetry at the end of Book VI ("Therfore do you my rimes keep better measure, / And seeke to please, that now is counted wisemens threasure") is in effect a condensed version of du Bellay's contemptuous *Poete courtisan* (ca. 1559). To these suggestions I tentatively offer two more possibilities: first, that well before compiling *Amoretti* (1595), Spenser had read du Bellay's abjectly Petrarchist but gracious *Olive* (1550); and, second, that he did so with an eye on structure.

The proem to Book III of *The Faerie Queene*, praising the inimitable beauty in the queen's chaste heart, polishes a flattering conceit that has as its best analogue *Olive* 19. Were Heaven to revive antiquity's best artists, says du Bellay, not even Lysippus, Apelles, or Homer could show her beauty. So he will use his own heart as marble, "table," and paper (ed. 1961, 1). The sonnet had already caught Nicholas Grimald's eye when he was writing the poems published in *Tottel's Miscellany* (ed. 1965, 1:99). Regendering the compliment, Grimald claims that antiquity's best artists, were they to be revived, could not frame a "noble prince" with such a visible and "lively shape" as Virgil has given his Aeneas. Some details suggest that Spenser had read Grimald's version: the image visible in Elizabeth's heart is "lively," both poets say "expresse," and both exempt another writer (in Spenser's case Ralegh) from the general artistic failure. Only Spenser and du Bellay, though, think beauty representable cardiacally, call the author's instrument a quill ("plume"; Grimald has "poyntel"), and speak of "color" (not Grimald's "paint"). Like du Bellay, Spenser specifies the artists'—and implicitly all artists'—inadequacies, merely changing one set of ancient names for another; to say that the painter's "daedale hand would fail" parallels du Bellay's "la main fault," while the adjective "daedale," together with the phrase "his error taint," recalls "L'art peut errer." Spenser also retains du Bellay's quasi-logical structure: "If . . . But . . . Then." It is perhaps ironic that even while assuring Elizabeth that he has no need to import "Forreine ensamples" from Fairyland to illustrate the virtue she already contains, Spenser is adopting for himself, if I am right, a model fetched from France.

By late 1589, then, Spenser had probably read *Olive*. And, once more, he may have read instrumentally, with an eye on the usable, for there, in *Olive*'s augmented 1550 version, he would have found precisely the same basic pattern on which he was to improve in *Amoretti* (1595) when he fashioned his love sonnets (some composed earlier) into a sequence with bilateral symmetry and calendrical curves. Let me explain.[16]

Du Bellay's Olive both pays homage to and rivals Petrarch's Laura— same style, different tree. Spenser would have had no difficulty in recog-

nizing the problem: granted that one wants to make the first French amatory sonnet sequence, how does one do so with some shred of originality
while writing après-Petrarch in every sense? Du Bellay's individual sonnets
are often derivative, but the poet has found a new leaf, if not written many
entirely fresh ones of his own, and he has woven his leaves into a new
shape. That shape, like Spenser's, incorporates or imitates an arc of the
year's circle even as carefully positioned allusions make his garland symmetrical. Thus, whereas an early sonnet (no. 2) tells how in a sort of floral
incarnation Olive came into our "bas lieux" during an Advent season of
peaceful seas and gracious winds, those near the end meditate an ascent of
the lover's imprisoned soul ("mon ame emprisonnée") back to the world of
ideas ("le clos des occultes Idées") and its "repos," love, and pleasure. As
one of du Bellay's modern editors says, the Ficinian *circuitus spiritualis*
superimposes itself on the Petrarchan matter.[17] The liturgical symmetry is
more precise. Revising Petrarch's Good Friday *Rime* 3, the fifth sonnet
recalls that Love first enslaved the lover on the very night ("c'etoit la nuyt")
that celebrates divinity's descent from heaven. Sonnet 111, fifth from the
end, exclaims that this is the day ("Voicy le jour") when by his death the
eternal lover ("l'eternel amant") made his beloved live. We have moved
from the past tense to the present, from night to day, from Advent and
Christ's birth to Easter season and his victorious death. But we hear no
more of Olive; perhaps the lover has in some sense won her or the peace
and victory her leaf represents.[18]

Du Bellay reinforces this pattern with seasonal allusions. Counting forward from the Christmas Eve sonnet to Good Friday brings us to 9 April,
a good time of year for Easter season, although I cannot find any relevance
to the date, and the sonnet that might correspond to Ash Wednesday (No.
67) hopes like Spenser's more explicitly Lenten *Amoretti* 22 to soften the
lady's "rigueur" with flames and thoughts. Less hard to ignore is the im-
provement of the weather as the sonnets pass by. Sonnet 73, which easy
calculation would put near the start of March, has seasonally suitable winds
and rain, while also beginning the spring and floral imagery that now ac-
cumulates and includes allusions to Zephirus. Sonnet 75 mentions that
the sun is not yet in Taurus—that is, not yet past 10 April, where the sun
will be going just in time for Easter on the eleventh day of that month.
Olive, then, has a calendrical aspect as well as a triptych shape with a large
central section and two stubby wings. Du Bellay even makes his olive leaves
connect at the ends by vowing in his first sonnet that he will make the
olive "Egal un jour au Laurier immortel" and asking in the last how to
make the olive "Jusq'à l'egal des Lauriers tousjours verd." The resulting

Figure 8. An olive wreath (or *stephanos*) like those often used by the the Stephanus (Estienne) family of printers. Dares Phrygius, *L'histoire veritable de la guerre des Grec, et des Troyens* (Caen: Benedic Macé, 1572). *By permission of the Department of Printing and Graphics Arts, The Houghton Library, Harvard University Library.*

poetic shape in effect combines two sorts of classical wreaths, the kind that goes round and round and the kind with two branches tied in the back that bend forward to mingle or touch leaves at the front (see Fig. 8.). As a segment of the year with a literary equivalent of glue or Velcro at its tips, du Bellay's triptych of sonnets is thus also a wearable coronal (in *Amoretti* 1, though, Spenser asks his lady to hold his book/wreath and study its happy "leaves"). No wonder *Rome* 33 calls du Bellay a "garland"; it is pleasant to suppose that even by then he had noticed *Olive*'s urge toward circularity.

When Spenser read *Olive* he could have found, then, a clear, obvious, simple scheme requiring only one hand's worth of fingers on which to do some minimal counting. *Amoretti*, of course, manages the same umbrageous feat, forming a triptych of leaves with a central group of forty-seven sonnets proceeding from the "holy day" Ash Wednesday, when it is fit we "fast and pray," to Easter, that "joyous day" when Christ triumphed over death and sin.[19] True, Spenser further steadies his calendar with a Lady Day allusion (*Amoretti* 62). And, in a polemical revision of post-Petrarchan tradition, his lover plans to marry, not to liberate himself from the flesh into the empyrean; in this he is unlike du Bellay who, although nearing the desired port (*Olive* 98; so, too, *Amoretti* 63), makes the lady vanish when Christ dies and who finally contemplates taking spiritual wing. Spenser also saves his anguish over slander and separation for after Easter: in terms of the sequence's scriptural echoes, it makes more sense there than in the middle of the sequence where du Bellay has it.

When did he read *Olive* in these structural terms, if he did? Granted how little we know, there can be no precise answer, but it seems likely, if indeed the proem to Book III owes something to *Olive*, that Spenser had been thinking about amatory sonnet sequences even while working on his epic. This would not be astonishing; anyone as well read as Spenser would early on have been familiar with Petrarch and his followers. Nevertheless, the hint of an interest in *Olive* before 1590 is a salutary reminder to treat with some skepticism a sense of Spenser's career that moves him smoothly from genre to genre or from a public and Virgilian *vates* to a disillusioned singer of personal love and inward withdrawal. Perhaps Spenser at some point read with fellow feeling Ronsard's defensive poem to his Cassandre on how he was partway through his *Franciade*—like *The Faerie Queene* an unfinished dynastic epic on the Trojan diaspora—when a shot by Cupid gave him generic pause and forced him to write love sonnets; Spenser's similar excuse is *Amoretti* 80.[20] One may suspect, though, that poets so professional as these two proceeded in private on a broad front, whether composing or reading, and that we should hesitate to interpret as developmental, or serial, interests that may have had considerable simultaneity.

Probably, then, even after Spenser was through translating the *Antiquitez*—or just pulling work already read off some shelf of Eumnestes in the back of his mind—du Bellay's works continued to help shape his verse. Certainly, to judge from its impact on *The Faerie Queene* and *Complaints*, his experience with the *Antiquitez* had a lasting effect on his imagination and verbal repertoire. Yet in effect what we hear, for the most part, are echoes of his own Roman poetry, not of du Bellay himself. For it may be the case that in fact Spenser's favorite reading matter, more vivid to him even than the works of Chaucer, Ariosto, Tasso, and du Bellay, or any text except possibly the Bible, was the poetry of Edmund Spenser. After all, of all major English poets he is perhaps the most given to recycling his own phrases.[21] If the woods ring with an echo in *Epithalamion*, they had already done so for Una when she visited the salvage nation in *The Faerie Queene* (I vi 14.2); if the lady of *Amoretti*'s light was first "kindled above" in heaven, so was that of Belphoebe in Book II (iii 23.2); and the overshadowed "Impes" that used to shoot up for Clio in *Teares* (75) thrive near Troynovant in *The Faerie Queene* IV xi 26. A few moments with a concordance of Spenser's verse produces many, many such examples.

All reading, as I have said, is a diachronic enterprise. The diachrony becomes more problematic, though, when the text being "read" is inside the memory. In deducing anyone's intellectual or affective biography it would be good to know if the evidence shows that he or she was reading, rereading, or remembering. Yet, even if we could be sure, inevitable shifts in circumstance and subjectivity would make the biographical implications hard to calculate. "The person who reads a text," remarks Robert Scholes, "is never the person who wrote it—even if they are the 'same' person" (1989, 50). In Spenser's case, though, the biographical importance of his self-imitation or verbally formulaic memory may rest just here: in the very fact of a lifelong fascination with fairly stable sets of phrases. It would be interesting to know what contexts activated the set originating in *Rome*. My own attempts suggest the obvious: giants, big oaks, Rome, Trojan progeny, cities, ambition, Britomart (because of her association with Trojans and the giant-killer Athena?), and praise of writers and statesmen. Nor was Spenser indiscriminate in using the diction he first learned from the *Antiquitez* and *Songe*. Its absence from *Muiopotmos*, for example, and from passages in *The Faerie Queene* that might invite it, shows that Spenser exerted, if intuitively, considerable control over his "Roman" phraseology.

Spenser's recycling is most poignant in the *Mutabilitie Cantos*: echoes of his translations from du Bellay, remembered or reread, seem to intensify after a pause in Book VI and give his epic if not closure then renewed recuperation of his early work. Mutabilitie is a giant, like those to whom du Bellay, among many others, compared Rome, and so understandably Spenser activated his *Rome* vocabulary for her; he had used it already for the giant Orgoglio who, like Rome, is "puft up" (cf. *Rome* 11, "puft up with pride of Romane hardiehead"), can cause trembles, threats the sky, recalls the hydra, collapses like a ruined castle's "heaped hight," and vanishes into nothingness.[22] Spenser's lexicon of aspiration has further developed, to be sure, so it would be wrong to exaggerate the echoes of *Rome* in his final cantos. Still, his aspiring Titaness has a curious subtextual kinship with Rome and its giants. I say "curious" because the relationship is not analogous or parallel but topologically inverted, so to speak: Spenser's early and persistent interest in Rome, time, ruins, dynastic descent (Romans are both enemies and Trojans, Brute's people), the collapse of greatness into the earth, aspiring giants, and complaining female cities appears again here in Book VII but twisted, turned, so that the *topoi*, while recognizable, assume new forms and affiliations. Now the protagonist is Mutabilitie herself, not the city or people she ruins and who, like her and her fellow giants or Titan siblings, had thrust skyward to challenge the gods.

In the last sonnet of *Bellay*, the Bellona-like sister of Typhoeus (both of these being Mutabilitie's Titan relatives) "did seeme to match the Gods in Majestie," setting up a trophy to symbolize Rome's imperial victory, when the "mazed" dreamer sees "the heavens in warre against her rize" and she "stricken fell with clap of thonder." This is in a sense the plot of Spenser's *Mutabilitie Cantos*, but now the Titaness—on the make, not yet unmade—is less the ambitious Rome than the forces that once helped destroy the city. Change, one of the several energies that had brought the empire low, merges with Rome into a single figure. As a teenager Spenser had read du Bellay's allegory of Rome's ruin in which an earthquake destroys a shining crystal structure with diamond pillars (*Songe* 2). Now it is Jove whose "eternall towers" (*Mutabilitie* vi 20) are under assault and Cynthia's palace that rests on a thousand crystal pillars (vi 10). Rome's fate, says du Bellay, shows how, subject to time, the "seeds" of everything "Shall in great *Chaos* wombe againe be hid" (*Rome* 22) while modern Rome's relapse into rusticity and its reversion to rule by a pastor (i.e., the pope) show how "all things turne to their first being" (*Rome* 18). Others, such as Boethius, had said something similar, but Spenser's goddess Nature uses his Roman diction, too: according to her, "all things . . . their being doe dilate . . . turning to themselves at length againe" (vii 58).

A full collection of *Rome*-like vocabulary applied to Mutabilitie in the stanzas describing her or her actions would further bring out the degree to which the Titaness recalls, but with remarkable ambiguity, that imperious city on whom Jove heaped seven hills lest she revive the giants' war against heaven (*Rome* 4). Language such as "reare," "uprear'd," "reare her trophy aloft and bear triumph" recalls Rome's hubris.[23] Yet other phrases complicate matters, for Spenser's beautiful giantess is no less polyvalent than the city du Bellay called both "the worlds sole ornament" and an "antique horror" (*Rome* 29, 17). *Rome* 27 laments "injurious time," but Time's ally, Mutabilitie, thinks—and she has a case—that the usurper Jove, who had supplanted his father and her brother, acts "injuriously."[24] Jove says he rules by "eternall doome of Fates decree" and has "Empire of the heavens bright"; in *Rome* 6, though, it is the gods who "by heavenly doome decree" that Rome would have no rivals. In a similar inversion, Mutabilitie boasts that "*Time* on all doth pray" (vii 47), whereas in *Rome* 3 Rome is "The pray of time, which all things doth devowre," and Jove fears lest the giantess plunge the world into the "eternall night" whence du Bellay had hoped to recover the Romans (*Rome* 5). The blasted Irish landscape of Spenser's foolish Faunus recalls, if vaguely, the *Theatre's* sonnet (no. 10) in which du Bellay's watery *locus amoenus* of bathing nymphs falls prey to a marauding "rout" of naked "Faunes"; now the nymphs' leader, Diana, punishes Faunus for seeing her naked and lays waste the countryside.

The very end of Spenser's fragmentary Book VII, however, may in some fashion recover Rome from the *Theatre* (and Cleopolis from *The Faerie*

Queene). Both *Bellay* and *Rome* lament that in this world there is no "stay," a word of which, in both its noun and verb forms, Spenser remained fond. At the end of the *Theatre*'s opening sonnet, the dreamer says that in view of this world's "unstedfastnesse," and "Sith onely God surmountes the force of tyme, / In God alone" he will "stay [his] confidence." In *Rome* 3, too, everything shows "inconstancie" except the flowing Tiber, which in its very mutability can "abide and stay" even as Roman arches and palaces "flit." It may not be too sentimental to think that a vocabulary opposing inconstancy to that which can "stay" (remain, or steady something), when combined with references to a palace's pillars—those of Rome or, here, those of Diana—renders more moving Spenser's anticipation of a changed world's "stedfast rest of all things firmly stayd / Upon the pillours of Eternity." Architecturally speaking, the *translatio imperii* that Spenser learned as much from du Bellay as from anyone else except Virgil can go no farther. Rome—like Jerusalem and maybe even Troynovant—has died and gone to heaven.

Although it is impossible to say if Spenser has been remembering or rereading du Bellay or himself, one can still note the tendency to recall, in 1595 or so, images and concerns, the very diction, of decades earlier. Perhaps he recalled them all the more urgently now because the threat from Roman pride had only enlarged, the city's relation to change become yet more ambiguous, and the need for something that would indeed be *semper eadem* grown both more intense and less likely to be found in this world. Had he lived, Spenser would very likely have continued to read, reread, or remember du Bellay as well as Edmund Spenser. Kent Hieatt (1988) has (to my mind persuasively) imagined for the later *Faerie Queene* the epic anti-Roman adventures of a now crowned Arthur; perhaps, as literary fashion changed, Spenser might also have found fresh interest in du Bellay's more personal and satirical *Regrets*. In neither case, one imagines, would the results have pleased the authorities. By now speculation has become wild surmise, but even the more quasi-documentable facts about his reading show several likelihoods. Each suggests how comfortably Spenser's mind dealt with imaginative and textual simultaneity and how as he got older he added to but did not replace his earlier loves and concerns. First, he could at times read instrumentally and with several texts nearby (or nearly memorized) so as to micromanage his diction and images; second, he had seen and paid attention to an erotic sonnet sequence shaped like *Amoretti* even before publishing the first part of his *Faerie Queene*. And, finally, at times it is a nice psychophilosophical question whether he was (re)reading du Bellay or himself; for, if he had once called du Bellay the "garland of free Poësie," he had early on made many legible leaves in that garland his very own.

145

The Earl of Cork's Lute

DAVID LEE MILLER

Nay, but his jesting spirit, which is now crept into a
lute-string . . .

Much Ado about Nothing

The earl of Cork had a lute. We know this because it speaks to us in an
epigram attributed to Spenser:

> Whilst vitall sapp did make me spring,
> And leafe and bough did flourish brave,
> I then was dumbe and could not sing,
> Ne had the voice which now I have:
> But when the axe my life did end,
> The Muses nine this voice did send.
> E. S. (Spenser ed. 1989, 779)

We don't know whether this epigram is really Spenser's, or whether it was
really written (as the headnote reports) "upon the said Earles Lute." We
don't even know whether Richard Boyle, created first earl of Cork in 1620,
owned a lute—only that he had the fiction of one.[1] This signifying lute is
a perfect metonymy for the author: it tells us why his life cannot be written.

Inscriptions do figure prominently among the kinds of epigram and
sometimes appeared on Renaissance musical instruments. The epigram
attributed to Spenser is a version of what one historian calls the "Brescian
legend" because of its early use by violin makers in the Italian city of Brescia,
though it also appears in Germany in the mid-sixteenth century (Henley
1959, 1:165; Borthwick 1970). At the same time, mock inscriptions are
common to the epigram form, and it can be hard to tell the difference.
Even an inscription read in situ could have been composed as a riddle or
epigram and then carved by some jesting spirit into an appropriate setting.
This is just what happened with the so-called Brescian legend: it derives

from a much older form, the "riddle of the tortoise and the lyre," and was revived in the nineteenth century to "authenticate" forgeries of the sixteenth-century instruments on which it first appeared (Borthwick 1970).[2] Since Spenser cannot have written the headnote referring to the earl of Cork, it is tempting to read the verses as a riddle whose answer is given in the initials "E. S." Epigram has always been a playful kind: graffiti with a classical pedigree.

The verses on the earl's lute have never been incorporated into the Spenser canon because they do not appear in any of the early editions on which most complete Spensers are based. They turn up for the first time in 1633, at the end of Ware's edition of the *View of Ireland* along with an epigram about wasting time.[3] Given their similarity to a riddle popular in the collections of the time (Borthwick quotes a version published in London in 1631), the attribution to Spenser may be erroneous, although James Ware is a pretty good source as such things go, and the lines do *sound* Spenserian. There is a sense in which a great deal hangs on this question, for if the lines are anonymous, then when we locate their provenance in the textual milieu of the riddle there isn't much more to be said. We have a deft but unremarkable English version of a common inscription whose history has been traced by Borthwick to classical sources. But once the same verses are ascribed to the author of *The Faerie Queene*, they pass into a much wider textual milieu, where they take on considerably more significance. The editors of the Spenser Variorum trace them not to a popular form like the riddle but to Homer's *Iliad*, remarking that "the verses on the lute follow a device time-honored from the scepter of Agamemnon down" (ed. 1932-57, 8.2:510).

This epic genealogy isn't quite right, but it's close. The conceit of the cut tree that will not grow again goes back not to Agamemnon's scepter in the second *Iliad* but to Achilles' staff in the first:

> But I will declare my word to thee, and will swear thereto a mighty oath: verily by this staff, that shall no more put forth leaves or shoots since at the first it left its stump among the mountains, neither shall it again grow green, for that the bronze hath stripped it of leaves and bark, and now the sons of the Achaeans that give judgment bear it in their hands, even they that guard the dooms by ordinance of Zeus; and this shall be for thee a mighty oath. (Homer ed. 1930-34, 1:21)

Hesiod recalls Achilles' "mighty oath" when he claims in the opening lines of *Theogony* that the Muses plucked a branch from a laurel "in full bloom . . . / and gave it to me as a staff, and then breathed into me divine song" (ed. 1983, lines 30-32). In these two passages the central elements of the topos are established. Homer contrasts the scepter of imperial authority with the rooted and growing tree it once was, while Hesiod extends the contrast to the Muses' laurel staff, given "in full bloom" to betoken the vitality of "the holy gift the Muses give men":

> Blessed is the man
> whom the Muses love; sweet song flows from his mouth.
> A man may have some fresh grief over which to mourn,
> and sorrow may have left him no more tears, but if a singer,
> a servant of the Muses, sings the glories of ancient men
> and hymns the blessed gods who dwell on Olympos,
> the heavy-hearted man soon shakes off his dark mood. (93, 96-102)

In making the earl's lute a figure of authorship, Spenser follows Hesiod, but he also turns Hesiod's innovation back toward its source, insisting on the discontinuity between life and voice rather than celebrating any lingering on of the life force in the powers of song. This sardonic Spenserian twist makes the lute a metonymy not just of the author but of the author's death: the writing subject's subjective extinction in the act of writing.

The topos of the cut tree that will not grow again has a complex history, working its way through Virgil, Ovid, Tasso, and *The Greek Anthology* before Spenser applies it to the earl of Cork's lute. Without pretending to review this history fully, I will sketch the way it repeatedly evokes related generic contrasts, one between epic and epigram and the other between epic and pastoral. Having established the epigram's link to the epic tradition, I will then discuss its link to *The Faerie Queene* and to the general interpretive and theoretical question of how we are to read the author function in any text attributed to "Spenser."

In Achilles' oath the heroic will asserts itself as a force of nature, irreversible like death. It asserts this force against the legitimate authority of Agamemnon, whose scepter was forged on Olympos, not hewn in the forest.[4] Virgil translates this simile with precision in Book 12 of the *Aeneid*—at the close of its "Iliadic" half, just before the single combat between Turnus and Aeneas. King Latinus swears that he will honor their pact:

> No force on earth
> Can make me swerve from my intent, no force,
> Though it embroil the earth and water in flood
> To pour land into sea, heaven into hell.
> Just as this scepter here in my right hand
> Will never put out foliage or shade,
> Once cut from the live tree-bole in the forest,

148

Torn from that mother, and laid bare by steel
Of branching arms and leaves. This one-time bough
The artificer's hand has fitted well
In a bronze sheath and given to our Latin
Lords to carry.

                          nec me vis ulla volentem
avertet, non, si tellurem effundat in undas,
diluvio miscens, caelumque in Tartara solvat;
ut sceptrum hoc (dextra sceptrum nam forte gerebat)
numquam fronde levi fundet virgulta nec umbras,
cum semel in silvis imo de stirpe recisum
matre caret posuitque comas et bracchia ferro;
olim arbos, nunc artificis manus aere decoro
inclusit patribusque dedit gestare Latinis. [5]

Virgil transvalues the simile with considerable irony. He transforms a gesture of defiance into a pledge of peace, as if returning to the Homeric text
to correct Achilles' error—for even as he throws his scepter down at
Agamemnon's feet, Achilles acknowledges it to be a symbol of law, borne
by the magistrates of Greece.[6] His oath announces strife within the Greek
camp, whereas that of Latinus signals an end to the "civil war" between
Latins and Trojans, allusively reuniting Achilles' scepter with Agamemnon's
at the inaugural point of Roman history. Yet Latinus and Aeneas have
scarcely finished invoking heaven and earth to witness their solemn treaty
before it is broken, collapsing the elaborate reversal of Achilles' wrath in
yet another outbreak of wild discord.

    In Spenser's hands, this same "device" reopens a space not of civil war
but of imperial reluctance and nostalgia. The tree's loss of "vitall sapp" is
irrevocable and a little sad, however beautifully the lute sings. In its compressed and diminished way, the epigram recalls Aeneas witnessing the
Trojan apocalypse:

I knew the end then: Ilium was going down
In fire, the Troy of Neptune going down,
As in high mountains when the countrymen
Have notched an ancient ash, then make their axes
Ring with might and main, chopping away
To fell the tree—ever on the point of falling,
Shaken through all its foliage, and the treetop
Nodding; bit by bit the strokes prevail
Until it gives a final groan at last
And crashes down in ruin from the height.

Tum vero omne mihi visum considere in ignis

149

Ilium et ex imo verti Neptunia Troia;
ac veluti summis antiquam in montibus ornum
cum ferro accisam crebrisque bipennibus instant
eruere agricolae certatim; illa usque minatur
et tremefacta comam concusso vertice nutat,
volneribus donec paulatim evicta supremum
congemuit traxitque iugis avolsa ruinam.
descendo ac ducente deo flammam inter et hostis
expedior; dant tela locum flammaeque recedunt. (2.624-33)

The image of the "ancient ash" naturalizes the imperial city, stressing its organic life, its rootedness in history—feelings proper to Aeneas as he sees his home destroyed. The simile elaborates an earlier and more powerfully compressed description of Priam's corpse: "On the distant shore / The vast trunk headless lies without a name" ("iacet ingens litore truncus, / avolsumque umeris caput et sine nomine corpus," 2.557-58). These lines close the terrible scene of Priam's murder by Pyrrhus, drawing back abruptly from "the altar step itself" ("altaria . . . ipsa," line 550) to view the body "on the distant shore." In this way Priam's headless corpse merges anonymously into the ruins of his decapitated city, the great tree a "vast trunk" receding now in the distance of an abrupt remove. Such passages invest the felling of the tree with immense pathos. Latinus's oath, like so much in the *Aeneid*, acknowledges the terrible finality of this loss even as it looks forward to an imperial *pax Romana*.

This sense of rootedness and organic growth as opposed to the fate of nations is elaborated in another passage of the *Aeneid*. The descent of Venus in Book 8 with her gift of armor is followed in Book 9 by Iris's visit summoning Turnus to attack the Trojan camp. The two scenes are elaborately parallel. Both warriors are alone at rest in ancestral groves when visited. Aeneas receives armor, including the shield through which he shoulders an imperial history he cannot understand:

> All these images on Vulcan's shield,
> His mother's gift, were wonders to Aeneas.
> Knowing nothing of the events themselves,
> He felt joy in their pictures, taking up
> Upon his shoulder all the destined acts
> And fame of his descendants.

> Talia per clipeum Volcani, dona parentis,
> miratur rerumque ignarus imagine gaudet,
> attollens umero famamque et fata nepotum. (8.729-31)

Turnus receives not armor but a call to arms. He attacks the Trojan fleet, however, with weapons also supplied by Vulcan, and like Aeneas he assumes the character of his weaponry:

> He rode for it, calling his cheering men
> To bring up fire, and he, himself enflamed,
> Took up a blazing pine torch in his hand.
>
> invadit sociosque incendia poscit ovantis
> atque manum pinu flagranti fervidus implet. (9.71-72)

The pine torch is meant to ignite the timbers of the Trojan fleet, but at this point Cybele intervenes, and so does Virgil: after the line "And Vulcan clouded heaven with smoke and ash" ("taeda et commixtam Volcanus ad astra favillam," 9.76) the narrator breaks off his description of the conflagration to insert a genealogy of the threatened timbers.

The break leads to a reinvocation of the Muse followed by a flashback to the building of the Trojan fleet. The timbers used to make the ships came from a "dusky place" ("lucus . . . obscurus," 9.86-87), a mountain grove sacred to the mother of the gods. Like Turnus and Aeneas, then—and the tree used to make the earl's lute—the wood is summoned from the obscurity of the forest. Happy at first to donate the grove, Cybele later has second thoughts and begs Jove to protect the pines from storms at sea. He promises instead that when their imperial burden is discharged he will "strip away their mortal shape" ("mortalem eripiam formam," 9.101) and turn them into sea nymphs. When the narrative turns back to the scene of combat, it is to describe this transformation: reversing the movement from isolation and repose to the labors of empire, the ships break their tethers, dive like dolphins, and resurface as nymphs swimming out to sea. The narrative in Virgil imitates this movement of withdrawal as it turns back to recount the ships' genealogy, but it does not follow the nymphs into the freedom of the watery element. Like Aeneas, the poem must resume the burdens of epic warfare, associated here with the element of fire.

By contrast, when Ovid retells the story in *Metamorphoses* 14 he omits Vulcan's shield, expanding the metamorphosis of the ships while abbreviating the narrative context. Barkan observes that Ovid's treatment of this episode belongs to the antiheroic, counterimperial tendency that pervades the *Metamorphoses*, though Ovid is amplifying an imperial reluctance already discernible in the *Aeneid*.[7] If Spenser's epigram likewise has its roots in Cybele's grove, then it too may participate in a submerged counterepic current in literary history.

A number of other vignettes in *Metamorphoses* 14 resonate suggestively against the lute. The sybil, for instance, tells us her body will waste away but that her voice will endure, although fated to deliver the words of the very god whose love she refused. Picus, turned into a woodpecker by Circe, leaves behind a wife named "Canens" (for her lovely voice) when he takes up a career felling trees. And just before the transformation of the Trojan fleet, we read of a shepherd who mocked the dance of the nymphs, "Nor did he cease speaking until the rising wood covered his mouth. For now he is a tree" ("nec prius os tacuit, quam guttura condidit arbor: / arbor enim est," Ovid ed. 1916, 2:336, 337). His metamorphosis reverses those of the ships and the lute.

From Ovid, then, Spenser inherits the topos of metamorphosis, its characteristic emphasis on identity-in-transformation focussed in Book 14 on the loss or survival of the voice. Another important precedent is *The Greek Anthology*, widely circulated and imitated throughout the sixteenth century.[8] With its playful gift of first-person utterance to all manner of objects, the anthology even more pointedly questions the "origin" of voice. Book 9 in particular is rich in "declamatory" epigrams, including inscriptions and mock inscriptions, in which everything from laurel trees to latrines speak about themselves and their histories. Trees are especially voluble: walnuts, pears, laurels, and olives lament their fortunes or warn axe-wielding readers to spare them, and—especially interesting in light of the passages from Virgil and Ovid—pine trees felled by storms demand, in several variations on the same theme, "Why, foolish carpenter, dost thou make of me, the pine-tree that am the victim of the winds, a ship to travel over the seas, and dreadest not the omen?" (9.376; cf. also 9.30-32, 105, and 131). It sounds as if Cybele has these omens in mind when she begs Jove to protect her pines, although it may be that the epigrammatists, many of whom are anonymous, were thinking of Cybele.[9] Another group of equally Virgilian pines reflects on the irony of having been made into ships and then having survived the seas, only to perish by fire (9.34, 36, 106, 398). An anonymous epigram in which a pen celebrates its transformation from "a reed, a useless plant," into an instrument of language might have been known to Spenser from several sources: it is clearly a version of the tortoise riddle and, given its wide circulation in the sixteenth century, a likely source for the "Brescian legend."[10]

Like its precedents in Ovid and *The Greek Anthology*, the indeterminate "I" of Spenser's epigram both celebrates the gift of voice and questions its origin. The instrument gains a song only at the cost of its "vitall sapp": as an allegory of authorship, the epigram instrumentalizes the poet even as it anthropomorphizes the lute. As an instrument of culture, it says, the poet loses his animate being like Cybele's sacred grove, but unlike the grove, he never gets it back. He remembers that before there was speech he had a rooted, organic being, but he knows this condition is irrecoverable, knows he will never escape being played upon by the Muse of history. Such a poet finds an image of his fate in the diphonic lute built by Thomas Mace in 1672 (Fig. 9). "Fairely written upon each belly" of this double lute were verses interpreting it as a three-dimensional emblem of imperial harmony:

> Let thus much suffice to be spoken by me, concerning this new instrument; but whosoever pleaseth, may hear it speak much better for it self.
> Yet only, because it is my beloved darling, I seem'd (like an old doting body) to be fond of it; so that when I had finish'd it, I be-deckt it with these fine rhimes, following; fairly written upon each belly; viz. first, round the Theorboe Knot, thus.

> I am of old, and of Great Brittain's fame,
>   Theorboe was my name.
>   (Then next, about the French Lute Knot, thus.)
> I'm not so old; yet grave, and much accute,
>   My name was the French Lute.
>   (Then from thence along the Sides, from one Knot to the other, thus.)
> But since we are thus joyned both in one,
>   Henceforth our name shall be The Lute Dyphone.
>   (Then again cross-wise under the Theorboe-Knot, thus.)
> Loe here a perfect emblem seen in me,
>   Of England, and of France, their Unity.
> Likewise that year they did each other aid,
>   I was contriv'd, and thus compleatly made.
>   Anno Dom. 1672.
>   (Then lastly under the French-Lute-Knot, thus.)
> Long have we been divided; now made one,
>   We sang in 7th's; now in full Unison.
> In this firm union, long may we agree;
>   No Unison's like that of Lute's Harmony.
> Thus in it's body, 'tis trim, spruce, and fine;
>   But in it's sp'rit, 'tis like a thing divine. (Mace 1676, 206)

A marginal gloss identifies the "year they did each other aid": "*Viz.* When they united both against the Dutch, and beat them soundly."

Mace's "Lute Dyphone" has an obvious source in Alciati's *Foedera* (Fig. 10). The epigram to Alciati's emblem asks Maximilian, duke of Milan, to "Accept . . . this lute . . . as you prepare to enter upon new alliances with your allies," and it develops an extended analogy between musical and political harmony. This emblem was, in Hollander's words, "the source of

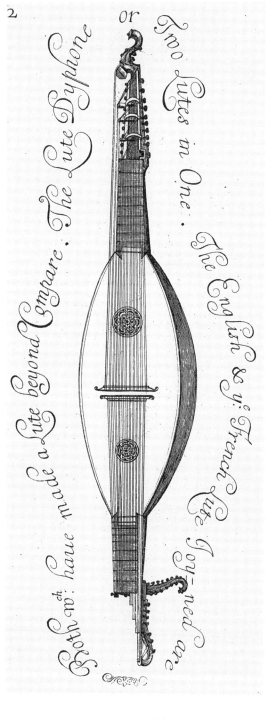

Both wch: haue made a Lute beyond Compare . The Lute Dyphone or Two Lutes in One . The English & ye French Lute Joy-ned are

Figure 9. "The Lute Dyphone." A signifying lute built by the English lutanist Thomas Mace in 1672, honoring the military alliance with France. *Musick's Monument* (1676), 32. *By permission of the Folger Shakespeare Library.*

154

6   ANDREAE ALCIATI

Fœdera.

Hāc citharā à lembī quæ forma halieutica fertur,
   Vendicat & propriam Mufa latina fibi,
Accipe Dux, placeat nostrū hoc tibi tēpore munus,
   Quo noua cum focijs fœdera inire paras.
Difficile est, nifi docto homini, tot tendere chordas,
   Vnáq; fi fuerit non bene tenta fides,
Ruptáue (qd' facile est) perit omnis gratia cōchæ,
   Illeq; præcellens cantus, ineptus erit.
Sic Itali coëunt proceres in fœdera, concors,
   Nil est quod timeas, fi tibi confiet amor.
At fi aliquis defcifcat (uti plerunque uidemus)
   In nihilum illa omnis foluitur harmonia.

Figure 10.   Andreas Alciati, *Foedera* [Alliance], from *Emblematum Libellus* (1534), 6. *By permission of the Folger Shakespeare Library.*

many subsequent allegorizations of stringed instruments."[11] Among these subsequent allegorizations is Peacham's 1612 emblem (Fig. 11), in which an Irish harp praises James I as a greater Orpheus for having restored its broken strings to harmony (Peacham 1612, 45). Peacham's Latin motto makes explicit the link I have been arguing for, between the musical instrument and the imperial staff of office: the harp refers to its "sceptre . . . defiled by native gore" ("Cum mea nativo squallerent sceptra cruore").

155

Hibernica Respub : ad Iacobum Regem .

WHILE I lay bathed in my natiue blood,
  And yeelded nought saue harsh, & hellish soundes :
And saue from Heauen, I had no hope of good,
Thou pittiedst (Dread Soueraigne) my woundes,
  Repair'dst my ruine, and with Ivorie key,
  Didst tune my stringes, that slackt or broken lay.

Now since I breathed by thy Roiall hand,
And found my concord, by so smooth a tuch,
I giue the world abroade to vnderstand,
Ne're was the musick of old Orpheus such,
  As that I make, by meane (Deare Lord) of thee,
  From discord drawne, to sweetest vnitie.

Basil : Doron.

Cum mea nativo squallerent sceptra cruore,
  Edoque lugubres vndique fracta modos :
Ipse redux neryos distendis (Phœbe) rebelles,
  Et stupet ad nostros Orpheus ipse sonos .

Pænitentia

Figure 11. Henry Peacham, *Hibernica Respub: ad Iacobum Regem* [The Republic of Ireland: To King James], from *Minerva Britanna* (1612), 45. *By permission of the Folger Shakespeare Library.*

Even more nakedly than Mace's jingoistic lute, Peacham's sycophantic "Irish" harp offers a ruthless instance of the harmonizing topos as a kind of imperial ventriloquism, projecting an acceptable voice and identity into a silence secured by force.[12] In contrast to the convention deriving from Alciati, Spenser's lute knows that something has been sacrificed for the sake of imperial harmony. In this respect it has more in common with Michele Carrara's 1585 engraving (Fig. 12). Vine leaves and branches sprout along the upper border of the lute's belly and fingerboard, as if a stylized band of ornamentation had set down roots and started to grow again. Birds alighting on the vine feed or sing; a dragonfly hovers nearby; a cluster of grapes dangles invitingly against the fingerboard; and a snail delicately surmounts the sprig that rises above the sixth fret. But below the rose, or sound hole, a human hand emerging from a cuff of lace lies spread and labeled as if for dissection: another part of the instrument, formed by its discourse, or what the ironically named Mace designates "the Language of LUTE'S Mysterie."[13] Central to this mystery is an exchange of properties whereby the instrument is reanimated as the performer is instrumentalized.

Carrara's engraving takes us back to Hesiod, where the poet's laurel staff is still blossoming in token of the healing powers of song. But, like Spenser's epigram, the engraving hints at the opposite effect as well, implying that the Muses' gift may deracinate the recipient. Given the convention of the lute as an emblem of political harmony, this irony implies a veiled complaint. For the literary allusion embedded in the topos of the cut tree returns us to the privileged symbol of imperial authority in classical antiquity—the scepter—and it returns us to just those passages in Homer and Virgil in which the unity of empire is decisively broken: Achilles' wrath in the opening books of the *Iliad* and Latinus's inability to reconcile Turnus and Aeneas at the close of the *Aeneid*. These passages are among the founding moments of the cultural myth of *translatio imperii*. Hesiod had substituted the poet's laurel staff for the imperial scepter in Homer, as if to say that the poet's staff, unlike the scepter, *will* bloom again. The emblem tradition deriving from Alciati restores a political context for Spenser and Carrara. Their lutes, alluding to Hesiod's Muses but also to the imperial scepter of antiquity and the Renaissance lute of state, suggest that imperial culture tends to appropriate the artist to its own ends. His instrument flourishes only as he surrenders his hand to a dominant discourse; if he sings at all, he does so with a voice not his own.

Spenser figures this cultural appropriation as the expense of "vitall sapp." This is the deepest irony of his hybrid epic-gram: thematic contrasts between art and empire, voice and silence, epic labor and shady repose, are

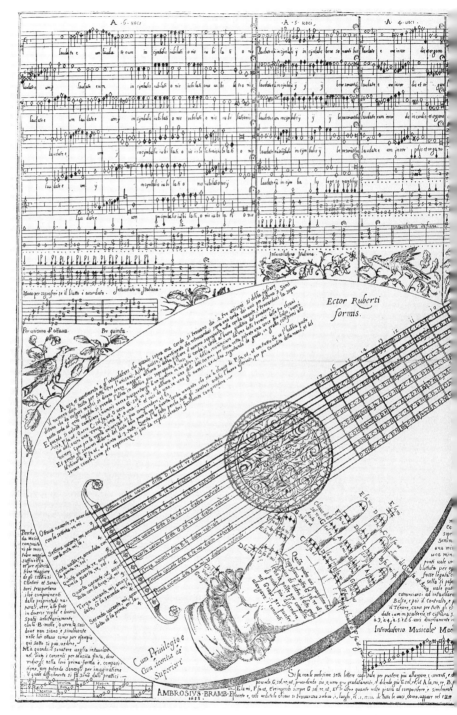

Figure 12. Italian engraving, with text by the lutanist Michele Carrara, depicting what Thomas Mace in *Musick's Monument* (38) calls "The Language of LUTE's

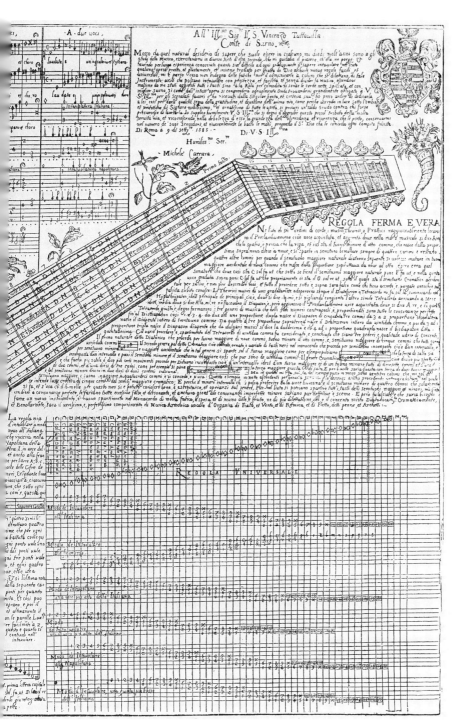

Mysterie." From a modern facsimile, *Intavolatura di liuto, 1585; a cura di Benvenuto Disertori. By permission of the Library of Congress, Music Division.*

grafted onto the radical translation from being into language. Traditionally the poet recalls his culture's roots in the past, but in Spenser's lines memory becomes a paradoxical figure for what cannot be remembered or represented, the rift between life and voice. Once spoken, prediscursive being is neither prediscursive nor being. Spenser's lute plays elegantly on this paradox, for when it pretends to remember a leafy origin, it pretends to forget the inaccessibility of such an origin to a voice materially wrought out of the tree's organic death. Using terms that Teskey has borrowed from Heidegger (1988; see also 1992, 1993), we could say that the epigram pretends to forget the forgetting of being. But it also sets this pretense forth as part of its wit. By staging the pronoun "I" so wittily *en abîme*, it implicitly remembers and makes the poet a figure for this memory of forgetfulness. If asked the Foucauldian question "Who is speaking?" the lute would reply not "What does it matter?" but rather "Who wants to know?" (Foucault 1977, 138).

This *mise en abîme* of the speaking voice is a pervasive feature of *The Faerie Queene*.[14] The poet as a figure of national memory appears most clearly in the chronicle sections of Book II. There (as I have argued before) Spenser makes the poet a figure not of historical truth but of the political desires that produce truths out of the historical record. Consider the passage that really does allude to Agamemnon's scepter, marked by its distinguished genealogy as the privileged symbol of imperial rule:

> Thy name O soveraine Queene, thy realme and race,
>   From this renowmed Prince derived arre,
>   Who mightily upheld that royall mace,
>   Which now thou bear'st, to thee descended farre
>   From mightie kings and conquerours in warre.[15]

It is conventional to distinguish the proems, where the poet speaks in his own person ("Lo I the man"), from the rest of the narrative, spoken by a narrator often subject to irony. But these lines from canto x of Book II are addressed directly to Elizabeth: are they spoken, then, by the poet and not the narrator? The chronicles themselves seem clearly enough to begin at stanza 5, and their end is marked by a dramatic break in midsentence, but in whose voice are they spoken? Or to put it another way, what is the relation between the text Arthur reads and the text in which he reads?[16]

The chronicles begin with a recitation of the "noble deeds" in "that old mans booke" (4.7-9), but the transition into another text is not marked. Spenser's narrator earlier spoke of *himself* as reciting the ancestry. Shall we assume then that the poet-narrator's voice is the only one and that *The Faerie Queene* has effaced *Briton moniments* so thoroughly that it is always the Spenserian poet speaking, if only to quote another text? Shall we assume further that scattered lines throughout the chronicles represent unmarked interruptions by this narrator into the text he is quoting? *Briton moniments* starts out as "that old mans booke" and concludes as the "it" of "it did end" (68.2), but the act of narration collapses the distance between the two texts, making the poet's voice indistinguishable from that of the chronicler.

This undecidability is strikingly marked when the *Moniments* breaks off "without full point, or other Cesure right" (68.3). The resulting fragment, "After him *Uther*, which *Pendragon* hight, / Succeeding," might be completed in any number of ways: "Succeeding whom that glorious Arthur rose"; "Succeeding to the auncient British throne"; "Succeeding from that honorable sire"; or even "Succeeding evils did quite overrule." "Succeeding," then—the key term of chronicle discourse, and never more so than in 1590—retains its greatest semantic indeterminacy, offering an exact textual equivalent of Elizabeth's notorious refusal to settle the royal succession. And yet the poetic "line" goes on without missing a beat: "Succeeding There abruptly it did end" is strictly unconstruable, lacking the phrasal closure that Lacan compares to an upholstery stud, but as pure signifier it is metrically unbroken. That is, it lacks a caesura, although modern editors often insert punctuation to create one.

The "cesure right" missing from Arthur's reading is thus both phrasal closure and a once and future king. Stanza 49 clarifies this pun, for the "reckoning" Arthur will defray is nothing less than British subjection to Roman rule, personified by "warlike *Caesar*" (47.6). Androgeus, we read, betrayed his uncle Cassibalane, and "by him *Caesar* got the victory," although in the battle Androgeus lost his sword, "yet to be seene this day" (49.1, 5). We may wonder which day is meant, Spenser's or Arthur's, especially since a similar phrase is applied in Book I to Arthur's weaponry, preserved by Gloriana in Faeryland, where "yet it may be seene, if sought" (I vii 36). These passages link the confusion of historical times to the indeterminacy of utterances, and they bring both questions to bear on the reader's relation to the text: will Arthur become the Caesar that the chronicles say he was? Will he sustain the genealogy of the imperial scepter, like Aeneas, or betray it as Androgeus did? Indeed, how distinct are betrayal and heroism in a *translatio* that carries empire from Agamemnon to his defeated rival Aeneas, and from Aeneas's descendant Caesar to the rebellious British?

Elizabeth Bellamy has pointed out the ambiguity of Spenser's answer to these implied questions: in the poem as we have it, Arthur does not become a British Caesar, and his armor ends up not in England but in Faeryland.[17] It is as if Arthur had somehow passed over from *Briton monuments* into the *Antiquitee of Faery Lond*. The armor that hangs there is not quite part of any epic destiny, for the voice of faery antiquity, like the signifying lute, remembers nothing but fiction.[18] In this way it remembers the massive forgetting upon which imperial history is written.

What does the lute tell us, then, about literary biography? It alludes to the fictionality of pretextual origins, whether we call them life, history, or politics: there can be no "life writing" if the Muses speak only in the swath of the axe. For Spenser studies today such a warning is apt. The biographical portrait of Spenser as colonial oppressor enjoys wide currency, and a politically charged historicism uses this portrait to discredit Spenser's writing as careerist or reactionary.[19] These arguments ignore the indeterminacy of texts in favor of the imagined certainties of politics, presumed to be more important, determinable, and real.

Such readings secure their conclusions in the first place by ignoring serious problems in the critical bibliography. The epigram on the earl's lute calls attention to such problems, reminding us how little we know about the production and circulation of texts attributed to Spenser. Brink puts the matter bluntly: "critical and bibliographical methods taken for granted in Shakespearean scholarship," she observes, have never been applied to Spenser's *View*.[20] There is no evidence that Spenser considered any manuscript of *A View* to be complete or final. No printed text in existence takes account of all known extant manuscripts, although these vary substantively. No extant manuscript used as a copytext for any modern edition is in Spenser's holograph, nor have efforts been made "to date or trace the provenance of most of the manuscripts" we do have. No contemporary reference to Spenser's authorship of the *View* has been found, nor is it clear that Spenser intended publication; the lack of a preface or dedication suggests just the opposite. In short, we don't know when, why, or for whom the treatise was composed. It is not even certain that publication of the *View* was officially suppressed, although the assumption that it was appears regularly in critical discussions.

The tendency to forget uncertainties in discussing the *View* may be seen in the most responsible historicist arguments. Montrose (1992) prefaces an analysis of the "autobiographical mythopoeia" in such late works as *Amoretti and Epithalamion* and *Colin Clouts Come Home Againe* by acknowledging that, "[w]hatever autobiographical circumstances we may specify or surmise as sources or originating conditions of this poetry, they have been conspicuously and elaborately shaped into an autobiographical fiction in the Spenserian text." Yet later in the same essay he asserts,

> The *View* manifests the darker side of Spenser's investment of his whole personal and family future in Ireland. In it, Spenser employs the conventions of dialogue toward a sweeping and systematic program for the eradication of traditional Irish culture and society, and the violent imposition, from the ground up, of a society and culture conformable with the dominant institutions, beliefs, and practices of Elizabethan England—one which would be controlled by transplanted Englishmen such as Spenser himself.
>
> The general end of the *View*, which was to fashion Ireland in virtuous and gentle discipline, was itself shaped and impelled by the circumstances of Spenser's own position there.

Here a different protocol governs Montrose's reading: personal and historical circumstance "shape" and "impel" an odious political program to which the treatise's explicit fictionality ("the conventions of dialogue") is wholly subordinated.

A similar contradiction marks Richard Rambuss's important study, *Spenser's Secret Career* (1993). Rambuss argues persuasively that

> Spenser's career as a secretary provided him with a discursive practice and professional model that had a shaping effect both on his poetry and on the professional role he envisioned for himself as a poet. In short, even as a poet, Spenser writes as a secretary—as one . . . who not only takes what appears to be a form of poetic dictation from his muse, but who also is busily employed in the management of secrets. (28)

Modified by the secretary-function, the author-function in Spenser constructs the poet as one who transmits another's messages. It also hollows him out, like the "excavated" pen in *The Greek Anthology*, to serve as a writing implement: the discourse of secretaryship "fashions a secretary who literally has become his office, has become the privy place where his master withdraws to store secrets" (30).[21]

Yet the secretary-function allows a countermovement to this elision of the person in the office. The indeterminate scope of the secretary's commission, in comparison with that of other functionaries, created unique opportunities for shaping the "voice" of power. Contemporary accounts cited by Rambuss describe a degree of intimacy between master and secretary exceeding that between father and son; Robert Cecil compares the relation to matrimony (40-41). In such a scenario the secretary's self and interests merge into his master's much as a wife's identity merges into her husband's, but in both relations the subordinate partner might wield considerable influence. Rambuss quotes a passage from Angel Day's *English*

Secretary in which the syntax becomes as ambiguous as the relation itself and may be read to imply either that the secretary is "the disposer of his [i.e., the master's] everie thought" or vice versa (43-44). In this passage, suggests Rambuss, we glimpse the possibility that "the secretary, having already displaced son and spouse, now looms to stand in place of the master himself, whom he imitates in all things" (44).

Rambuss develops an incisive account of the relation between Spenser's poetic and bureaucratic careers, and of the poetics of secrecy informing much that Spenser wrote. Yet the sharp outlines of this account reduce the irreducible ambiguity of the scenario Day and Cecil sketch. The most radical implication of a scriptive economy in which master and secretary are functionally and syntactically indistinguishable is not a scenario of suppressed rivalry, in which the secretary may advance his own interests by supplanting the master; it is a scenario lacking the very distinctness of persons and interests upon which rivalry depends. To speak in this context of "careerist negotiations" and "strateg[ies] for self-promotion" (4) is to fix the play of self and interest in a way contrary to the secretarial relation's unmooring of these in a powerful and erotically charged homosocial intimacy.

Rambuss sees Spenser most fully realizing the secretary's potential reversal of position with the master in Book V of *The Faerie Queene*: "Spenser," he writes, "is not the state instrument he here claims to be. Inasmuch as he is rewriting history in Book 5 with a political agenda that is not exactly Elizabeth's (so that in actuality the book's allegory is anything but transparent), he is dictating to the queen even as he claims to be taking her dictation" (1993, 114). This recuperation of agency and intentionality in the figure of the poet may reflect the political agenda of modern historicist criticism as much as it does Spenser's. Citizens of a world empire whose benefits we enjoy with a dubious conscience, we tend to reduce the difference between culture and politics so as to magnify, by implication, the political value of cultural work, especially ours. Rhetorically this reduction of difference often proceeds by denying an extreme form of its contrary. Thus Spenser's "vocational aspirations and agendas as a poet are never cordoned off from his professional pursuit as a secretary of office, status, and political influence" (9). Or in the words of Ciaran Brady, quoted with approval, "The attempt to distinguish the poet Spenser from any of his presumed personae in Ireland is . . . futile" (Rambuss 1993, 127 n.10).

What cannot be distinguished cannot be related. Brady's influential re-assessment of *A View* nevertheless attempts precisely to formulate interrelations among Spenser's indistinguishable personae, including the Virgilian poet, the messianic Elizabethan, the disappointed courtier, the cultivated humanist, and the ruthless colonial landowner. The problem as Brady defines it is to understand "the poet's moral sensibility": "How could the principal poet of the English Renaissance not merely tolerate or even defend, but actually celebrate the use of merciless and unrestrained violence against large numbers of his fellow men?" (1986b, 18). Brady raises the issue of "moral sensibility" in order to judge Spenser as a writer. But to do that we have to forget how little is known about when, why, or for whom the unpublished manuscript was written. Without such a context the *View* is like the unpunctuated line in the chronicles, lacking the upholstery stud that would anchor a reading. Inevitably, critics establish their views of the *View* by supplying the missing context, just as modern editors punctuate Spenser's unreadable line. Textual royalists, such scholars cannot help supplying an author, an Arthur, a Caesar: a figure who can guarantee the orderly succession of reading.

Unlike the "Briefe Note of Ireland," composed in the aftermath of rebellion, the *View* is no simple plea for military intervention. For Brady, though, its contradictions reflect the author's "persistent but concealed attempt to marry expediency with morality" and so resolve themselves into uncontradictory evidence that "the *View of the Present State of Ireland* is nothing short of a sustained exercise in bad faith" (41). At the same time, Brady argues that "such a conclusion would . . . be quite unhistorical" (41), and attributes some of the inconsistency to Spenser's "genuine commitment" to the "moral development" of the English, "an element of intrinsic sincerity" among "motives [that] were in good part manipulative" (47). Referring the contradictions of a "clotted and ambiguous" argument to the moral sensibility of the writer, he constructs a clotted and ambiguous moral sensibility.

Whatever their provenance, though, Brady sees contradictions in the *View*, together with its signs of fictionality, as forms of "decoy" that "allow[ed] Spenser to retain the mantle of the conscientious humanist scholar while he urged a brutal and desperate policy" (41). Spenser's motives for developing such a rhetorical strategy may hover undecidably between sincerity and bad faith, but the strategy itself is internally coherent as an effort to paper over the damaging contradiction between humanist values and political expediency.

This reading assumes that Spenser could not have intended contradictions in his argument to be read as contradictions, or that he could not have intended his dialogue to be read dialogically. In a strong riposte to Brady, Patterson argues that "Spenser, too, was from the start conscious of the limitations of abstract principle as an intellectual response to life in the early modern world" (1992, 106). She argues that Book V of *The Faerie Queene*, far from confirming an ideologically closed reading of the *View*, "is the hard core of Spenser's inquiry into the ideological moves a society makes when it encodes as platonic forms necessary protocols and procedures" (106). The opening sections of the *View*, she says, "make fully explicit the conceptual problems that the poem renders fantastic" (115). Once we acknowledge the dialogue form as more than a "decoy," it is easier to see Eudoxus as more than a straight man or a straw man: "the fact that he is usually persuaded to change his mind under 'strong constraint' does not necessarily eradicate from the reader's mind the justice of his position" (120). At the same time it becomes less clear that Irenius is a transparent spokesman for the author: Patterson argues persuasively that in the celebrated passage where Irenius demands reform "even by the sword," Spenser is showing him "caught in the act of apologetic icon making" (125).

Like Brady, then, Patterson anchors her reading of Book V and the *View* in a plausible model of authorial intention:

> I am not suggesting that Spenser was opposed to the policy of Irish subjugation that the *View* as a whole promotes. . . . But it is a mistake to believe he was comfortable with this final solution or only inadvertently revelatory of the contradictions in the ideology of Justice that appear in both the Legend of Justice and the *View*. He is prepared to argue for violent suppression, but only on the naked grounds of necessity. (94)

This intentional model is surprisingly close to Brady's; far from arguing that Spenser was comfortable with the brutal logic of his treatise, Brady sees him writing in "a tortured and distorted manner" (1986b, 41) that expresses not a coherent political doctrine but "an acute sense of crisis" (49). The difference between the models (and the opposed readings they sustain) lies in how contradictions internal to the intention are characterized. Where Brady sees inadvertent traces of ideological crisis which nonetheless serve strategically as decoys, Patterson sees deliberate ironies reflecting the way iconographic representation will always betray into visibility the contradictions internal to an ideology. Thus, in the egalitarian giant episode of Book V, "the strains within justice as a theory are exhibited as strains on the allegorical system itself" (112). The agency that sponsors such representations is complexly but not haplessly at odds with itself, for it intends an "internal critique" of its own intentionality (112). The *View* in this view is so far from obscuring the contradiction between humanist culture and "the naked grounds of necessity" (Brady's contention) that it conscientiously stages their rupture in order to prevent exactly the mystification Brady thinks the treatise was written to perform.

Finally, the difference between these readings lies in the readers, both those who produce the readings and those whom the readings presume. Patterson argues for an irreverent author writing at least in part for irreverent readers; the broad thesis of her essay is that skeptical, antiauthoritarian reading is no mere invention of modernity but a common practice of early modern subjects. Brady argues for a conflicted and devious author, one who writes for an audience of humanists who need as he does both to believe in humane reason and to do what is politically necessary. Neither assumption is inherently implausible, but neither can be empirically proven. Nor can either claim to be the origin of Spenser's text, although each demonstrably generates the interpretive "evidence" of its own validity by imagining an audience and the historical scene of its reading.

There is, however, evidence throughout *The Faerie Queene* that when critique cannot declare itself openly it is exhibited as a strain on the allegorical system, as if the poem were "assuming" and exacerbating ideological flaws it dare not name. Such a politics of naming is memorialized in the spectacle of "Malfont," which edifies Arthur and Artegall at the threshold of Mercilla's court in Book V. The image of the poet with his tongue nailed to a post has often been discussed, so let me simply emphasize that in context it belongs to a subtle allegory of guile. It is preceded in canto ix by Talus's annihilation of a figure *named* Guyle, and is followed in cantos x-xi by a guileful allusion to Elizabeth's guile in executing Mary, Queen of Scots. Arthur and company approach Mercilla's court by way of "Awe." This proto-Hobbesian figure recalls the egalitarian giant, especially since Artegall's inability to grasp Guyle in the previous episode has just reenacted the earlier Giant's inability to weigh "the winged words" of "right or wrong, the false or else the trew" (ii 44). Awe is charged with performing the task at which Artegall and the egalitarian giant have both failed—his job is to "keepe out guyle" (ix 22.7)—and he is stationed for this purpose at the threshold of the royal court. Yet he is himself a work of guile, not exactly a giant but, in Spenser's canny phrasing, a "gyantlike resemblance" (22.6), an illusion whereby statecraft dissimulates its guile.

This pattern must raise questions about the author's own guile when, after passing by Awe and Order, we come upon a poet whose tongue has been crucified because he accused the queen of "forged guyle" (25.5): the word seems to have winged its way past giantlike resemblances to reappear at the center of the court, where it lights on the royal majesty. Such "winged words," Malfont reminds us, are arrested by the politics of naming. Who has the power to fix meaning? Stanza 25 asserts that the punished figure "on himselfe had ta'en" the "bold title of a Poet bad" (8-9). But stanza 26 gives a different account of how this name was imposed:

> . . . high over his head,
> There written was the purport of his sin,
> In cyphers strange, that few could rightly read,
> BON FONS: but *bon*, that once had written bin,
> Was raced out, and *Mal* was now put in:
> So now *Malfont* was plainely to be red;
> Eyther for th'evill, which he did therein,
> Or that he likened was to a welhead
> Of evill words, and wicked sclaunders by him shed.[22]

This poet is literally written under erasure: "the purport of his sin" is a strangely ciphered, hard to read *BON FONS*, whereas the "title of a Poet bad," overwritten by the invisible hand of power (the Star Chamber?), is "plainely to be red." To read this poet accurately, to divine the real "purport" of his sin, we must decipher his "raced" character. The official acts of naming are more legible; every title they confer is "bold" (easily read). Explicit, reiterated, and authorized, they label the good and the bad as if truth were self-evident: as if the victim really had labeled him*self* "a Poet bad."[23]

The devious economy of naming evoked in these lines calls for strategies of decipherment that will let us recover the element of critique encoded in what look like strains on the allegorical system. At the same time, it suggests that we can never get back to the origin. A "bon font" is a wellhead, and a well head is a *mens sana*, but one that has been deviously encrypted. What Spenser in the "Letter to Ralegh" calls the "welhead" of his fable is an intention to skirt "the daunger of envy, and suspition of present time."[24] This may be as much of the well head as we are likely to recover, since between us and the Helicon there is always a printer's font. *All* labelings of the origin, therefore, all models of authorial intention—including this one—are reinscriptions of an erased cipher. Taken together with the lute epigram, this passage implies that the poet can neither write his own life nor speak with his own voice. The most he can do is encrypt his name, the trace of an inestimable loss, beneath the boldface imprinted on him from beyond.

In the poetic scales that measure out the due proportions of *The Faerie Queene*, this passage from Book V is poised against Arthur's and Guyon's visit to the castle of Temperance. Book II, canto ix, stanza 25—like its numerical counterpart in Book V—shows us an allegory of the human tongue. Here it occupies the watchtower of the well head:

> Within the Barbican a Porter sate,
>   Day and night duely keeping watch and ward,
>   Nor wight, nor word mote passe out of the gate,
>   But in good order, and with dew regard;
>   Utterers of secrets he from thence debard,
>   Bablers of folly, and blazers of crime. (1-6)

As we pass from Book II to Book V, from the well head of temperance to the wellhead of the body politic, this warden of "good order" is subjected to the "Awe" of the political "Order," which changes his name from "Porter of good speech" to "source of evil." Rechristened with a hammer and nails, his "crime" blazed in "bold" letters over his head, even the temperate tongue becomes an utterer of secrets, his speech polarized between the extremes of blazon and crypt.

I have argued before that Spenser's name is encrypted in Book II in the figure of Diet (ix 27) and again in the unnamed figure who occupies the middle chamber in the turret of Alma's castle (54).[25] In each case the poet is a "dispenser," a weigher-out of wisdom and safe diet. His name thus contains an allegory of his function, an allegory that, like the lute poem, makes "Spenser" the instrument of another's voice. There is no evading this constitutive ventriloquism: like his political critics, I am rewriting the author's name. In tracing an allegory of deracinated authorship, I risk mistaking my own voice for that of the earl's lute. My argument must therefore advance seemingly contradictory claims: first that this allegory of authorship is intentional and, second, that its argument, correctly deciphered, deconstructs intentionalist reading. The result is an allegory of authorship under erasure.

A final illustration of this deconstructive allegory may be found in the closing lines of *The Faerie Queene*. The Beast of Slander, "supprest and tamed" by Sir Calidore in the final canto of Book VI, has broken loose again:

> Ne spareth he most learned wits to rate,
> Ne spareth he the gentle Poets rime,
> But rends without regard of person or of time.
>
> Ne may this homely verse, of many meanest,
>   Hope to escape his venemous despite,
>   More then my former writs, all were they clearest
>   From blamefull blot, and free from all that wite,
>   With which some wicked tongues did it backebite,
>   And bring into a mighty Peres displeasure,
>   That never so deserved to endite.
>   Therfore do you my rimes keep better measure,
> And seeke to please, that now is counted wisemens threasure. (xii 40.7-9; 41)

If "style," as Lacan would have it, is not "the man" but "the man to whom one addresses oneself" (Gallop 1985, 116), then Spenser's style in these lines must be William Cecil, Lord Burghley. In the imago of that mighty peer, the passage concentrates the intensely politicized register of awe and guile, secrecy and blazon, within which Spenser wrote. It does so through a strategy of double writing, appropriating the jargon of the treasury. "Rate," in stanza 40, means not only to scold but to appraise and measure out; "learned wits to rate" thus condenses the figures of slanderer and Treasurer. "Counted" in the final line slides between the enumeration of syllables or wealth and the more complex exchange called patronage in which rhymes and pleasures are rewarded: the scene of reading, rating, and arithmetic.

In evoking this exchange the poet gives himself the last word. That word is threasure, in 1596 literally the last word of the poem. Spenser had closed *The Shepheardes Calender* in 1579 with similar wordplay: a Latin motto (*Merce non mercede*, "[judge] by the goods, not the price") reinscribes the authorial pseudonym Immerito, implying that the text of the poem, which falls between the two, has produced "goods"—that it has, by being read, created value *ex Immeritione*. In 1596, however, Spenser purloins the very letter of Burghley's title from the word-hoard of the bureaucracy. Hidden in plain view, this reinscription of "Treasurer" implies that Burghley, like the cynic in *Lady Windermere's Fan*, knows the price of everything and the value of nothing. In combination with the references to rating, measuring, and counting, it casts him as a sort of Bureaucratic Giant, whose balance is no better at weighing words than that of his egalitarian counterpart.

Silently but unmistakably, the passage also opposes Lord Burghley to "the Muses' dispenser." The sardonic admonition to "keep better measure" glances at the standardization of weights and measures under Elizabeth, who "impaneled special commissions to supervise the examination of weights and measures everwhere in the realm. The commissioners destroyed any standards that did not conform to Crown specifications and constructed new sets which they distributed to the Exchequer and to various local authorities."[26] Such commissions were impaneled twice during the latter part of the century, as the requirements of an increasingly national economy reinforced the centralizing tendencies of the royal bureaucracy. In theory, then, every act of measurement imposed a royal standard, although it proved impossible in practice to destroy all local variation. The first series of royal standard-weights, bearing a crowned monogram, was cast in gunmetal in 1558 and kept at the Exchequer. In 1582 a new series was cast, and over the next four years fifty-eight copies were distributed throughout the realm. A royal proclamation, posted in every market and church and "read to parishioners twice a year for four years," called for nationwide acceptance of these standards (Zupko 1977, 92).

Against this elaborate promulgation, a government's program for standardizing terms of exchange, Spenser quietly poises the "threasure" of poetic wisdom. This threasure differs from royal treasure by the barest of aspirations, an archaic "h" that may not even have been pronounced. This "h" is the trace left in treasure by "thesis," for treasure like thesaurus has its Latin roots in *thesis aurum*, or the placing of gold. It is a thesis that places Spenser, the Muses' t(h)reasurer, where we are always invited to seek him: everywhere and nowhere, under erasure throughout the massive thesaurus of his work.

Afterword

DONALD CHENEY

Writing—and reading—at a time when "we know less than earlier generations thought they did," in Jon Quitslund's words, we should not be surprised if the essays in this volume lack the shapeliness of earlier biographies and instead dwell insistently on what Judith Anderson calls the "ambiguous subject of biography" itself. It seems axiomatic today that all evidence is questionable, that nobody's life can be written truly or "factually": it is not the novelty of these axioms that accounts for their prominence here but the fact that Spenser insists on them. Whether or not the epigram on the earl of Cork's lute that was attributed to Spenser in 1633 is really his, it *sounds* like the postmodern Spenser we know, acutely aware of the Death of the Author; it would almost be more interesting if it were not authentic, since it would seem to show (as do many items already listed in *Spenser Allusions*, ed. Wells, 1972) how close our sense of the poet is to that of his earliest readers.

The evidence for Spenser's life is questionable, then—not merely doubtful but calling its own authority into question and demanding that we question it. This is immediately obvious in those early texts associated with Gabriel Harvey—the gossipy, coy, perhaps deliberately misleading notes to the *Calender* and the equally mystifying *Letters* pamphlet of 1580. The strategies of authorial self-presentation, of Spenserian "autobiography," are certainly complex here, but they are not completely unintelligible or indecipherable. The new poet is allowing himself to be seen trying to make a name for himself; he and his singular friend Harvey document the anxieties of emergence both from personal obscurity and from manuscript to print culture. Immerito as Homo Prototypographicus: publication offers a heady opportunity for social advancement, but it is fraught with risks that necessitate framing fictions of well-wishers who urge on the timid author and remind us and him of the multifaceted cultural work being advanced by his published words.

172

The conventions of the Renaissance dialogue confront us at every point: in the poet's dialogic intertextuality and in his invention of personae that refract elements in his sense of self, and in the debates among readers who seek a theoretical perspective from which to write the poet's life. From the outset of Spenser's career, prior texts provide a context, a palimpsest to which he lends a hand. This is obvious in his earliest work, his anonymous contributions to the already overinscribed, overtranslated *Theatre* of van der Noot; and as Anne Lake Prescott has shown in this volume and elsewhere, Spenser continues to read and transmute these poems of vision and ruin, and the readers and pre-texts of the poems, that he first confronts in these youthful translations. Gascoigne's *Adventures of Master F. J.* (1575) similarly provides a fertile precedent for the epistolary framework by which these intertextual encounters can be deployed in the dialogues of *Calender* and *Letters*, with a panoply of mysterious contributors whose initials continue today to resist identification. We cannot know (and are little inclined today to guess) how much basis F. J.'s adventures may have had in Gascoigne's life story, but it is clear that the persona of feckless lover and courtier figured prominently in the self that Gascoigne presented to the world; so we can say that there is as much of "Gascoigne" in the F. J. who loses Elinor to her "secretary" as there is of "Spenser" in the Colin who can never have his Rosalind. And when one considers the two authors' playing with naïveté and sophistication, and their self-amused recognition of the limits (at times, even, the irrelevance) of persuasive speech in the pursuit of desire, Gascoigne's fiction seems so prophetic of Spenser's four years later that it is tempting to wonder if E. K.'s initials may not allude to, and embrace, F. J.'s at one remove in the alphabet.[1]

Dialogues with other texts, and the elaboration of Spenser's text as itself a dialogue, are everywhere central to Spenser's self-presentation. Joseph Loewenstein shows in his discussion of the dedicatory sonnets to *The Faerie Queene* how Spenser in 1590 associates manuscript culture with a "fiction of privacy"; and the same can be argued for the interruption of Calidore's (and Colin's) quest in 1596, the abandonment of one Elizabeth's poem for another's, the "happie leaves" of the *Amoretti*. Yet "privacy" is an elusive concept if we try to import it with all its present-day baggage for application to Spenser's contemporary sense of identity;[2] perhaps we need to back up and reconsider the terms of Spenser's dialogues. As a *pastoral* fiction, the songs of Colin Clout that Rosalind has rejected scarcely exist even as part of manuscript culture; it will be left to a later Rosalind to mock the leaves that her suitor has pinned to the trees of Arden. The relation of song to singer is rendered problematic from the opening lines of the *Calender*, when the reader overhears Colin lamenting and sees him making good on his promise to break his pipe; the rehearsing by Hobbinol of Colin's earlier song to Elisa and Colin's improvising of a new lament for Dido in "November" similarly call attention to love songs that have been lost.

The *Calender* might be called an academic pastoral, not only because of its convoluted allusiveness but because it invokes a fiction of rejecting the security of academe, Hobbinol's sheltering love for Colin. The irony noted by F. J. Levy, "which charity would make us suppose accidental," in Spenser's celebration of Harvey's happiness as "a looker-on / Of this worldes stage" in a 1586 sonnet to his friend, echoes Colin's words to Hobbinol in "June": "O happy *Hobbinoll*, I bless thy state, / That Paradise hast found whych *Adam* lost." However conscious Spenser may have been of Harvey's insecure position at Cambridge, in 1579 or 1586, he is bidding a definitive farewell to that world, as figured both in Colin's rejection of Hobbinol for Rosalind and in the journey imagined in his Latin epistle "Ad ornatissimum virum . . . G. H."

C. S. Lewis (1954, 361) responded with mocking skepticism to the portrayal of Colin and Hobbinol in "Januarye": "Note the suggestion of pederasty advanced to show that we are classical, and withdrawn in the gloss to show that we are Christians." Yet there is more at stake here than a conflict between classical and Christian dispensations; and E. K.'s characterization of Hobbinol as the poet's "very speciall and most familiar freend, whom he entirely and extraordinarily beloved," generates anxieties from which the suggestion of pederasty is not entirely withdrawn. E. K. denies any "savour of disorderly love, which the learned call paederastice," but he goes on to cite approvingly Socrates' love for Alcibiades' soul as showing that "paederastice [is] much to be praeferred before gynerastice, that is the love which enflameth men with lust toward woman kind." And then, turning once again, he tries to distance himself from "Lucian or hys develish disciple Unico Aretino,"[3] whose defense of fleshly lust "is fully confuted of Perionius, and others."

Questionable evidence, indeed: all this protestation has the effect of complicating the tone of amused affection that Spenser-Colin seems to show toward Harvey-Hobbinol. It would be easier to accept unquestioningly the spiritual and altruistic love of Hobbinol for Colin, and the benign seclusion of Cambridge, if we were not being reminded repeatedly of a scandalous undertow. The *Letters* show Spenser wagering Harvey for an edition of the forbidden Lucian, and Harvey reporting that Aretino and other Italians are overly popular at Cambridge. A Protestant might claim that he could safely and profitably read Aretino, the scourge of Italian,

Catholic princes; but it is just as well to show one has prophylactically read Perionius too. And as Loewenstein has noted, in the 1580s John Wolfe, the printer of *The Faerie Queene*, publishes several volumes of Aretino's most scandalous works with a false foreign imprint (the imaginary city of Bengodi, "Jouissance").[4]

E. K.'s anxious attempt to invoke a reformed and pure pederasty thus comes close to enacting the degenerations of language and desire that Aretino himself satirizes: the mix of buggery and humbuggery that (a Protestant might argue) adheres to the cloistered donnishness of university life. Prescott has shown with respect to Spenser's use of French writers that one can never be certain just how Spenser's own Englishness or Protestantism is being compared or contrasted to the other's real or presumed allegiances. I think it plausible that he should be intentionally obscure on this matter; that he invokes their voices as parts of a more expansive culture than his contemporary society can wholly define or embrace at present. The old religion and its internationalism continue to speak through him.

The question of the national language, its cost and its rewards, remains a seriously underconsidered aspect of Spenser's art, and one that has bearing on Spenser's construction of identity. It is difficult today to grasp the emotional valences of the struggle for dominance between Latin and the vernacular, although the nostalgia felt by some Catholics for the Latin mass may give us a partial insight into them. But nothing (with the possible exception of the fading tradition of British schoolboy immersion in a Latinity that is profoundly class- and gender-bound) prepares us to appreciate the degree to which Latin, most notably in the Spenser-Harvey letters, is the chosen language both of learning and of intimacy, of truths to be kept secret and veiled. As Quitslund points out, when Spenser first names himself in print he does so in Latin, as the "Edmundus" whose absence his friend laments.

Judith M. Kennedy has examined (1980, 1990) the ways in which the *Calender* invokes the humanists' taste for mottos or *symbola* that summarize a position, riddlingly or ambiguously. Spenser frequently is bilingual in these mottos: as Kennedy notes (1990, 652), the motto to "Januarye," *Anchôra Speme*—"[There is] still hope" in Italian—puns on the familiar printer's device figuring Hope as an anchor, Latin *Anchora spei;* and the concluding motto, *Merce non mercede*, seems to suggest a Latinate grammar for words being used in their evolved Italian senses.[5] A similar bilingualism is found, I think, in the new poet's name, Immeritô. He is a poet *immeritus*, not yet worthy or recognized, at the opposite pole from an *emeritus*. In calling himself Immerito he adopts the Italian form of the nominative case. Yet he signs himself Immeritô; does the accent call attention to the long vowel in the Latin adverb for "unfairly"? It would be hard to claim this for any occurrence of the name in the *Calender*; but when he is writing quantitative verses, in the "Iambicum Trimetrum," it is just this long vowel which crowns his experiment in attempting linguistic dominion, the "kingdom of our language," by observing quantity:

> And if I starve, who will record my cursed end?
> And if I dye, who will saye: *this was, Immerito?*

"Immerito" is imagined as a proper noun that cannot be turned into an adverb of lamentation ("It's not fair") precisely because the poet has no identity yet. As much so as the verses on the earl's lute, these iambics tell us why the poet's life cannot be written.

Yet they do so ironically, embedded as they are in the career-advancing correspondence of two university men and in an attempt to "illustrate" (in the sense of du Bellay's defense of the vernacular) their local and contemporary language, to give it the permanence enjoyed by the classics. Recent biographers of Spenser have speculated on the "scenes and signs of desire" suggested by Harvey's relationship to Spenser as it is portrayed in the *Calender* and *Letters;*[6] prominent among them, I would claim, is the desire for linguistic and intertextual plenitude that recognizes and affirms the origins of our words and modes of thought, even at the risk of undercutting Protestant and national allegiances. That project would be quite dissolute and regressive enough to be figured by a shared bed in Westminster, without invoking visions from Unico Aretino.

The characterization of Spenser as poet's (or poets') poet has been invoked by too many critics, in too many outmoded styles, to seem useful today; but we shall continue to need some such term to refer to his pervasive allusiveness, the way his references, to nature or to art, seem always to refer to an earlier reference. Spenser's text is radically and relentlessly dialogic, and in writing about such a text (and trying to write the life that such a text figures at one or more removes) we must be dialogic as well. The preceding essays constitute one such piece of dialogue within and among themselves; and they engage earlier commentary most clearly when they claim to break with it. If Judson's life of Spenser seems dated and inadequate today, it is in large measure because the academy and its privileged terms have changed: feminist, postcolonialist, queer perspectives on culture call into question some of the terms in both Spenser and Judson that a white, Protestant, male academy considered secure. We are beginning to reconsider the ways in which Spenser's secretary hand, like the dyer's, may have been subdued—or may have subdued his text—to what it worked in. We are demanding fuller and seemingly harder-headed answers to the question of Spenser's commitment to his career in Munster; we are coming to see that Colin was a colonist and a *colon* as his name suggested. But like Judson, we are still trying to write, in our new terms, the balance that the interplay of voices, languages, and genres in Spenser's text achieves. Absurdly, like characters in Samuel Beckett, we know we can't go on writing biography; we shall go on.

Notes

Spenser's Lives, Spenser's Careers

1. The inscription on his Westminster funerary monument accords Spenser the place of "the prince of poets." He is named "Englands Arch-Poet" on the title page of the 1611 folio edition of his collected works. "[O]ur new Poete" is one of E. K.'s designations for the unnamed author of *The Shepheardes Calender*. The nomination of Spenser as "the poet's poet" is discussed by Paul Alpers in an entry under that heading in *The Spenser Encyclopedia* (1990). According to Alpers, the phrase, although traditionally credited as the coinage of Charles Lamb, was first used by Leigh Hunt in *Imagination and Fancy*, his anthology of select English poetry complete with commentary. My concern with this nomination has to do with the ways it has accorded Spenser and his poetics a (unique) measure of aesthetic transcendence at the cost of effacing some of the historical and material contexts in which his verse was produced. Also relevant here is the figuration of Spenser as "the *poets'* poet"—that is, a poet for poets—which may be taken to mean that his verse is much cited and much imitated by other poets, or that his verse is so densely allusive and so encyclopedically intertextual that it can best be appreciated by poets. That these two figurations are closely related is evident in Hunt's formative account, which signals both how much Spenser is esteemed by other poets and how he "is the farthest removed from the ordinary cares and haunts of the world of all the poets that ever wrote, except perhaps Ovid" (1845, 74).

2. Thus Eliot's glowing introduction to Knight's Shakespearean-derived but Wagnerian-sounding *The Wheel of Fire* commends the book in its "search for the pattern below the level of 'plot' and 'character,'" its efforts to discern the "subterrene or submarine music" of each play (Eliot 1946, xviii-xix). With the plays now being treated in terms of what John Dover Wilson calls "dramatic symphonies" (1936, 12), the new vocabulary of Shakespeare criticism became musicalized as that of theme (and variation), exposition, melody, counterpoint, rhythm, tone, and dissonance.

3. See Henley 1928, Carpenter 1921-22, Gray 1930, Gottfried 1939, Judson 1933, and Hulbert 1936-37 for other representative examples of historicist scholarship from this period focused on Spenser in Ireland.

4. Consider in this framework one of the most recent scholarly endeavors in the field of Spenserian biography, the work of Willy Maley. Eschewing "inference, surmise, and conjecture" (Maley 1994, xiv-xv), Maley doesn't compose a biography but instead plots *A Spenser Chronology*, a reference work rather than a narrativized "life of the poet." In this respect, he revives and updates the form of Carpenter's 1923 *Reference Guide*.

5. "On this journey through Wexford, Spenser, who like Shakespeare seems ever to have had an eye for profitable investments, probably examined the castle and manor of Enniscorthy as well as the monastery of St. Augustine's in New Rosse" (Jenkins 1937, 346). Compare Taylor 1989, 215-16, on how Shakespeare's life became in the hands of a

number of Victorian biographers and critics an exemplary demonstration of the virtues of entrepreneurial self-help.

6. On the Nugent case, see Judson 1945, 104-5, as well as Maley 1994, 32.

7. See also Jenkins's "Spenser and Ireland" (1952), a kind of summation of his work on the Irish contexts that shaped Spenser's work. In this late, postwar essay, Jenkins's tone is more dour: "The many accidents by flood and field which Spenser underwent in Ireland awakened the imagination and hardened the sensibilities of a very sensitive poet" (53). Yet Jenkins remains divided on where to place Spenser in relation to the campaigns of colonialism and war, as we can see in the following representative passage: "The poet must have been shocked and hardened by the callous attitude of his English associates toward this constant strife. The intensity of his feelings on such occasions made him a vehement exponent of the repressive policies of Grey, for he yearned to see internecine strife blotted out from Irish history forever" (53). The first sentence of this passage places "the poet" (as Jenkins recurrently hypostatizes Spenser in this essay) at a horrified remove from his fellow English colonizers, while the second makes him a committed propagandist of wartime repression and violence. "Spenser," Jenkins notes later, "like most of us, was able to reconcile the conditions incident to his advancement with his idealism" (55).

8. Here I follow the informative account of Morley and his cultural agendas provided in Gross 1969, 99-112. See also Morgan 1944, 115-18.

9. This endorsement is cited from the back-page advertisement included in each volume of the English Men of Letters series.

10. See Lerer 1992, 1139-40, on early-twentieth-century fashionings of Chaucer along similar lines.

11. None of this is meant to minimize the real and important differences in practice, intention, and politics that set apart new historicism from earlier "historical background" or "world picture" approaches to historicizing literary studies. For more on those differences, see Montrose 1986a, 303-7.

12. For a related critique of Helgerson, see Venuti 1989, 215-19. Interestingly, Gary Waller's new *Literary Life* of Spenser, although offered from a perspective somewhat removed from new historicism, likewise at times follows Helgerson in positing a convention-bypassing uniqueness to Spenser's poetry and poetic careerist (e.g., Waller 1994, 7, 79).

13. It appears that it was in the first instance historians, not the historicists, who were principally responsible for renewing interest in the "Irish Spenser." See, for instance, the debate played out by Brady (1986b and 1988) and Canny (1988) in the pages of *Past and Present*, as well as the work of Bradshaw (1978). The revival of interest in Spenser in Ireland has now begun to make inroads through literary studies. See, among others, Patterson 1993, Lupton 1987 and 1993, Baker 1985 and 1993, Jardine 1990 and 1993, Rambuss 1993, Cavanagh 1993, Waller 1994, Hadfield 1994, and Maley 1994, as well as the essays collected in Coughlan 1989.

This is not to suggest, however, that all the critical and historical work which is now foregrounding the Irish contexts of Spenser's work and career has proceeded according to the same methodology or politics. Patterson, for example, interrogates what she finds to be a simplistic, if widely held, notion that the *View* "is a disgraceful instance of colonial prejudice" (1993, 82), reflective of Spenser's unflinching advocacy of whatever means necessary to subdue the perpetually rebellious Irish. Against this consensus, Patterson argues for a Spenser who is, if not positively egalitarian, at least a far more ambivalent colonial operator and apologist. Patterson makes this case both from the *View* itself and from the poetry, and, like so many other Spenserians, comes up with a Spenser who is presciently contemporary: "It is probably impossible to operate without a prejudice of one's own. Mine is for assuming less difference between Spenser and ourselves, by postulating both that he might have been embarrassed by the ethical conflicts posed by the colonial experience, and that he was strong-minded enough to give expression—troubling expression—to the contradictions he perceived" (88).

14. That is, Greenblatt does situate Spenser in relation to English imperialism, including the colonization of Ireland. But this contextualization is made chiefly in the interests of an application of Freud's thesis in *Civilization and Its Discontents* concerning the production of culture by means of repression and the violent repudiation of pleasure to *The Faerie Queene*'s announced aim of "fashioning a gentleman," specifically as that project is played out in terms of Guyon's exorbitantly violent destruction of the Bower of Bliss.

15. My chief concern here has been to point up contiguities between the positivistic historicism of Church, Jenkins, and Judson and the prevailing new historicist articulations of Spenser's career. But I do not mean to suggest that new historicism is the only force at work in current Spenser studies to make it seem as though Spenser sought his place in the world solely in terms of his poetic endeavors. For instance, Patrick Cheney's recent book, *Spenser's Famous Flight* (1993), whose critical protocols are chiefly thematic and comparativist, not historicist, offers what may be the most detailed taxonomy yet of the literary contexts (genres, tropes, image patterns, relations with previous poets, and so on) in which Spenser's poetic career took its impressive shape. But missing here is, first, the registration that his poetic career was not Spenser's only career (which is, as I see it, a crucial recognition in any careerist account) and, second, any discussion of relations between his two careers (both dependent, after all, on Spenser's humanist training and skills). Interestingly, Cheney strategically excludes from his discussion Spenser's *Complaints* and *Colin Clouts Come Home Againe*, arguing "that they do not belong to the generic progression organizing the fiction of the New Poet's career" (3). The omission of the latter volume—to my mind a kind of "career autobiography" that locates Spenser's poetic practice in terms of a number of split subjectivities and hybrid positionalities (he is the Englishman who returns home to Ireland; he is an Elizabethan poet who writes outside the court in the Irish "wilds"; he is of the producer of national epic who is writing "private" love lyric; etc.)—allows Cheney's streamlined career narrative to efface Spenser's Irish contexts and to fashion him as the court poet he never entirely was.

Disenchanted Elves

1. This view finds eloquent expression in Miller 1979: e.g., Spenser "has come to see his art not as the shaping of culture but as its refuge" (190). Compare similar tales of career rejection or loss in Helgerson 1983, 53, and Goldberg 1981, 171. Goldberg sensibly recalls that these claims of disappointment really lack credibility since Spenser in fact gets on fairly well in what Helgerson terms "the literary system." Kenneth Gross presents a much more carefully nuanced account of these issues, especially in his chapter "Enchantment and Disenchantment" (1985, 210-45).

2. Spenser's roles as colonial official or would-be courtier figure regularly in accounts that infer the poet's mentality from those of the court or of a colonial administration. Helgerson 1983 has more particularly developed Spenser's laureate status in an emerging institution of letters, and Rambuss 1993 has recently made a fascinating case for Spenser in the habitus of the Elizabethan "secretary."

3. Very roughly, what undermines the poet's traditional aspirations to authority, autonomy, and creativity is in Goldberg 1981 Lacan's "other"; in Montrose 1986a it is Foucault's "other." Both accounts respond to an old concern: "the adulation, sometimes offensive, into which the pursuit of reward too often tempted" Spenser (Dodge 1936, xxi).

4. For criticism focused on history, on an Elizabethan hegemony, or on global epistemic questions, the close textual crawl through a writer's impersonated voices may produce

insignificant distinctions. However, biography's insistence on individual ethnography can give a helpful corrective to the generalizing, typifying drift of historical anthropology.

5. Both new and old Spenser portraits show a Spenser not distinctive but typical, a Spenser figuring the age in all its virtues and vices. In Judson, this figure lacks the convincing fullness that is the hallmark of biographies of better-documented subjects. A further problem for both Judson and Greenblatt, though perhaps inevitable, is the circularity that creeps into the conclusion. The individual is typical in large part because he has been reconstructed from generalizations about the Tudor or Renaissance or laureate type— generalizations needed for covering gaps in the documentary record as well as for defeating the ambiguities of poetic fictions. The displacement of an author's personality by a critic's personification is a true hazard for the biographer committed to history with a human face. The individual must always compete with the types, the ideas, the ideology it bears; without a concept like Greenblatt's "internal distantiation" (1980, 192), it is impossible to tell Spenser from the uniform he wears, perhaps because—to extend one of Greenblatt's Guyonesque metaphors (174)—this would be like separating the face from the skull in one's search for the true portraiture.

6. A picture in lieu of 1,000 words: Dante's great image of secularity, the "old man" of Crete in *Inferno* XIV, who weeps the rivers of hell through his fractured baser metals, while his golden head, intact like Astraea, yearns for the imperial west.

7. Hunting "after fame and honour" (V iv 29), Terpine underestimates Radigund. Instead of an easy conquest, he finds an opponent of "great successe . . . and famous, more than is believed; / Ne would I it have ween'd, had I not late it prieved" (V iv 33). Terpine's great expectations play perfectly into the double bind Radigund imposes on her conquests, so he chooses "to die in lives despight" (V iv 32).

8. Despite Hamilton (Spenser ed.1977, 592), "for forged guyle" must mean "on account of [her] forged guyle" (a sense of *for* already used twice in the stanza), not "*through* forged guyle."

9. I offer Kant's article, written in 1784, as a version of early modern humanism and idealism as instructive for thinking about Book V as, say, Pico's discourse on "The Dignity of Man."

10. In this paragraph I don't intend an argument for "modernism" so much as a caution against the naturalizing power of biography or history, insofar as these seem relatively commonsensical, immediate, or unproblematic compared to the unfamiliar discourses of literary interpretation. Biography has always been a powerful limiter of reading, a way both of accommodating difficult texts to common readers and of routinizing or desublimating those texts within contemporary economies. Such reduction is a special risk with poorly documented, richly inventive writers like Spenser, whose biographies are, as I have tried to suggest, at many points no more than displaced, refigured interpretations of their fictions.

11. See the *Charmides* of Plato for the source of this allusion.

Factions and Fictions

1. By November 1579 Grey was once again being considered for the Irish post; see Walsingham to Nicholas Malbie, Pelham to Walsingham, and Pelham to Burghley, 6, 26, 28 November 1579 (Public Record Office, London, State Papers, Ireland, 63/70/7, 24, 35; hereafter referred to as S.P. 63).

2. Grey to Leicester, 7 April 1580 (S.P. 63/72/36); Grey to Leicester, 12 May 1580 (S.P. 63/73/11).

3. See especially 29 June-15 July, *Acts of the Privy Council, England, 1580-81* (1974), 75, 86, 102-3; and "Articles between Lord Grey and Jonas Ladbroke," 10 July 1580,

"Memorial of directions to be given to Grey," "Certain points to be resolved by the council touching Grey's dispatch," "Grey's petitions concerning [the] service in Ireland," 10-15 July 1580 (S.P. 63/74/16, 37, 38, 39, and 41).

4. 15 July 1580, *A.P.C., England, 1580-81*, 102-3, 106-7; and "Burghley's memorandum," 8 July 1580 (S.P. 63/74/13).

5. "Grey's petitions concerning [the] service in Ireland," 15 July 1580 (S.P. 63/74/41).

6. Greville to Walsingham, 2 July 1580 (S.P. 63/74/3); 15 July 1580, *A.P.C., England, 1580-81*, 97-98.

7. See especially the letter from Sir Philip Sidney "To my welbeloved friend Mr. Edward Denny," 22 May 1580 (Bodleian Library, Phillipps MS 9014), reproduced as Appendix 5 in Osborn 1972, 535-40; and Edward Denny to Walsingham, 8 September 1580 (S.P. 63/76/18).

8. Sidney had a stake in each of Frobisher's voyages of 1576, 1577, and 1578 (Wallace 1915, 195-96); Greville's interests in Ireland in this period are outlined in Greville to Walsingham, 2 July 1580 (S.P. 63/74/3).

9. Fenton to Leicester, 8 September 1580 (S.P. 63/76/19).

10. Fenton to Leicester, 10 July 1580 (S.P. 63/74/17); Thomas Wingfield to Walsingham, 5 August 1580 (S.P. 63/75/14); Henry Sheffield to Burghley, 5 August 1580 (S.P. 63/75/13); Fenton to Leicester, 8 September 1580 (S.P. 63/76/19).

11. Sheffield to Burghley, 5 August 1580 (S.P. 63/75/13).

12. Earl of Leicester to the earl of Kildare, 23 May 1580 (B.L., Cotton Titus B III(ii), fol. 310v,); Grey to Walsingham," 22 December 1580 (S.P. 63/79/24); Deputy to the Queen, (S.P. 63/79/24, enclose i).

13. All quotations from *The Shepheardes Calender*, *Complaints*, and *Colin Clouts Come Home Againe* are from *Poetical Works* (Spenser ed. 1912). See McLane 1961, 36-40, for a reading of Menalcas as Spenser's protest against a French marriage project. David Quint comments that McLane's reading of the *Calender* made him "posit a late date for the composition of the eclogues in question in order to have them reflect the events of 1579— quite a rush job for a poet who obtained a license for his book in December of that year" (1992, 420). Donald Cheney has claimed that there is no clear mandate for such a topical reading of this passage but concedes at the same time that it is E. K. who tries to move us in this direction. Menalcas as an anagram for Alençon is only one of many possible readings. While the poet may not have initially planned the poem to have this specific reference, the comment of E. K. that by Menalcas "is meant a person unknowne and secrete, agaynst whome he often bitterly invayeth" (Spenser ed. 1912, 443b), certainly seems to invite such topical decoding.

14. Hieatt 1990 has argued that Spenser originally planned *The Faerie Queene* to include Arthur's defeat of Rome. In a rejoinder to Thomas Roche's response to his essay, Hieatt 1991, 247, suggests that the dedicatory sonnet to Essex describes him as the type of Arthur. This dedicatory sonnet echoes the lines to Leicester in "October": "when my Muse, whose fethers nothing flitt / Doe yet but flagg, and lowly learne to fly / With bolder wing shall dare aloft to sty / To the last praises of this Faery Queene, / Then shall it make more famous memory / Of thine Heroicke parts" (Spenser ed. 1912, 411b).

15. See his forthcoming article in *Spenser Studies*.

16. Brink's caution (1991) that we should not necessarily assume that Spenser authorized publication of the text contrasts with the critical tradition from the Oxford (1912) to the Yale edition (1989) that builds a case for Spenser's involvement in its publication. McCoy 1989, 132, cites *Teares of the Muses* (lines 94-97) as evidence that "Spenser's devotion to the major figures and ideals of Elizabethan chivalry was qualified by a surprising skepticism towards many of its pretensions." But when we consider that the lines critical of the nobility in this poem make no reference to the Leicester circle and that Sidney and Leicester were both dead in 1591 at the time of the poem's publication, then it seems hard

to see the poem as critical of them. Indeed, the elegiac tone and sense of a decayed present expressed throughout much of the *Complaints* is reminiscent of the proem to *Faerie Queene* V, a book that reaches its climax in praise of the idealized exploits of Leicester and Grey.

"All his minde on honour fixed"

1. Judson 1945; Welply 1922, 1924a, 1924b, 1927, 1932; Hamer 1932; Welply 1933a, 1933b, 1940, 1941a; Hamer 1941; Welply 1941b, 1944a, 1944b. Ray Heffner (1938-39) detected a connection between Elizabeth Boyle, Spenser's wife, and the Spencers of Althorp. Spenser dedicated *Mother Hubberds Tale* to the third Spencer sister, Anne, Lady Compton and Monteagle, but without reference to benefits received.

2. Philipp Camerarius, *Operae horarum subsicivarum* (Frankfurt, 1591); quoted from the English version in *The Living Librarie*, trans. John Molle (London, 1621), 98-99. Portions reprinted in Osborn 1972, 464-66.

3. Sidney also writes, "I have spent more lynes then I thought to have done words. but good will carries mee on to this impudence to write my councell to him, that (to say nothing of yourselfe) hath my Lord Grayes company." Osborn (1972, 536) suggests that the man "having [Grey's] company" is Spenser. A less likely candidate would be Fulke Greville, who had already left for Ireland. Lodowick Bryskett, who was closely connected with the Sidneys, was in England when Grey landed and did not return to Ireland until six months after the force had arrived (Plomer and Cross 1927, 14).

4. Documentary evidence of Spenser's connection with Leicester House is by no means as compelling as we could wish. Arguing against the Greenlaw hypothesis, as early as 1916 Percy Long pointed out that Spenser was not Leicester's secretary (720); see also Brink 1991, 155, and Woudhuysen 1981, 47-49.

Spenser and Court Humanism

1. The disadvantages faced by the nongentle were spelled out by Mulcaster in ed. 1888, 150-51.

2. The "generational" approach was adumbrated by Esler 1966, though some aspects of the effects of changing generations on literary men had been worked out by Hunter 1962, esp. chap. 1. Hunter's insight, in its turn, was applied to Spenser by Neuse 1968. Something of the same approach lies behind Helgerson 1983, to which I am much indebted. My own belief, however, is that all these men may best be understood from the point of view of their political aspirations, to which their literary aims were subordinated; see, e.g., Levy 1972a and 1972b.

3. Mulcaster 1582, 12. On Mulcaster, see DeMolen 1991, which incorporates the material in his earlier articles on the subject.

4. Mulcaster 1582, 16. The repressive aspects of this educational scheme have been brought out by Grafton and Jardine 1982.

5. Cicero ed. 1959, 1:109. Note Harvey's view that "no one can be a Ciceronian complete in all points and particulars who rests content with oratorical embellishments of speech and does not lay the rest of the subjects of learning under contribution" (ed. 1945, 97). There is a useful discussion of this in Grafton and Jardine 1986, esp. 210-20. On the meaning of *De Oratore* in the courtier tradition, on the Continent and in England, see Javitch 1978.

6. Harvey ed. 1884, 78-79. The letter is ostensibly written to Spenser, though Bennett 1931 has raised doubts about whether the correspondence ever took place. The letter does, however, remain pertinent evidence for Harvey's opinions, nor is there reason to

doubt that Spenser knew of Harvey's views. On Harvey's reading and its relation to his career, see Jardine 1986.

7. See Harvey 1578b. Song VII especially praises the variety of Smith's learning.

8. Bryskett 1606, 8. Bryskett's book is largely a translation of a part of G. B. Giraldi's *Ecatommiti,* but the framing sections, upon which I am drawing, are not in Giraldi's original Italian text of 1565 or in the French translation of 1583. See Lievsay 1961, 83-88. On Bryskett's career, see Plomer and Cross 1927, and Jones 1933.

9. Osborn 1972, 536. On Denny's career, see *The House of Commons, 1558-1603* 1981, 2:29-30; Denny 1904; and MacCarthy-Morrogh 1983, 414-16.

10. Jenkins 1937 and 1938. On Smerwick, see O'Rahilly 1938 and Maley 1994, 14-15. See also Jenkins's general article (1952).

11. West 1988 casts some amusing doubts on the knowledge of military realities of Spenser and his contemporaries; the Privy Council apparently did not share them.

12. Spenser ed. 1912, 463b. On Gascoigne's career as a court poet, see McCoy 1985 and Javitch 1982. My discussion of the learned poet owes much to the help of G. W. Pigman III, who kindly took the time to e-mail me a long letter on the subject (25 September 1992); he is not responsible for my "politicization" of the topos.

13. Heninger 1988 argues that the book imitates editions of the ancients by way of Sansovino's edition of Sannazaro.

14. Sir Kenelm Digby, "A discourse concerning Edmund Spenser" (B.L. Harl. MS. 4153), quoted in *Spenser: The Critical Heritage* 1971, 150. There is an interesting discussion of Virgil's learning in Perkell 1989, 64-65. Spenser's learning is the subject of a fascinating examination in Roche 1989.

15. The distinction is drawn by, e.g., Sir Thomas Elyot in his *Book Named the Governour,* quoted in Gilbert 1962, 237.

16. Jonson, *Poetaster* V ii, in ed. 1925-52, 4:294.

17. Heninger 1987 is rather skeptical about any close relations between the two poets, arguing that they hardly had time to say much to each other; Heninger 1989, 1-16, is not so rigorously negative.

18. The precise nature of Spenser's Protestantism has been much debated: see most recently Hume 1984 and King 1990. Bradshaw 1987 relates to our theme but is overly reductive. The arguments would be clearer if there were any sort of general agreement on the nature of the Puritan tradition to which Spenser did (or did not) belong. However, Puritanism had a political as well as a religious side. This involved adherence to an activist foreign policy, dedicated to helping Protestants abroad (e.g., by intervention in the Netherlands) and to continuing warfare with Spain. The details of this political Puritanism can be found spelled out in Fulke Greville's biography of Sir Philip Sidney. I have no doubt that Spenser shared this view.

19. Norbrook 1984, 129 ff., explores the relationship between Spenser and Essex's politics.

20. Brink 1991 argues that Spenser had nothing to do with the setting forth of *Complaints* and so cannot be blamed for *publishing* the attack on Burghley, or even authorizing it. This may well be so; nevertheless, it is worth recollecting that *The Faerie Queene* originally appeared without a dedicatory sonnet to Burghley, and one had hurriedly to be added as a "stop-press."

21. The issues are discussed in the general context of English views of gentility in Javitch 1978, 132 ff.

22. Even Gabriel Harvey thought the poem went too far: "Mother Hubbard, in heat of choller . . . wilfully over-shott her malcontented selfe" (ed. 1966, 15).

23. Brady 1986a takes the position that Spenser's lack of success at court during the 1590 visit led not only to *Colin Clout* and *Mother Hubberds Tale* but also to the repressive-

ness of the *View*. I am inclined rather to attribute the excesses of the *View* to Spenser's gradual realization that his haven in Ireland was also undergoing siege.

24. Lennon 1981, Part 1, describes this scene and makes clear how separate Bryskett's world was from Stanyhurst's.

25. On undertakers in Munster, see MacCarthy-Morrogh 1986 and 1983, Appendix 2. Herbert ed. 1887 also exists in an English translation (British Library, Harley MS 35, fols. 145-78). Other tracts attributed to Herbert have been summarized in *Calendar of State Papers, Ireland, 1586-88*, 527-47. Richard Beacon wrote *Solon His Follie; or, A Politique Discourse, Touching the Reformation of Common-weales Conquered, Declined or Corrupted* (Oxford, 1594); a useful commentary, pointing out his debts to Machiavelli, is Anglo 1990. Brady 1989 sees both Herbert and Beacon as defending the use of violence, with Spenser (in the *View*) more ruthless still. Bradshaw 1988 examines all these works as part of the humanist tradition, arguing that Spenser is less "humanist" than the others, and more inclined to follow the lead of the members of the Sidney circle, "who strove to combine the ideals of protestantism and neo-chivalry, and to put military arms at the service of social renewal, the protestant cause, and the greater glory of England" (162).

26. Quinn 1945, Morgan 1985. Quinn 1976 treats the point more generally, while Canny 1976, 129 ff., sets Smith's venture into the wider context of English settlement of Ireland. See also Jardine 1993.

27. On sixteenth-century notions of barbarism, see Pagden 1982, 24ff. On Spenser's use of such ideas, see Coughlan 1989 and McCabe 1993, which examines Spenser's entire career in terms of his residence in Ireland. McCabe's section on *Colin Clout* (91 ff.) is particularly interesting, though he sees Spenser as more "anti-Irish" than I do.

28. On all this, see Oram 1990. I find Patrick Cheney 1990 oddly unhistorical in its working out of the relationships among Queen, courtier, and poet.

29. Indeed, it spilled over (rather inappropriately) into the very late *Prothalamion*, when the poet complains of his "long fruitlesse stay / In Princes Court, and expectation vayne / Of idle hopes" (lines 6-7).

30. In Marston 1598, Satyre 1. See also Pincombe 1993, which notes that a sneer began to accompany late sixteenth-century usage of the word "humanist."

Questionable Evidence in the *Letters* of 1580

Extensive comments by the editors on an earlier version of this essay, and a reading both scrupulous and generous by Anne Lake Prescott, have saved me from many errors, infelicities, and obscurities. Needless to say, such defects as remain, and others introduced *de novo* in the course of revision, are all my own.

1. There is no satisfactory text for the *Letters* of Spenser and Harvey. The Variorum *Prose Works* (ed. Rudolf Gottfried, 1949) offers a reliable and well-annotated text of the various items but presents them out of sequence, relegating much of the collection to an appendix. The one-volume Oxford *Poetical Works* (ed. 1912) includes the *Letters* entire and in order, and for many purposes this text is preferable to that in the *Prose Works*.

2. I quote from the glosses on Colin's friendship with Hobbinol, at "September" 176 and "Januarye" 59. These and related passages in the *Calender* and *Letters* pertaining to Spenser's friendship with Harvey are discussed by Goldberg 1992, 63-81, in terms that provide a frame of reference for other scholars (Smith 1991, Rambuss 1993) and the basis for several points in my argument.

3. Rambuss 1993 studies Spenser's career(s) as a poet and a secretary with reference to the discourse of secrecy in which someone holding or seeking a secretary's office was supposed to be proficient. In this connection, Jardine and Grafton 1990 on Gabriel Harvey's

methods as a reader and his services to members of the Leicester/Sidney circle is quite relevant.

4. In a few years generalists in Renaissance studies have gone from knowing less than nothing on this subject to an embarrassment of riches, both in the archives of information now available to us and in strategies for its interpretation. For my purposes, the most useful socioliterary study is Smith 1991; Goldberg 1992 is by design more "exorbitant," but as already noted it offers more detailed and original attention to Spenser and Harvey. Rambuss 1993, 40-48, explores the homoerotic aspect of secretaryship, and see the comments on secrecy in Smith 1991, 114-15, 234-36. Readers of either Smith or Goldberg will be led to relevant earlier work of Michel Foucault, Alan Bray, and Eve Kosofsky Sedgwick.

5. It is generally accepted that Spenser left London with Arthur, Lord Grey, in July of 1580 (see Judson 1945, 71-72), but he may have gone to Ireland earlier. In one of the best recent discussions of Spenser's involvement with the English colonial enterprise in Ireland, Lisa Jardine treats this posting with Lord Grey as a "return." The months in which the *Calender* and *Letters* were published become, then, an interval with an indeterminate significance: perhaps they were a hiatus in his public career rather than steps upward to laureate status (Jardine 1990, 70 n.8; cf. Judson 1945, 46, and Rambuss 1993, 25-28).

6. In this I concur with the skepticism voiced by Heninger 1987, 241-42, 245; cf. Oruch 1990, 738, and Rambuss 1993, 53-56. Heninger 1989, 5-6, is more inclined to wishful thinking about "the 'lost works'" and other mysterious business.

7. Kinney 1983 notes how, in the absence of clear distinctions between truth and falsity, training in rhetoric emphasized plausible eristic arguments, which play an important part in the prose fiction that was contemporary with the *Familiar Letters*. Both Lyly and Gascoigne, using epistolary conventions for fiction and discourse on literary matters, offer precedents close in time to the unusual project undertaken by our two University men.

8. Goldberg 1990a, a study of the conventions governing handwriting in the Renaissance, is relevant here, as is Miller 1990, a review essay pertaining specifically to Spenser's writing. See also Crane 1993: the subject-forming strategies of gathering and framing found in sixteenth-century commonplace books are also apparent in the *Letters*.

9. *Prose Works*, 484-85, quoting from Nashe's *Strange Newes* (1592): "for an Author to renounce his Christendome to write in his owne commendation, to refuse the name which his Godfathers and Godmothers gave him in his baptisme, and call himselfe *a welwiller to both the writers*, when hee is the onely writer himselfe; with what face doe you thinke hee can aunswere it at the day of judgement?"

10. Except for his *View of the Present State of Ireland,* which appears to have been "published" in manuscript form for a select audience, next to none of Spenser's writing survives in manuscript copies. The other notable exception is the sonnet eventually printed as *Amoretti* 8, which appears in several manuscript miscellanies with other courtiers' poems composed circa 1580. Spenser's poem is intertextually related to Greville's *Caelica* 3 and Sidney's *Astrophel and Stella* 42, serving as evidence of the "familiarity" with Sidney and his circle which Spenser claims in the course of these letters to Harvey (Cummings 1964; Quitslund 1973, 238-39).

11. This is not, however, the only instance of Spenser's playing with his readers' awareness that printed texts are derived from manuscript copies that may get out of the author's hands: in the epistle prefacing the *Fowre Hymnes,* he refers to earlier poems that he had been unable to "call in," because "many copies thereof were formerly scattered abroad." No manuscript copies of the first two *Hymnes* have been found, and this cryptic passage probably refers to passages in *Colin Clouts Come Home Againe,* which is the kind of poem that may have circulated in manuscript before it was revised and printed in 1595 (years after the occasion that prompted its writing and the dedication to Ralegh).

12. McKitterick 1981, 350-53, provides a full account of Harvey's annotations in a copy found in the Peterborough Cathedral Library; I have incorporated these corrections where appropriate in subsequent quotations. McKitterick comments, "Most, but not quite all, of the corrections and alterations are to Harvey's part of the correspondence, and thus present him actually at work at his own texts" (351). In fact, only the first of the changes he records pertains to Spenser's part, and that amends a comment attributed to Harvey: introducing the subject of "your late Englishe Hexameters," Immerito says that he too has been writing "in that kinde," finding it, "as I have heard you often defende in worde, neither so harde, nor so harshe, [but] that it will easily and fairely, yeelde it selfe to our Moother tongue" (*Prose Works*, 16; ed. 1912, 611).

13. "Self-fashioning is always, though not exclusively, in language" (Greenblatt 1980, 9; cf. Greenblatt 1990). Bellamy 1992, 19-22, adds some pertinent nuances, commenting on "a subjecthood that is specifically *literary*," inscribed within a narrative of events.

14. For Harvey's letter, see *Prose Works*, 449-62; ed. 1912, 613-22. On the earthquake and responses to it in print, see *Prose Works*, 263, 477-79: immediately after the event five items were entered in the Stationers' Register, with a dozen or more ballads and pamphlets appearing in the next three months.

15. At the end of his discourse on the earthquake, Harvey's brief account of the state of learning at Cambridge builds its satire similarly on tropes of collapsing distinctions; for example, "*David, Ulysses,* and *Solon,* fayned themselves fooles and madmen: our fooles and madmen faine themselves *Davids, Ulysses,* and *Solons*" (*Prose Works*, 461; ed. 1912, 621b).

16. A full discussion of "Ad Ornatissimum virum" is beyond the scope of this essay, but a few comments will appear in the next section. Here I would note that, with regard to love and marriage, in his Latin poem Spenser can be observed in transition from a view limited by pastoral conventions to the larger ideals appropriate to a quest romance. In addition, foretastes of Book II—allusions to Horace and Cicero, for example—are especially interesting, since it has not been assumed that the Legend of Temperance contains much material from the earliest stages in Spenser's evolving plans for *The Faerie Queene*.

17. Here and subsequently, translations of passages from "Ad Ornatissimum virum . . . G. H." are my own, and I refer to the Latin text in the Oxford *Poetical Works*. The Variorum *Prose Works* provides a text with notes and a translation by Rudolf Gottfried (8-11, 255-61). A new text and an annotated translation of the Latin poem, alone or in concert with the *Letters*, is to be desired.

18. My reading differs from Goldberg's: "Immerito's veil is *almost* dropped" (1992, 73; emphasis added). Having made much of the author's absence from *The Shepheardes Calender* (1986, 38-67) and the presence of Harvey in Hobbinol (1992, 72-78), Goldberg seems loath to allow Edmundus a footing in reality similar to Gabriel's.

19. For reasons having more to do with our culture than that of Spenser's time, readers will differ in their interpretations of Spenser's sleeping with Harvey: for some, sexual intimacy is definitely *not* implied, while for others the question of its significance deserves both a shrug and a smirk. I regard the issue as undecidable, and not unrelated to the appearance of various aporias in this and other Spenserian texts.

20. See the Variorum commentary (*Prose Works*, 259); on Horace's poem, Kilpatrick 1986, 43-48; on Harvey's poem, Barnett 1945, and cf. Stern 1979, 43-44. It is not irrelevant that Castiglione's *Courtier* was one of the books Harvey was studying in 1580; see Ruutz-Rees 1910, 634-35.

21. Spenser's allusion to Ceres' search for Proserpina recalls the account in Ovid, *Metamorphoses* 5.341-486, but my colleague Patrick Cook aptly suggests that Ariosto (*Orlando Furioso* 12.1-4) is uppermost in Spenser's mind here.

22. Bruce R. Smith (1991, 31-77) provides an account of this literature and the forces at work in society that rendered sexuality problematic, yet central to the definition of social roles: women regarded as objects of sexual desire threatened masculinity and the

solidarity of all-male institutions, yet the interests of a patriarchal culture required most men to found families, and affectionate bonds within marriage might be threatened by a husband's continuing emotional involvement with an old friend.

Spenser's Retrography

1. Cited in the introduction to Sidney ed. 1973a, xl.

2. Brennan 1983 remarks that Ponsonby's texts "could almost always be connected with influential court circles, particularly those of the Dudley and Sidney families" (91), but his evidence (92) for a Leicester connection prior to 1586 seems to me to be tenuous. See also Brennan 1988.

3. See the account in Judge 1934, 100-111. It bears noting that the dispute ended up before the Court of Assistants.

4. Judson, for example, takes the conventional line in his *Life of Spenser* for the Variorum edition (1945, 140).

5. Ponsonby may have been anticipated in this practice. Since 1586 John Wolfe had been publishing the works of Robert Greene with considerable frequency. (It may be observed that Wolfe is usually designated as printing Greene for other stationers, though it is not unprecedented for a printer to locate a manuscript, to offer it to another stationer who will bankroll the publication, and to reserve, as a kind of finder's fee, the right to print the edition. Wolfe also regularly printed and published the editorial productions of Scipione Gentile, though this sort of publishing simply sustains a slightly different, and older, practice of adopting "house *scholars*" (one recalls Aldus's relations with Erasmus), a practice rather unlike Ponsonby's "line" in Sidney or Spenser.

6. Wolfe used four skeleton formes in regular recurrence for most of the text. Though evidence from skeleton formes is far less conclusive than bibliographers once thought, this certainly suggests that Wolfe was using at least two presses for the job; the corroborating fact that he seems to have kept printing even when his copy is defective — in other words, that he didn't proceed to different formes (or switch print jobs) when difficulties presented themselves—implies, at least, an unfussy interest in sustaining *pace*.

7. For a lively study of the editorial and critical problem thus presented, see Teskey 1990. It bears remarking that Elizabethan printers usually printed the front matter to a book last.

8. Nashe, *Pierce Pennilesse,* in ed. 1904-10, 1:243-44.

9. I rely here on F. R. Johnson 1933. Despite the ease with which Wolfe's compositers might have skipped ahead in their setting, they seem to have set sequentially by gathering; they worked their copy not only with speed but with a dogged inflexibility.

10. The commendatory poems include the only example with which I am familiar of a sonnet in poulter's measure couplets; attributed to W. R.—presumably Ralegh—it cunningly reflects on Spenser's long lines and his archaism. More to the point of this essay, this poem, like the one that precedes it (also by W. R.), knowingly reflects on the relation between Spenser's epic line and the sonnet, recognizing how critically Spenser's epic practice engages with the traditions of amatory sonneteering.

11. The protocol of dedications is difficult to ascertain. In the next century it had become customary for an author or some intercessor for an author to consult dedicatees before printing dedications, but evidence for such a practice does not survive from the sixteenth century, to my knowledge. In one of Spenser's published letters to Harvey, he remarks on Gosson's folly in dedicating the *School of Abuse* to Sidney, who, it turned out, disapproved of the work. This hardly proves that Gosson had not secured Sidney's approval for the dedication, though it strongly suggests that if such approval had been secured, Sidney had not actually read the book when the approval was granted. In the case

of *The Faerie Queene*, it simply cannot be proved that Spenser did or did not secure permission to make his various dedications.

12. For a census of copies and a discussion of this bibliographically critical group of variants, see Johnson 1933, 13-16.

13. It is therefore not surprising that the last new poem of the dedicatory sequence, the poem to the countess of Pembroke, attempts to make sense of endings. As in the poem to Northumberland, the present to which the sonnet refers is essentially commemorative, in this case commemorative of the countess's brother, Philip Sidney:

> Remembraunce of that most Heroicke spirit,
>> The hevens pride, the glory of our daies,
>> Which now triumpheth through immortall merit
>> Of his brave vertues, crownd with lasting baies,
> Of hevenlie blis and everlasting praies;
>> Who first my Muse did lift out of the flore,
>> To sing his sweet delights in lowlie laies;
>> Bids me most noble Lady to adore
> His goodly image living evermore,
>> In the divine resemblaunce of your face.

But the countess's "resemblaunce" is a compound; the sister embodies the brother, whose image "with your vertues ye embellish more, / And native beauty deck with hevenlie grace"(lines 11-12). Compound compounded: this family resemblance recurs to and reconfigures the conclusion to Book III. Not only is Amoret, she who "had deathes owne image figurd in her face," redeemed here, but the representation of the countess as a hermaphroditic compound of her brother and herself, of native beauty and heavenly grace, recapitulates the transfiguration together of Amoret and Scudamour. The last stanzas of Book III would be erased in 1596 (as would the errata of 1590), but they are first rewritten here in the dedicatory sequence which was Spenser's nearly handwritten envoy to his printed book.

The hermaphrodite of the canceled stanzas manages the boundary anxieties, the crisis, of concluding a legend of chastity, and it achieves its effect precisely by a dissolution of boundaries that blurs conclusion. In an earlier essay (Loewenstein 1987), I pointed out that Busyrane's threat, the threat of a highly ritualized, isolating eroticism, persists in the wedding volume that intervenes between *The Faerie Queene* of 1590 and that of 1596. That the 1595 *Amoretti and Epithalamion* responds to the conceptual issues left hanging at the end of the 1590 *Faerie Queene* is by no means a startling assertion: it is not surprising, after all, that a sequence of love poems should grapple with the same issues as were taken up in the Legend of Chastity and do so in much the same idiom. On the other hand, this instance of recursion is not unrevealing. Since autobiography crowds the wedding volume as it crowds no other Spenserian text, since the great project of the *Epithalamion* is the publication of the private, it is especially fitting that the volume pick up where the published epic left off, that it respond to conditions specific to print culture. A good deal more of the epic had been written by the time that Spenser came to compose the wedding volume, but the sequence in which these poems most richly signify is a sequence of printed books.

14. It might be said that Book I of *The Faerie Queene* should be read as a St. Georgic; one might also argue that the emphasis on disciplined effort suffuses the epic—from below, as it were—with the ethos of georgic.

15. Perhaps "dysonymous" would be more accurate, since the title page of the first five editions of *The Shepheardes Calender* invigorates the very idea of titling as it disturbs our ideas of authorship. It advertises the eclogues as "*Entitled* / TO THE NOBLE AND VERTU- / *ous Gentleman most worthy of all titles* / both of learning and chevalrie M. Philip Sidney."

16. In the *Theatre,* van der Noot actually seems to claim the work of translation as his own, but in terms that point how very casually the language of attribution could be handled in the sixteenth century, how uncertainly the grid of modern proprietary authorship applies to Renaissance writing: "oure visions the learned Poete M. Francisce Petrarche Gentleman of Florence, did invent and write in Tuscan the six firste, after suche tyme as hee had loved honestly the space of .xxi. yeares a faire, gracious, and a noble Damosell, named Laurette, or (as it plesed him best) which bicause they serve wel to our purpose, I have out of the Brabants speache, turned them into the Englishe tongue" (F3r-v). Marot has disappeared from this account; small wonder that the French-Dutch translator (and the fact of that translation) has all but dropped out, too. This passage is further muddled by the heading printed twenty-four pages earlier—"A BRIEFE DE- / claration of the Authour / upon his visions, take[n] out of the holy scrip- / tures, and dyvers Orators, Poetes, / Philosophers, and true histories. Tran- / slated out of French into En- / glishe by Theodore Roest" (D7r)—since, at the risk of excessive fastidiousness, "translated" may modify visions, declaration (surely), or both. Of course, this makes it unclear to whom the "I" of F3r refers. The consensus among Spenserians is that van der Noot wrote the commentary in Dutch and translated Marot and du Bellay for *Het Theatre* in 1568 (printed by John Day, and quite possibly with John Wolfe as one of the printshop workers), that he translated the commentary into French in the same year for *Le Theatre* (again, printed by John Day), that Roest translated the commentary from French into English in 1569, and that Spenser translated Marot and du Bellay into English in the same year—that no one undertook to translate Petrarch "out of the Brabants speache . . . into the Englishe tongue." (The same odd fiction, of a translation from Dutch into English, is put forward on F4v: "The other ten visions next ensuing, ar [*sic*] described of one Joachim du Bellay, Gentleman of France, the which also, bicause they serve to our purpose, I have translated them out of Dutch into English.") And we might reformulate this consensus thus: that the work of verse translation is systematically misrepresented in the *Theatre*, the translators of verse systematically forgotten.

17. However much the cultural historian wishes to attend to the modulated onymity, the editor will wish to attend to attribution, to the question of whether the poems from the *Theatre* may be admitted into the canon of authentic Spenserian work. Certainly there are good reasons to associate these poems with Spenser—connections between Spenser's schoolmaster, Richard Mulcaster, and van der Noot; the manifest resemblance of the *Complaints* texts and those of the *Theatre*; Spenser's apparent indebtedness, in *Complaints*, to other texts by du Bellay (and his indebtedness to Marot in the *Calender*), evidence of an interest in French translation (and, more specifically, in the work of the Pléiade, to whom van der Noot is also obviously indebted). Still, the attribution of these poems is irreducibly awkward: that G. L. Craik (1843, 1:17-18) could challenge Ponsonby's attribution of the *Visions of Bellay* and the *Visions of Petrarch* to Spenser—and thereby dismiss the attribution of the *Theatre* translations to Spenser—suggests how clumsily the editorial operation that distinguishes attributable from anonymous texts functions in Spenser's case.

18. Jonathan Crewe has performed a similar operation in his fine study of *Mother Hubberds Tale* (1986, 55-65), concerning himself more with the semantics of the poem at the moment of its deferred publication than with those that would have prevailed at the moment of its composition.

19. The passage is intriguing: E. K. is glossing the phrase "Nectar and Ambrosia": "Ambrosia they liken to Manna in scripture and Nectar to be white like Creme, whereof is a proper tale of Hebe, that spilt a cup of it, and stayned the heavens, as yet appeareth. But I have already discoursed that at large in my Commentarye upon the dreames of the same Authour." The referent of the *that* on which E. K. claims to have commented is unclear, whether it be nectar and ambrosia or the legend of Hebe. All three are loosely conjoined in *The Ruines of Time*, in a passage that could easily have been adapted from a *Stemmata*

Dudleiana, said to have been in existence in 1580 and conceivably itself a dream-vision like *The Ruines of Time*. Lovers feed on nectar in the company of Hercules and Hebe in the *Hymne in Honour of Love* (lines 282-83), poems also said to have been composed "in the greener times of my youth."

20. There may be some wishful thinking in Spenser's description of the readiness of the volume. As described in the letter to Harvey, *Dreames* would have been an elaborate and even glamorous book. Most emblem-books used recycled or recyclable images, but if Spenser hoped to be able to reuse the woodcuts from Bynneman's 1569 edition of the *Theatre*, he would have been disappointed, since the woodcuts were probably in Germany, having been used in 1572 for a German translation of the *Theatre*. The copper engravings used in Day's 1569 Dutch and French versions may still have been serviceable and available, though this is intrinsically unlikely, given the relatively low yield of a copper plate. The letter suggests that new illustrations had been prepared, and here Spenser's description may be getting ahead of reality. New illustrations would have made the book an especially costly production, particularly if all the poems in the volume were to have been illustrated. (Illustrated books of this period would typically cost 75-100 percent more than unillustrated books of equal length; see Johnson 1950, 84, 90, 93.) If the illustrations had indeed been cut, the nonappearance of the volume is even more mysterious, since money spent on preparing the blocks (or plates, though this is less likely) would have been wasted. Spenser's letters may be a way of stirring up enough interest to warrant the expense of cutting blocks for a volume the text of which was ready or nearly so. That *Dreames* failed to appear may be a sign that sufficient interest never materialized. Of course, to focus on the expense of producing illustrations is to explain little more than that an **illustrated** *Dreames* never appeared, but we have the 1591 *Complaints* as evidence that the visions can stand without accompanying illustrations. It is true that Spenser's early print career is as an anonymous or pseudonymous writer of primarily illustrated poems, and it may be that he had no enthusiasm for publishing merely textual visions.

21. Harvey's letter may indicate a far sharper opposition between Spenser's visionary and his epic projects than scholars have previously alleged; it depends on how one construes the conclusion of Harvey's assessment of Spenser's epic efforts: "But I wil not stand greatly with you in your owne matters. If so be the *Faerye Queene* be fairer in your eie than the *Nine Muses*, and *Hobgoblin* runne away with the Garland from Apollo: Marke what I saye, and yet I will not say that I thought, but there an End for this once, and fare you well, till God or some good Aungell putte you in a better minde" (ed. 1912, 628b; Variorum *Prose Works*, 472). Pity that Harvey breaks off. He casts Spenser as both vulgar author and vulgar judge, both Pan and Marsyas—that is clear enough—but the opposition of the Faerye Queene and the Nine Muses constitutes a crux. Harvey may be proposing the Nine Muses as figures of some alternative mode or source of inspiration, the serene classical alternative to the hectic Ariostan romance manner of the draft epic, the compositional stratum that Bennett plausibly associates with the Florimell-Marinell plot (Bennett 1942, 101-3, 138-43, 237). On the other hand, the Nine Muses may be more than a modal alternative; they may be the subjects of an alternative poem. Scholars have failed to date *The Teares of the Muses*, arguing for dates of composition from 1580 to 1590, but, oddly, this passage from Harvey's letter has never been cited as possible evidence for an early date of composition. This poem shares the idiom of complaint found in Spenser's visions. If the *Dreames* to which Harvey refers in this letter include the visions published in *Complaints*, they may also include *The Teares of the Muses*, to which work he may be referring as instancing an idiom that he preferred to that of the draft epic.

22. Sometimes the constraint of rhyming drags Spenser farther from his source: in sonnet 11, the "sodain dropping of a golden shoure" ("degout d'une pluie doree") is softened (or muddled) as a "sudden dropping of a silver dew." This "silvering" is not isolated,

however, and may entail an evocation of lunar symbolism or something of the sort: the entirely unqualified "aelles" of sonnet 4, rendered as "golden wings" in the *Theatre*, are given less dazzling sheen in *Complaints* as "wings of silver."

23. Singleton transferred his copyright in the *Calender* to John Harrison in October of 1580 (Arber 1875-94, 2:380).

24. Indeed, not just the vatic mode but the allegorical manner of these sonnets was tainted. Van der Noot had returned to the Low Countries, had reconverted to Catholicism; Day's Flemish edition of *Het Theatre*—and Bynneman's edition of the companion miscellany, *Het Bosken*—had been printed for van der Noot with unpaginated sheets and no imprints, making it possible for van der Noot to bind up collections of his work that could be tailored for presentation to Catholic or anti-English patrons. For van der Noot, then, the allegorical manner of the poems and the gnomic quality of the illustrations made possible a deferral of decryption. Spenser, however, was writing for publication and not presentation, and the allegorical manner was, at this moment, a dangerous invitation to "application."

25. The recovery of "Afrike" seems to have inspired a reconsideration of the aesthetics of the edifice and of the sonnet. Spenser forgoes the purity of "plus fin or d'Afrique" on behalf of its gorgeous exoticism. (He will lose the reduplicating "dorez du . . . or" but will compensate to an extent with "Gold . . . / . . . gold" [lines 9-10] in precise imitation of the French original.)

26. For a general, and brilliant, statement of this problem, see McKenzie 1969.

27. McKenzie's arguments—and they have been well supplemented by those of Peter Blayney (1982, 188-205)—must be respected: we simply do not know what constitutes a norm for press correction. The survival of multiple variant states may indicate especially fastidious correction during normal printing, or it may indicate a printer's unusual reluctance to dispose of sheets from customary preliminary proof-pulls. Nonetheless, the four surviving states of the inner forme of Y are unusual, and they evidence an interest in minute rectification that is inconsistent with what we know of Elizabethan proofing. Of course, even if we accept the multiple variants of evidence of press correction while printing off, we cannot identify the person who called for the rectifications.

28. Margaret Ferguson has brilliantly charted the aggressivity, the hostility to Rome, past and present, of du Bellay's *Deffence* (1983, chap. 2). That aggressivity is latent in *Songe* and almost blatant in the *Antiquitez*.

29. Jebb is quoted in Gollancz 1907, 99.

30. See Variorum *Minor Poems*, 2:419-20.

Spenser (Re) Reading du Bellay

1. See, e.g., Jardine and Grafton 1990; Kintgen 1990; Darnton 1991, although I doubt that many in the Renaissance thought reading "a sacred activity" putting them "in the presence of the Word" (153); and Crane 1993, who explores the impact on the literary imagination of a pedagogy stressing the collection of textual fragments for rearrangement in commonplace books. Sherman 1995, chaps. 2-3, speculates on the dynamics of John Dee's great library at Mortlake and explores the relevance of modern theories of reading to what we can deduce of Dee's practice.

2. Noakes 1988, ix.

3. I take seriously, although I would apply them less relentlessly, the arguments of Goldberg 1990b against a delusionary precision in dating texts.

4. Higgins 1990.

5. Du Bellay and Spenser were too ironic and vigorous for any simple view of their relationship, and both had mixed feelings toward Rome (du Bellay, who saw much to

despise in the modern city, was more a Gallican than a Roman Catholic). Cf. Pigman 1982 on du Bellay's ambivalence toward Rome.

6. "L'Envoy," in ed. 1912. *Ruines of Rome* (henceforth *Rome*), published in *Complaints* (1591), translates *Les antiquitez*. If Spenser alludes to *La premiere sepmaine*, the compliment's *terminus a quo* is 1579; if he means the also famous *Muse chrestienne*, it is 1574, before Spenser published *The Shepheardes Calender* (1579).

7. Ferguson 1984, Prescott 1978.

8. Although she may exaggerate the moral equivalence of du Bellay's and Lucan's oaks, Johnson 1990, 69-70, rightly notes that in "Februarie" Spenser sets up "an elaborate literary dialogue" with those two poets; for her, the eclogue's old Thenot misreads this emblem of political pride and decay.

9. Spenser ed. 1932-57, vol. 7.

10. Greene 1982, 225-26, compares the two oaks (perhaps exaggerating du Bellay's sarcasm). For more trees and their classical and Neo-Latin contexts, see Tucker 1990.

11. I quote the edition by Chamard (du Bellay 1961, 2:26).

12. Few admire *Rome*, but Stapleton 1990 ably defends it.

13. Illustrations of Daniel in the great 1568 Bishops' Bible may have helped fix Spenser's "ruins" aesthetic. In the Bishops' translation, the tree "reached unto the heaven," provided "meate" (i.e., food), and gave "shadowes" to the beasts of the field, details found, if only by explicit negation, in Spenser's various doomed trees. In Daniel, though, it is "a watcher and a holy one" from Heaven who "cryed mightily, saying thus: Hew downe the tree." L. Johnson 1990, 71, cites Luke 3:9: "Now also is the axe laid unto the roote of the trees."

14. Furthermore, the argument in "Maye" that "long prosperitie" corrupts shepherds recalls *Rome* 23; the phrase "long prosperitie" is in *Rome* 31. In "Julye" the Roman shepherds who "heapen hylles" of wrath echo the *Rome* style, as does the envoy's claim that this calendar "time in durance shall outweare" (cf. *Rome* 27).

15. Also lexically syncretic, combining *Rome* 6 and *Aeneid* 6.777-87; Spenser's "they say," furthermore, may recall the nostalgic-cum-skeptical "sic feruntur" in Lucretius's set piece on Cybele (*De Rerum Natura* 2.598-654).

16. My discussion expands a note in Prescott 1985, 58.

17. Saulnier 1968, 63, says Henri II's sister Marguerite, *Olive*'s dedicatee, bore the olive branch as her sign; for the significance of the olive (gift of the wise giant-killer Athena, biblical sign of peace, worn by conquerors), see Coleman 1990.

18. On *Olive*'s structure and religious implications, see Saulnier 1968, 63; Katz 1985, chap. 2; and Nash 1991, although none quite ties the symmetries to the liturgical allusions.

19. Dunlop 1980 describes the calendrical structure.

20. *Amours de Cassandre* 71 ("Ja desja Mars").

21. The oak, too, is recycled: in *Teares* 67 ff., Clio laments that insolent growth with "spredding armes" "underkeep[s]" the "learned Impes" below, hurting the buds of those once "the worlds chief ornament," while in *Rome* 29, Rome was "the worlds sole ornament"; cf. *Amoretti* 53 ("the worlds most ornament") and *Prothalamion* ("the worlds faire ornament").

22. FQ I vii and viii; cf. *Rome* 4, 6, 9, 10, 12, 15-16, 18, 20, and 27. Orgoglio falls like an aged tree, a particularly evocative simile if one recalls "Februarie"'s papist oak and the Roman oak of *Rome* 28: now fully declined into Catholicism, the tree has met the ruin that Lucan and du Bellay foresaw.

23. Cf. *Rome* 12; also found in *Rome* are Mutabilitie's *aspire*, *shoulder* as a verb, *presumption*, *bold*, *haughty*, a connection with Typhoeus, and *decay* as a noun and object of a cycle. Mutabilitie objects that Jove has "the whole worlds reign," "the worlds whole

soverainty" (vii 15-16), a pattern of words found elsewhere in *Visions of Bellay* 10, *Rome* 26, and *Teares* 74.

24. Ferguson 1984 reads *Antiquitez*, and to some extent *Rome*, in terms of a Freudian and Bloomian family romance. As Jove's aunt and Earth's daughter, Mutabilitie has a family romance of her own, one that inverts the gender and generational lines; within her complaint, that is, are rivalries and vexations not unrelated to those in Lucan and "Februarie."

The Earl of Cork's Lute

A summer fellowship at the Folger Shakespeare Library let me finish the research for this essay. The Hudson Strode Program in Renaissance Studies at the University of Alabama provided additional support, as did the University of Kentucky.

1. Nor do we know anything of Spenser's relation to Boyle, an English colonist who came to Dublin in 1588. They are presumed to have met during the poet's courtship of Boyle's niece Elizabeth (Hamilton et al. 1990, 109). We can be certain only that Spenser did not write the lemma (headnotes) to the epigrams, which must postdate 1620. On Boyle's career, see Canny 1982.

2. Borthwick traces the tortoise riddle to the Homeric "Hymn to Hermes," citing numerous classical, medieval, and Renaissance versions. A 1562 engraving of the German lute maker Gaspard Duiffoprugger includes a version of the Brescian legend as the craftsman's motto, which also appears on the neck of "an apparently genuine *viola da gamba* of Duiffoprugger"; Borthwick suggests that the early-seventeenth-century riddlebooks he cites may have gotten the text from the instruments.

Hollander 1993 identifies the lute as "the most important stringed instrument of the Renaissance" (46). I find no empirical evidence for inscriptions on Elizabethan lutes, few of which survive, although, as Hollander notes, Gynecia in the third book of Sidney's 1593 *Arcadia* inscribes a veiled complaint on the belly of a lute (139-40). Many were rebuilt in the seventeenth century, when new fashions in design and construction prevailed (Gill 1959). Fig. 9, dating from 1676, records an elaborately inscribed double lute made in England. Hollander 1993 discusses both the "explicit association of the lute with the Muse," including "the figure of the instrument as the self," that develops in sixteenth-century English lyrics (128-45), and the traditional topos of "the self as stringed instrument" (266-74); the absence of Spenser's epigram from this learned study is a revealing mark of its obscurity (see n. 3, below). Thanks to Bruce Boehrer and Donald Cheney for suggestions that led me to these and other materials, and to Charles Sens of the Library of Congress Music Division for help with the illustrations.

On mock inscriptions, see the translator's headnote to *The Greek Anthology*, Book 9: "the latter part, from no. 582 onwards, consists mostly of real or pretended inscriptions on works of art or buildings." On the English epigram, see Coiro 1988, especially the discussion in part 2 of strategies employed by different English epigrammatists to finesse the central problem of flattery versus honesty in the praise of rulers. See also Hudson 1947, Colie 1973, and A. Fowler 1982. Hollander 1993 raises "the question of the relative authenticity of the occasional character" of commendatory and complimentary epigrams in praise of a lady singing and playing (364-66)—a direct analogue to the question I am raising about the reference value of Spenser's epigram.

3. Spenser's Irish treatise was published in various issues with differing title pages (see Johnson 1933, 48-53). I cite the title that heads Spenser's treatise in the version containing the epigrams (Ware 1633a, 1633b, and 1971). The usual form in which Spenser's title is cited derives from Spenser 1633, a separate issue of part 3 of Ware 1633a which does not include the epigrams. Ware 1633a (STC 25067) and 1633b (STC 25067a) also give

different titles to different issues of the entire volume; the epigrams appear in both. The modern facsimile edition of this text, published in 1971, is based on 1633a. Otherwise, the epigrams (so far as I can determine) appear only in Variorum 8.2 and in ed. 1989, both of which classify them, oddly, as "Fragments"—a term better suited to the *Mutabilitie Cantos* and *The Faerie Queene*. They are omitted from such standard research tools as the *Concordance* and *The Spenser Encyclopedia*.

A critical edition of the *View* is in preparation by Dr. Christopher L. Ridgeway, Librarian at Castle Howard, York, who has examined all extant MSS of the *View* and informs me that none of them contains the epigrams, or indeed any poetic material (personal communication, 6 June 1993).

4. In chap. 16 of *Laocoön*, Lessing contrasts the two descriptions, intended, he says, "to give us a clear image of the difference in power which the two staffs symbolized" (1984, 83).

5. Virgil ed. 1934, 12.203-11. English translation Fitzgerald 1983. Subsequent citations give parenthetical book.line references to Latin text.

6. Lessing (1984) comments that Achilles' staff identifies him as one "to whom, with others, the guardianship of the laws had been entrusted," adding that the "real difference" in legitimate authority signaled by the contrasting staffs of office was one "which Achilles himself, in spite of all his blind rage, could not help but acknowledge" (83).

7. Barkan 1986, 85-86, 304-5, n. 60. Wofford reads extensively in the epic tradition to establish the presence in Homer, Virgil, Spenser, and Milton of a tacitly counterepic perspective, a "disjunction between action and figure" that "allows an implicit, if unarticulated, demystification of the heroic ideology that shapes the epics—a demystification of the concept of kleos and of Virgil's imperial celebration, of the affirmations of royal power in Spenser's poem, and of Milton's assertions and justifications of 'providence'" (1992, 9). Suzuki offers a specifically feminist oppositional reading of epic tradition, focusing on "the male poet's representation of woman as a figure that questions and at times subverts continuity, hierarchy, and order" (1989, 3). I am grateful to Professors Barkan and Suzuki for calling my attention to a number of the passages I discuss.

Counterimperial readings of Virgil generally develop Adam Parry's 1963 critique of what he calls "the simple glorification of Rome interpretation." Johnson 1976, 8-12, contrasts an "essentially optimistic European school" of Virgil criticism with the "somewhat pessimistic Harvard school" of Parry and others, "pessimistic" meaning skeptical about imperial glorification. Anderson 1968 describes Virgil's use of pastoral imagery to measure Aeneas's "degeneration" (11). I am suggesting a limited point: that the kinds of oppositional strains these critics discern in classical epic are topically associated in Virgil (and thereafter) with the motifs of the cut tree and the sacred grove. (Although we do not discuss the same passages, support for this suggestion may be found in Thomas 1988.) A fuller account of sacred groves and their violation would involve more works than I have space to discuss, chief among them Tasso's *Gersalemme Liberata*.

8. I cite Paton's 1917 Loeb edition, specifying epigrams parenthetically by book and number. Like other modern editions, Paton's is based on the Palatine manuscript, whereas Spenser's knowledge of the anthology would come directly or indirectly from the Planudean manuscript. The epigrams I cite do appear in the first book of the Planudean anthology and were widely imitated during the sixteenth century; two of the pine tree epigrams, for instance, were translated by Thomas More in his *Epigrammata* (see More ed. 1963-, 3.2:121). For discussion of the anthology's tangled manuscript history and a "repertory of translations and echoes . . . in modern letters," see Hutton 1935 and 1946. The quoted phrase appears in the preface to the latter (vii); p. 95 lists "the contents of the first book of the Planudean Anthology in the Aldines or in Badius' edition." See also the discussion by the editors of More (3.2:38-56 and 695-754). I am grateful to Kenneth Gross for suggesting *The Greek Anthology* as a possible source for Spenser's lute poem.

9. The anthology contains verses from many different periods, some unattributed and some attributed unreliably; sixteenth-century readers would not have been able to tell which was the earlier text. Hutton implies that Virgil had at least some acquaintance with the Greek epigrams and concludes that Ovid had clearly studied them but does not mention the pine-tree group among the parallels he cites for either poet (1935, 13, 18-19). The presence of Homer and Virgil is felt often in the anthology, implying an amused kinship between great forms and small.

10. 9.162. Hutton 1935, 537, lists five translations of this epigram that predate Spenser, including one by Alciati that appears in Cornarius 1529, 40. Hutton 1946, 686 lists four translations published in the sixteenth century.

11. Translation of Alciati's epigram is from Alciati ed. 1985, 2: Emblem 10. The phrase quoted from Hollander 1993 appears in the caption to his unpaginated reproduction of a version of Alciati's emblem; see pp. 47-50 on "the political use of the lute as a sixteenth-century image," and pp. 387-89 on Mace's "rather antiquarian position with respect to his subject."

12. For help with the Latin motto, my thanks to Patricia Harris Stäblein, who suggests that the ambiguity of its Neo-Latin constructions may harbor a veiled critique of James's power not unlike the ironies I attribute to Spenser and Carrara—a point on which I lack the expertise to form an opinion.

13. On similar illustrations in Renaissance writing manuals and on the general tendency for writing instruction in the period to emphasize character formation in both senses, see Goldberg 1990a. On the musical instrument as an image of castrated or politically dominated poetic voice, see Parker 1987. I have reservations about Parker's development of the psychosexual allegory in *The Faerie Queene*, especially her adaptation of Mulvey 1978. For a lucid critique of the Foucauldian distortions of Lacan put into circulation by film criticism, see Copjek 1989.

On the distinctiveness of the lute's "mystery," see Hollander 1993: "the lute's importance [in the sixteenth century] can be partially measured by the fact that it alone (aside from the keyboard instruments) possessed a unique kind of notational system . . . while other kinds of instruments were simply employed at will to play any unspecified vocal parts that might fall within their ranges" (46). Hollander notes that Mulcaster (Spenser's schoolmaster) in *The First Part of the Elementarie* recommends instruction in the notational system for lute and virginal and (interestingly) that "his whole argument and exposition of the musical curriculum follows the model of basic grammar, and enforces an analogy by the use of grammatical terms throughout" (115-16).

14. On dynamics of voice and authority in Spenser, see especially Goldberg 1981; 1986, 38-67; and 1983, 1-12. The most authoritative recent treatment of these issues is Berger 1991, which identifies the term "Spenser" with a principle of ironic reading that pervasively undermines ideological elements such as misogyny: "if the narrator and his story are working for the government," Berger remarks, "the poem is not" (48). In practice, however, this solution tends to make the text's social and political views coincide with those of American English professors in the late twentieth century. As Montrose has written, "By adapting to his present purposes a strict New-Critical distinction between the writer and his characters, Berger's [recent] essays strongly imply that . . . linguistic slippages are not so much a general condition of discourse as manifestations of the author's ironic mastery over the imaginative world of his text—a mastery that the critic expounds and thereby shares" (1988, 16).

15. *FQ* II x 4.1-5, in ed. 1912. My reading of Spenser is generally informed by Hamilton's annotations (Spenser ed. 1977).

16. In what follows I refer to the reading given in Miller 1988, 191-214, partly by way of response to the important discussion in Bellamy 1992, 189-233. On the "untimely breach" in stanza 68, see also Fried 1981.

17. Bellamy 1992: "the trajectory of Tudor destiny [in *The Faerie Queene*] continually struggles to interpellate its Briton subjects into imperial ideology, even as these same knights suffer a *méconnaissance*, misrecognizing their own destiny as they wander aimlessly through Faerie" (193); "in an oddly misplaced elegiac moment, the poet adds, almost parenthetically, 'But when he dyde, the Faerie Queene it [Arthur's shield and arms] brought / To Faerie lond, where yet it may be seene, if sought' (I vii 36.8-9). Thus we are presented with a brief and evanescent foreshadowing of the deadly termination of Arthur's 'prophetic moment'— a moment reduced to a memorial fetish through his enervate armor" (247).

18. Anderson 1984 argues that life writing in the English Renaissance conceives the relation between truth and fiction differently than post-Enlightenment culture does. Following Teskey (1988, 1992, 1993), I am making a different kind of argument about a different group of texts. In Spenser, the thematic contrast between truth and fiction plays ironically and perhaps even subversively against the imperial theme, and along with the counterimperial theme of retreat or escape, it is grafted onto a more fundamental dualism, that of meaning and being. Spenser implies that to assume or be given meaning is, prima facie, to be stamped with an image that comes from elsewhere. To resist this imposition even marginally, the author must produce a doubly written text.

19. Shepherd's "vulgar Marxist" introduction to Spenser (1989) illustrates the politics of not reading closely. Aimed at students, this account opens with a view of Spenser as "penpusher in the service of imperialism," developed in a discussion of the *View* which barely notices its dialogue form, attributing quoted passages not to their fictional speakers but directly to the author. Greenblatt 1980, 186-92, illustrates by contrast how subtly biography may be deployed in the service of reducing Spenser's textual politics. Greenblatt argues that the text "worships" royal power, deflecting all its iconoclastic and interrogatory force onto its own status as art; he does not read its dissemination of imperial ideology (see the critique in Berger 1991).

Waller 1994 represents the latest effort to write what the author calls Spenser's "literary life." This study, which appeared after the present essay was in its final form, is interesting and informative on many topics but is not (as Waller recognizes) the writing of a life. Rather, it is the selective reinscription of an Elizabethan textual milieu in terms of what Waller refers to as the "stories" of "criticism and the reading of 'literature' in the late twentieth century" (189). As such, it is an extended, self-conscious exercise in the sort of appropriation the Earl of Cork's lute prefigures. Preferable in my view are the deconstructive strategies Goldberg 1992 employs "to read texts into the world" (74), though I would sharply distinguish these from the reductively polemical and sometimes abusive way he reads his own contemporaries. Goldberg writes, "it seems to me important not to allegorize and thematize the text so entirely that its sole function is to read the world at the expense of the text, to decide beforehand that the world is real and that the only reality that a text might have would be its ability to translate the world in terms that need to be translated back into the social, historical, or political" (74-75).

20. Brink 1993; the rest of my paragraph summarizes and quotes from this essay. I am grateful to Professor Brink for sharing with me her work in progress.

21. Anderson 1989 traces connections between the "everlasting scryne" of Eumnestes and the Muses (I proem 2.3) and the medieval church or monastery's "secretum, or 'secret place,' the treasury of the institution and, prior to the establishment of libraries, the depository for books" (18).

22. For this stanza I depart from Spenser ed. 1912 to cite the text as printed in 1596. The reinscription of BON FONS is already underway in editions that substitute the reading "BON FONT."

23. This reading owes something to Gross 1987. Goldberg 1983, 1-12, discusses the passage in the context of James's demand that Spenser be punished and notes that the claim to be speaking "beyond oneself" is a characteristic recourse of power: "Denying

itself, contradiction defines the essence of the discourse of power" (7). Goldberg compares the Malfont passage to the ensuing trial of Duessa; my emphasis here on its link to the previous episode (the destruction of Guyle) leads to a somewhat different account of the passage's relation to the trial scene and, more generally, to the discourse of sovereign power. Goldberg comments on the language in Book V and *A View* of "cutting off," "racing," and "replanting," which he reads as metaphors for the operations of sovereign power. The lute epigram tacitly applies these metaphors to the poet, whose voice is thereby represented as having been colonized much like Ireland.

24. Spenser ed. 1977, 738. My remarks on the "wellhead" as a punning *mens sana* are indebted to John Barrett.

25. Miller 1988, 176-77, 185. See also Miller 1990, 23. Puns on Spenser's name may refer to his days as a "sizar" at Cambridge, where the would-be laureate's duties included serving meals. If so, these puns treat Spenser's use of poetry for social advancement with more wit than most modern critics who discuss the topic: once a butler, always a butler, even on Parnassus.

26. Zupko 1977, 86. Anderson 1989 notes a link between the word-hoard and the scrine: "repeatedly and specifically *scrine* is associated with secrecy or seclusion (*secerno, secretum*), with the need to guard or preserve, and with the word and idea of a *thesaurus*, a treasure or a treasury of writing and, more fundamentally, of words" (19). The "wisemens threasure" of the poem's close thus glances sardonically at the "everlasting scryne" of its opening.

Afterword

1. Or, by the same token, one can move another step forward and backward in the alphabet (assuming that I and J are a single letter) and complete a progress from E. K. to F. J. to G. H. There is of course no way of verifying this surmise: my point is, first, that it is no more speculative, no less provable, than other claims for Edward Kirke or Edmundus Kalendarius; and second, that such speculation is invited by the implicit voyeurism of any genre in which private writing is made public by another. The publisher and published pass the burden of deciphering meaning to the reader, who can never be sure there is anything to be deciphered. A twentieth-century analogue is HAL, the dysfunctional computer in Kubrick's film *2001*, who has been popularly taken to allude to IBM by a similar process of decoding, despite the denials of director and author. *Se non è vero, è ben trovato.*

2. Ferry 1983 provides a useful overview of this problem.

3. The epithet properly belongs to another native of Arezzo, Bernardo Accolti, who figures in Castiglione's *Courtier*, but Harvey obviously applies it here and in the *Letters* to the far more eminent Pietro.

4. Literally, "Enjoy yourself," or "Have a nice orgasm" (It. *godere*; cf. Fr. *gaude-michi*, dildo). Wolfe gives this imaginary place of publication to three volumes of the *Ragionamenti* (STC 19911.5-12-13); his editions of Machiavelli bear false imprints of real cities, Rome, Palermo, or Piacenza (Fr. Plaisance), the last of which may have inspired the more explicitly sexual site for the Aretino. Although the false imprints are presumably meant to protect Wolfe (or to suggest, at least, that these are dangerous foreign works), the choice of Bengodi advertises the contents as pornographic. Wolfe further attributes the notes by Annibale Caro in one of the Aretino volumes to a bawdy-sounding "ser Agresto da Ficaruolo."

5. The Yale edition (Spenser ed. 1989) translates the motto as "[judge by] the goods, not the price," and others have tried slightly different meanings for Latin *merx* and *merces* which do not evolve distinctly until the words become Italian *merce* and *mercede*, at which point the ablative form needed for an elliptical construction is lost. Kennedy plausibly

argues for Spenser's invocation here of the separate Italian word *mercé*, grace, as either the primary or secondary meaning in the motto, which like many Latin *symbola* is finally too ambiguous to be translatable satisfactorily.

6. See especially Goldberg 1989. Ellis 1994 (the source of the quotation in the text) remarks that, in E. K.'s gloss to "Januarye" and in Harvey's letter, "translation figures prominently, both as the scene of desire and its 'cover' or shadow." Rambuss 1993 provides the fullest survey of the role of such cover or "secrecy" in Spenser's self-promotion. My remarks here are directed to the (relatively) narrow question of intertextual and interlinguistic cohabitation.

Works Cited

Unless otherwise noted, all citations of Spenser's works refer to
The Poetical Works of Edmund Spenser ed. 1912.

Acts of the Privy Council of England, 1542-1631. 1974. 46 vols. Nendeln, Liechtenstein: Kraus reprint.

Alciati, Andrea. 1534. *Emblematum Libellus*. Paris.

Alciati ed. 1985. *Andreas Alciatus*, ed. Peter M. Daly, et al. 2 vols. Toronto: Univ. of Toronto Press.

Alpers, Paul. 1988. "Pastoral and the Domain of Lyric in Spenser's *Shepheardes Calender*." In *Representing the English Renaissance*, ed. Stephen Greenblatt, 163-80. Berkeley: Univ. of California Press. First pub. in *Representations* in 1985.

Alpers. 1990. "the poet's poet." In *The Spenser Encyclopedia*.

Anderson, Judith. 1984. *Biographical Truth: The Representation of Historical Persons in Tudor-Stuart Writing*. New Haven: Yale Univ. Press.

Anderson. 1989. "'Myn auctor': Spenser's Enabling Fiction and Eumnestes' 'immortal scrine'." In Logan and Teskey 1989, 16-31.

Anderson, William S. 1968. "Pastor Aeneas: On Pastoral Themes in the *Aeneid*." *Transactions of the American Philological Association*, 99:1-17.

Anglo, Sydney. 1990. "A Machiavellian Solution to the Irish Problem: Richard Beacon's *Solon His Follie* (1594)." In *England and the Continental Renaissance. Essays in Honour of J. B. Trapp*, ed. Edward Chaney and Peter Mack, 153-64. Woodbridge: Boydell and Brewer Press.

Arber, Edward. 1875-94. *A Transcript of the Register of the Company of Stationers of London, 1554-1640*. 5 vols. London and Birmingham.

Archer, John Michael. 1993. *Sovereignty and Intelligence: Spying and Court Culture in the English Renaissance*. Stanford: Stanford Univ. Press.

Attridge, Derek. 1990. "quantitative verse." In *The Spenser Encyclopedia*.

Baker, David J. 1985. "'Some Quirk, Some Subtle Evasion': Legal Subversion in Spenser's *A View of the Present State of Ireland*." *Spenser Studies*, 6:147-63.

Baker. 1993. "Off the Map: Charting Uncertainty in Renaissance Ireland." In Bradshaw et al. 1993, 76-92.

Bald, R. C. 1970. *John Donne: A Life*. Oxford: Oxford Univ. Press.

Banks, Theodore. 1937. "Spenser's Rosalind: A Conjecture." *PMLA*, 52:335-37.

Barkan, Leonard. 1986. *The Gods Made Flesh: Metamorphosis and the Pursuit of Paganism*. New Haven: Yale Univ. Press.

Barnett, George L. 1945. "Gabriel Harvey's *Castilio, sive Aulicus* and *De Aulica*: A Study of Their Place in the Literature of Courtesy." *Studies in Philology*, 42:146-63.

Beacon, Richard. 1594. *Solon His Follie; or, A Politique Discourse, Touching the Reformation of Common-weales Conquered, Declined or Corrupted*. Oxford: Joseph Barnes.

Bellamy, Elizabeth J. 1992. *Translations of Power; Narcissism and the Unconscious in Epic History*. Ithaca: Cornell Univ. Press.

Bellay, Joachim du. 1961. *Oeuvres Poétiques*, ed. Henri Chamard, vols. 1-2. Paris: Didier.

Bellay ed. 1974. *Olive*, ed. E. Caldarini. Geneva: Droz.

Bennett, Josephine Waters. 1931. "Spenser and Gabriel Harvey's *Letter-Book*." *Modern Philology*, 29:163-86.

Bennett. 1937. "Did Spenser Starve?" *Modern Language Notes*, 52: 400-401.

Bennett. 1942. *The Evolution of "The Faerie Queene."* Chicago: Univ. of Chicago Press.

Berger, Harry, Jr. 1988. *Revisionary Play: Studies in the Spenserian Dynamics*. Berkeley: Univ. of California Press.

Berger. 1991. "Narrative as Rhetoric in *The Faerie Queene*." *English Literary Renaissance*, 21:3-48.

Bernard, John D. 1989. *Ceremonies of Innocence: Pastoralism in the Poetry of Edmund Spenser*. Cambridge: Cambridge Univ. Press.

Berry, Edward. 1989. "The Poet as Warrior in Sidney's *Defence of Poetry*." *Studies in English Literature*, 29:21-34.

Birch, Thomas. 1751. "Life of Spenser." In *The Faerie Queene*. London: J. Brindley.

Blayney, Peter. 1982. *The Texts of "King Lear" and Their Origin*. Vol. 1; *Nicholas Okes and the First Folio*. Cambridge: Cambridge Univ. Press.

Borthwick, E. K. 1970. "The Riddle of the Tortoise and the Lyre." *Music & Letters*, 51: 373-87.

Bradbrook, M. C. 1982. "No Room at the Top" (1960). In *The Artist and Society in Shakespeare's England: The Collected Papers of Muriel Bradbrook*, 1:19-36. Brighton, Sussex: Harvester Press.

Bradshaw, Brendan. 1978. "Sword, Word, and Strategy in the Reformation in Ireland." *Historical Journal*, 21:475-502.

Bradshaw. 1987. "Edmund Spenser on Justice and Mercy." In *The Writer as Witness*, ed. Tom Dunne, *Historical Studies*, 16 (Cork): 76-89.

Bradshaw. 1988. "Robe and Sword in the Conquest of Ireland." In *Law and Government under the Tudors*, ed. Clair Cross et al., 139-62. Cambridge: Cambridge Univ. Press.

Bradshaw, Brendan, et al., eds. 1993. *Representing Ireland: Literature and the Origins of Conflict, 1534-1660*. Cambridge: Cambridge Univ. Press.

Brady, Ciaran. 1985. "Conservative Subversives: The Community of the Pale and the Dublin Administration, 1556-86." In *Radicals, Rebels, and Establishments*, ed. P. J. Corish, 11-32. Belfast: Appletree Press.

Brady. 1986a. "Court, Castle, and Country: The Framework of Government in Tudor Ireland." In *Natives and Newcomers: The Making of Irish Colonial Society, 1534-1641*, ed. Ciaran Brady and Raymond Gillespie, 22-49. Dublin: Irish Academic Press.

Brady. 1986b. "Spenser's Irish Crisis: Humanism and Experience in the 1590s." *Past and Present*, 111:17-49.

Brady. 1988. "Debate: Spenser's Irish Crisis: Humanism and Experience in the 1590s—Reply." *Past and Present*, 120:210-15.

Brady. 1989. "The Road to the *View:* On the Decline of Reform Thought in Tudor Ireland." In Coughlan, ed. 1989, 24-45.

Brennan, Michael. 1983. "William Ponsonby: Elizabethan Stationer." *Analytical and Enumerative Bibliography*, 7:91-110.

Brennan. 1988. *Literary Patronage in the English Renaissance: The Pembroke Family.* London: Routledge.

Brink, Jean R. 1991. "Who Fashioned Edmund Spenser?: The Textual History of *Complaints*." *Studies in Philology*, 88.2:153-68.

Brink. 1993. "Constructing the *View of the Present State of Ireland*." *Spenser Studies*, 11: 203-28.

British Library. Lansdowne MS 22, item 83, fol. 194.

Bryskett, Lodowick. 1606. *A Discourse of Civill Life.* London.

Calendar of the State Papers Relating to Ireland, of the Reigns of Henry VIII, Edward VI, Mary and Elizabeth. 1974. 24 vols. Nendeln, Liechtenstein: Kraus reprint.

Camden, William. 1635. *Annales; or, The History of the Most Renowned and Victorious Princesse Elizabeth.*, trans. R[ichard] N[orton] 3rd ed. London: Benjamin Fisher.

Camerarius, Philipp. 1621. *Operae horarum subcisivarum*, trans. John Molle, in *The Living Librarie.* London: Adam Islip.

Canny, Nicholas P. 1976. *The Elizabethan Conquest of Ireland: A Pattern Established, 1565-76.* New York: Barnes and Noble.

Canny. 1982. *The Upstart Earl: A Study of the Social and Mental World of Richard Boyle, First Earl of Cork, 1566-1643.* Cambridge: Cambridge Univ. Press.

Canny. 1983. "Edmund Spenser and the Development of an Anglo-Irish Identity." *Yearbook of English Studies*, 13:1-19.

Canny. 1988. "Debate: Spenser's Irish Crisis: Humanism and Experience in the 1590s — Comment." *Past and Present*, 120:201-9.

Carpenter, Frederic Ives. 1921-22. "Spenser in Ireland." *Modern Philology*, 19:405-19.

Carpenter. 1923. *A Reference Guide to Edmund Spenser.* Chicago: Univ. of Chicago Press.

Carrara, Michele. 1956. *Involatura di liutu, 1585; a cura di Benvenuto Disertori.* Florence: L. S. Olschki.

Cavanagh, Shelia T. 1933. "'The fatal destiny of that land': Elizabethan Views of Ireland." In Bradshaw et al. 1993, 116-31.

Chambers, E. K. 1930. *William Shakespeare: A Study of Facts and Problems.* 2 vols. Oxford: Clarendon Press.

Cheney, Donald. 1966. *Spenser's Image of Nature: Wild Man and Shepherd in "The Faerie Queene."* New Haven: Yale Univ. Press.

Cheney. 1983. "Spenser's Fortieth Birthday and Related Fictions." *Spenser Studies*, 4:3-31.

Cheney, Patrick. 1990. "The Laureate Choir: The Dove as a Vocational Sign in Spenser's Allegory of Ralegh and Elizabeth." *Huntington Library Quarterly*, 53:257-80.

Cheney. 1993. *Spenser's Famous Flight: A Renaissance Idea of a Literary Career.* Toronto: Univ. of Toronto Press.

Church, R. W. 1879. *Spenser.* In the English Men of Letters series, ed. John Morley. London: Macmillan.

Churchyard, Thomas. 1579. *A Generall Rehearsall of Warres.* London: Edward White.

Cicero ed. 1959. *De Oratore*, ed. E. W. Sutton and H. Rackham. 2 vols. Loeb Classics. Rev. ed. Cambridge, Mass.: Harvard Univ. Press.

Clements, Robert J., and Lorna Levant. 1976. *Renaissance Letters: Revelations of a World Reborn.* New York: New York Univ. Press.

Coiro, Ann Baynes. 1988. *Robert Herrick's "Hesperides" and the Epigram Book Tradition.* Baltimore: Johns Hopkins Univ. Press.

Coleman, Dorothy. 1990. "Minerve et l'*Olive*," in *Du Bellay: Actes du Colloque International d'Angers du 26 au 29 Mai 1989*, ed. Georges Cesbron, 161-69. Angers: Presses de l'université d'Angers.

Colie, Rosalie. 1973. *Resources of Kind: Genre-Theory in the Renaissance,* ed. Barbara K. Lewalski. Berkeley: Univ. of California Press.

Collins, Arthur, ed. 1746. *Letters and Memorials of State [of the Sidney family].* 2 vols. London: T. Osborne.

Copjek, Joan. 1989. "The Orthopsychic Subject: Film Theory and the Reception of Lacan." *October* 49:53-71.

Cornarius, Janus. 1529. *Selecta Epigrammata.* Basel.

Coughlan, Patricia. 1989. "'Some secret scourge which shall by her come unto England': Ireland and Incivility in Spenser." In Coughlan, ed. 1989, 46-74.

Coughlan, ed. 1989. *Spenser and Ireland: An Interdisciplinary Perspective.* Cork: Cork Univ. Press.

Covington, Frank F., Jr. 1924-25. "Biographical Notes on Spenser." *Modern Philology,* 22:63-66.

Craik, G. L. 1843. *Spenser and His Poetry.* 3 vols. London: Knight.

Crane, Mary Thomas. 1993. *Framing Authority: Sayings, Self, and Society in Sixteenth-Century England.* Princeton: Princeton Univ. Press.

Crewe, Jonathan V. 1982. *Unredeemed Rhetoric: Thomas Nashe and the Scandal of Authorship.* Baltimore: Johns Hopkins Univ. Press.

Crewe. 1986. *Hidden Designs.* New York: Methuen.

Cummings, L. 1964. "Spenser's *Amoretti VIII*: New Manuscript Versions." *Studies in English Literature,* 4:125-35.

Darnton, Robert. 1991. "History of Reading." In *New Perspectives on Historical Writing,* ed. Peter Burke, 140-67. University Park: Pennsylvania State Univ. Press.

Davis, Natalie Zemon. 1987. *Fiction in the Archives.* Stanford: Stanford Univ. Press.

DeMolen, Richard L. 1991. *Richard Mulcaster (c. 1531-1611) and Educational Reform in the Renaissance.* Nieuwkoop: DeGraaf.

Denny, H. L. L. 1904. "The Biography of Edward Denny." *Transactions of the East Hertfordshire Archaeological Society,* 2.3:247-60. Hertford: Stephen Austin and Sons.

Dodge, R. E. Neil, ed. 1936. "Biographical Sketch." In *Edmund Spenser: The Complete Poetical Works,* xi-xxiii. Boston: Houghton Mifflin.

Du Bellay, Joachim. See Bellay, Joachim du.

Duncan-Jones, Katherine. 1991. *Sir Philip Sidney, Courtier Poet.* New Haven: Yale Univ. Press.

Dunlop, Alexander. 1980. "The Drama of *Amoretti*." *Spenser Studies,* 1:107-20.

Egerton, Philip. See Grey 1847.

Eliot, T. S. 1946. Introduction to G. Wilson Knight, *The Wheel of Fire* (1930). Rpt. London: Oxford Univ. Press.

Ellis, Jim. 1994. "Desire in Translation: Friendship in the Life and Work of Spenser." *English Studies in Canada,* 20:171-85.

Ellis, Steven. 1985. *Tudor Ireland: Crown, Community, and the Conflict of Cultures, 1470-1603*. London and New York: Longman.

Esler, Anthony. 1966. *The Aspiring Mind of the Elizabethan Younger Generation*. Durham: Duke Univ. Press.

Ferguson, Margaret. 1983. *Trials of Desire: Renaissance Defenses of Poetry*. New Haven: Yale Univ. Press.

Ferguson. 1984. "'The Afflatus of Ruin': Meditations on Rome by Du Bellay, Spenser, and Stevens." In *Roman Images: Selected Papers from the English Institute, 1982*, ed. Annabel Patterson, 23-50. Baltimore: Johns Hopkins Univ. Press.

Ferry, Anne. 1983. *The "Inward" Language: Sonnets of Wyatt, Sidney, Shakespeare, Donne*. Chicago: Univ. of Chicago Press.

Foucault, Michel. 1977. "What Is an Author?" In *Language, Counter-Memory, Practice: Selected Essays and Interviews*, trans. Donald F. Bouchard and Sherry Simon, 113-38. Oxford: Basil Blackwell.

Fowler, Alastair. 1982. *Kinds of Literature: An Introduction to the Theory of Genres and Modes*. Cambridge, Mass.: Harvard Univ. Press.

Fowler, Joanne Ellis. 1982. "Edmund Spenser's Presentation of the Political Philosophy of the Earl of Leicester's Progressive Party." Ph.D. diss., Emory Univ.

Fried, Debra. 1981. "Spenser's Caesura." *English Literary Renaissance*, 11:261-80.

Gallop, Jane. 1985. *Reading Lacan*. Ithaca: Cornell Univ. Press.

Gilbert, Allen H., ed. 1962. *Literary Criticism: Plato to Dryden*. Detroit: Wayne State Univ. Press; orig. pub. 1940.

Gill, D. 1959. "The Elizabethan Lute." *Galpin Society Journal*, 12:60-62.

Goldberg, Jonathan. 1981. *Endlesse Worke: Spenser and the Structures of Discourse*. Baltimore: Johns Hopkins Univ. Press.

Goldberg. 1983. *James I and the Politics of Literature: Jonson, Shakespeare, Donne, and Their Contemporaries*. Baltimore: Johns Hopkins Univ. Press.

Goldberg. 1986. *Voice Terminal Echo: Postmodernism and English Renaissance Texts*. New York: Methuen.

Goldberg. 1989. "Colin to Hobbinol: Spenser's Familiar Letters." *South Atlantic Quarterly*, 88:107-26.

Goldberg. 1990a. *Writing Matter: From the Hands of the English Renaissance*. Stanford: Stanford Univ. Press.

Goldberg. 1990b. "Dating Milton." In *Soliciting Interpretation: Literary Theory and Seventeenth-Century English Poetry*, ed. Elizabeth D. Harvey and Katharine Eisaman Maus, 199-220. Chicago: Univ. of Chicago Press.

Goldberg. 1992. *Sodometries: Renaissance Texts, Modern Sexualities*. Stanford: Stanford Univ. Press; ch. 3, "Spenser's Familiar Letters" is a revision of Goldberg 1989.

Gollancz, Israel. 1907. "Spenseriana." *Proceedings of the British Academy*, 3:99-105.

Gottfried, Rudolf. 1937. "Spenser's *View* and Essex." *PMLA*, 52:645-51.

Gottfried. 1939. "Irish Geography in Spenser's *View*." *ELH*, 6:114-37.

Grafton, Anthony, and Lisa Jardine. 1982. "Humanism and the School of Guarino: A Problem of Evaluation." *Past and Present*, 96:51-80.

Grafton and Jardine. 1986. *From Humanism to the Humanities; Education and the Liberal Arts in Fifteenth- and Sixteenth-Century Europe*. London: Duckworth.

Gray, M. M. 1930. "The Influence of Spenser's Irish Experiences on *The Faerie Queene*." *Review of English Studies*, 6:413-28.

The Greek Anthology. 1917. Trans. W. R. Paton. The Loeb Classical Library. Cambridge, Mass.: Harvard Univ. Press.

Greenblatt, Stephen. 1980. *Renaissance Self-Fashioning from More to Shakespeare.* Chicago: Univ. of Chicago Press.

Greenblatt. 1990. "identity." In *The Spenser Encyclopedia.*

Greene, Thomas. 1982. *The Light in Troy: Imitation and Discovery in Renaissance Poetry.* New Haven: Yale Univ. Press.

Greenlaw, Edwin A. 1910. "Spenser and the Earl of Leicester." *PMLA*, 25:535-61; rpt. 1932 as Greenlaw 1932, chap. 3.

Greenlaw. 1932. *Studies in Spenser's Historical Allegory.* Baltimore: Johns Hopkins Univ. Press.

Greville, Fulke. 1986. *The Prose Works of Fulke Greville, Lord Brooke*, ed. John Gouws. Oxford: Clarendon Press.

Grey, Arthur, Lord Grey of Wilton. 1847. *A Commentary of the Services and Charges of William, Lord Grey of Wilton*, ed. Sir Philip De Malpas Grey Egerton. Camden Society. London: J. B. Nichols and Son.

Gross, John. 1969. *The Rise and Fall of the Man of Letters.* London: Macmillan.

Gross, Kenneth. 1985. *Spenserian Poetics: Idolatry, Iconoclasm, and Magic.* Ithaca: Cornell Univ. Press.

Gross. 1987. "Spenser's Malfont: Reflections on Renaissance Self-Immolation." Paper given at the 1987 meeting of the Modern Language Association of America.

Guillén, Claudio. 1986. "Notes toward the Study of the Renaissance Letter." In *Renaissance Genres; Essays on Theory, History, and Interpretation*, ed. Barbara Kiefer Lewalski, 70-101. Cambridge, Mass.: Harvard Univ. Press.

Guy, John. 1988. *Tudor England.* Oxford: Oxford Univ. Press.

Hadfield, Andrew. 1994. "Spenser, Ireland, and Sixteenth-Century Political Theory." *Modern Language Review*, 89:1-18.

Hamer, Douglas. 1931. "Spenser's Marriage." *Review of English Studies*, 7:271-90.

Hamer. 1932. "Edmund Spenser: Some Further Notes." *Notes and Queries*, 162:380-84.

Hamer. 1941. "Some Spenser Problems." *Notes and Queries*, 180:165-67, 183-84, 206-9, 220-24, 238-41.

Hamilton, A.C. 1977. See Spenser ed. 1977.

Hamilton, A.C., et al. 1990. See *The Spenser Encyclopedia.*

Harman, Edward George. 1914. *Edmund Spenser and the Impersonation of Francis Bacon.* London: Constable.

Harvey, Gabriel. 1578a. *Gratulationum Valdinensium Libri Quatuor.* London: Henry Bynneman.

Harvey. 1578b. *Smithus vel Musarum Lachrymae.* London.

Harvey ed. 1884. *The Letter-Book of Gabriel Harvey, A.D. 1573-1580*, ed. Edward John Long Scott. Camden Society, n.s. 30, London. Rpt. 1965.

Harvey ed. 1945. *Gabriel Harvey's "Ciceronianus,"* ed. Harold S. Wilson. Univ. of Nebraska Studies in the Humanities, 4 (November).

Harvey ed. 1966. *Foure Letters and Certeine Sonnets* (1592), ed. G. B. Harrison. Edinburgh: Edinburgh Univ. Press; orig. pub. 1922.

Harvey, Gabriel, and Edmund Spenser. 1580. *Three Proper, and wittie, familiar Letters: lately passed betwene two Universitie men: touching the Earthquake in Aprill last, and our English refourmed Versifying.* London: H. Bynneman.

Harwood, Ian. 1975. *A Brief History of the Lute*. The Lute Society Booklets, no. 1.

Heffner, Ray. 1931. "Spenser's Acquisition of Kilcolman." *Modern Language Notes*, 46:493-98.

Heffner. 1938-39. "Edmund Spenser's Family." *Huntington Library Quarterly*, 2: 79-84.

Helgerson, Richard. 1983. *Self-Crowned Laureates: Spenser, Jonson, Milton, and the Literary System*. Berkeley: Univ. of California Press.

Helgerson. 1992. *Forms of Nationhood: The Elizabethan Writing of England*. Chicago: Univ. of Chicago Press.

Henderson, Judith Rice. 1983. "Erasmus on the Art of Letter-Writing." In Murphy 1983, 331-55.

Henderson. 1990. "letter as genre." In *The Spenser Encyclopedia*.

Heninger, S. K., Jr. 1987. "Spenser and Sidney at Leicester House." *Spenser Studies*, 8:239-49.

Heninger. 1988. "The Typographical Layout of Spenser's *Shepheardes Calender*." In *The Word and the Visual Imagination*, ed. Karl Josef Höltgen et al, 33-71. Erlangen-Nürnberg: Universitätsbibliothek.

Heninger. 1989. *Sidney and Spenser: The Poet as Maker*. University Park: Pennsylvania State Univ. Press.

Henley, Pauline. 1928. *Spenser in Ireland*. Dublin: Dublin Univ. Press.

Henley, William. 1959. *Universal Dictionary of Violin and Bow Makers*. 5 vols. Brighton, Sussex: Southern Publishing.

Herbert, Sir William. 1887. *Croftus sive De Hibernia Liber*, ed. W. E. Buckley. London: Nichols and Sons for the Roxburghe Club.

Hesiod. 1983. *Theogony, Works and Days, Shield,* trans. with introduction and notes, Apostolos N. Athanassiakis. Baltimore: Johns Hopkins Univ. Press.

Hibbard, G. R. 1962. *Thomas Nashe: A Critical Introduction*. Cambridge, Mass.: Harvard Univ. Press.

Hieatt, A. Kent. 1988. "The Passing of Arthur in Malory, Spenser, and Shakespeare: The Avoidance of Closure." In *The Passing of Arthur: New Essays in Arthurian Tradition*, ed. Christopher Baswell and William Sharpe, 173-92. New York: Garland.

Hieatt. 1990. "The Projected Continuation of *The Faerie Queene: Rome Delivered?*" *Spenser Studies*, 8:335-42.

Hieatt. 1991. "Arthur's Deliverance of Rome? (Yet Again)." *Spenser Studies*, 9:243-48.

Higgins, Anne. 1990. "Spenser Reading Chaucer: Another Look at the *Faerie Queene* Allusions." *Journal of English and German Philology*, 89:17-36.

Hollander, John. 1993. *The Untuning of the Sky: Ideas of Music in English Poetry, 1500-1700*. Princeton: Princeton Univ. Press, 1961, Rpt. Hamden, Conn.: Shoestring.

Homer. 1930-34. *The Iliad*, trans. A. T. Murray. 2 vols. The Loeb Classical Library. New York: Putnam.

The House of Commons, 1558-1603. 1981. Ed. P. W. Hasler. 3 vols. London: Her Majesty's Stationery Office for the History of Parliament Trust.

Hudson, Hoyt Hopewell. 1947. *The Epigram in the English Renaissance Tradition*. Princeton: Princeton Univ. Press.

Hulbert, Viola Blackburn. 1936-37. "Spenser's Relation to Certain Documents on Ireland." *Modern Philology*, 34:345-53.

Hulse, Clark. 1988. "Spenser, Bacon, and the Myth of Power." In *The Historical Renaissance: New Essays on Tudor and Stuart Literature and Culture*, ed. Heather Dubrow and Richard Strier, 315-46. Chicago: Univ. of Chicago Press.

Hume, Anthea. 1984. *Edmund Spenser: Protestant Poet*. Cambridge: Cambridge Univ. Press.

Hunt, Leigh. 1845. *Imagination and Fancy: Selections from the English Poets*. London: Smith, Elder.

Hunter, G. K. 1962. *John Lyly*. London: Routledge and Kegan Paul.

Hutson, Lorna. 1993. "Fortunate Travelers: Reading for the Plot in Sixteenth-Century England." *Representations*, 41:83-101.

Hutton, James. 1935. *The Greek Anthology in Italy to the Year 1800*. Cornell Studies in English, 23. Ithaca: Cornell Univ. Press.

Hutton. 1946. *The Greek Anthology in France and in the Latin Writers of the Netherlands to the Year 1800*. Cornell Studies in Classical Philology. Ithaca: Cornell Univ. Press.

Jameson, Thomas Hugh. 1941. "The 'Machiavellianism' of Gabriel Harvey." *PMLA*, 56:645-56.

Jardine, Lisa. 1986. "Gabriel Harvey: Exemplary Ramist and Pragmatic Humanist." *Revue des Sciences philosophiques et theologiques*, 70:36-48.

Jardine. 1990. "'Mastering the Uncouth': Gabriel Harvey, Edmund Spenser and the English Experience in Ireland." In *New Perspectives on Renaissance Thought: Essays in the History of Science, Education, and Philosophy: In Memory of Charles B. Schmitt*, ed. John Henry and Sarah Hutton, 68-82. London: Duckworth.

Jardine. 1993. "Encountering Ireland: Gabriel Harvey, Edmund Spenser, and English Colonial Ventures." In Bradshaw et al. 1993, 60-75.

Jardine, Lisa, and Anthony Grafton. 1990. "'Studied for Action': How Gabriel Harvey Read His Livy." *Past and Present*, 129:30-78.

Javitch, Daniel. 1978. *Poetry and Courtliness in Renaissance England*. Princeton: Princeton Univ. Press.

Javitch. 1982. "The Impure Motives of Elizabethan Poetry." *Genre*, 15:225-38.

Jenkins, Raymond. 1932a. "Spenser and the Clerkship in Munster." *PMLA*, 47:109-21.

Jenkins. 1932b. "Spenser's Hand." *Times Literary Supplement*, 31 (7 January): 12.

Jenkins. 1933. "Spenser at Smerwick." *Times Literary Supplement*, 32 (11 May): 331.

Jenkins. 1935. "*Newes out of Munster*, a Document in Spenser's Hand." *Studies in Philology*, 32:123-30.

Jenkins. 1937. "Spenser with Lord Grey in Ireland." *PMLA*, 52:338-53.

Jenkins. 1938. "Spenser: The Uncertain Years, 1584-1589." *PMLA*, 53:350-62.

Jenkins. 1952. "Spenser and Ireland." In Mueller and Allen 1952, 51-62.

Johnson, Francis R. 1933. A *Critical Bibliography of the Works of Edmund Spenser Printed before 1700*. Baltimore: Johns Hopkins Univ. Press.

Johnson. 1950. "Notes on English Retail Book-prices, 1550-1640." *The Library*, 5.2: 83-112.

Johnson, Lynn Staley. 1990. "*The Shepheardes Calender*": *An Introduction*. University Park: Pennsylvania State Univ. Press.

Johnson, W. R. 1976. *Darkness Visible: A Study of Virgil's "Aeneid."* Berkeley: Univ. of California Press.

Jones, Deborah. 1933. "Lodowyck Bryskett and His Family." In Sisson 1933, 243-362.

Jonson, Ben. 1925-52. *Poetaster* and *Timber*. In *Ben Jonson*, ed. C. H. Herford and P. and E. Simpson. 11 vols. Oxford: Clarendon Press.

Judge, C. B. 1934. *Elizabethan Book-Pirates*. Cambridge, Mass.: Harvard Univ. Press.

Judson, Alexander C. 1933. *Spenser in Southern Ireland*. Bloomington, Ind.: Principia Press.

Judson. 1934. "A Biographical Sketch of John Young, Bishop of Rochester, with Emphasis on His Relations with Edmund Spenser." *Indiana University Studies*, 26:3-41.

Judson. 1942-43. "Another Spenser Portrait." *Huntington Library Quarterly*, 6:203-4.

Judson. 1945. *The Life of Edmund Spenser*. Baltimore: Johns Hopkins Univ. Press.

Kant, Immanuel. 1949. "What Is Enlightenment?" In *The Philosophy of Kant: Immanuel Kant's Moral and Political Writings*, ed. Carl J. Friedrich, 132-39. New York: Modern Library.

Katz, Richard. 1985. *The Ordered Text: The Sonnet Sequences of Du Bellay*. New York: Peter Lang.

Kennedy, Judith M. 1980. "The Final Emblem of *The Shepheardes Calender*." *Spenser Studies*, 1:95-106.

Kennedy. 1990. "*The Shepheardes Calender*, mottos in." In *The Spenser Encyclopedia*.

Kilpatrick, Ross S. 1986. *The Poetry of Friendship: Horace, Epistles I*. Edmonton: Univ. of Alberta Press.

King, John N. 1990. *Spenser's Poetry and the Reformation Tradition*. Princeton: Princeton Univ. Press.

Kinney, Arthur F. 1983. "Rhetoric and Fiction in Elizabethan England." In Murphy 1983, 385-93.

Kintgen, Eugene R. 1990. "Reconstructing Elizabethan Reading." *Studies in English Literature*, 30:1-18.

Knights, L. C. 1973. *How Many Children Had Lady Macbeth? An Essay in the Theory and Practice of Shakespeare Criticism*. New York: Haskell.

Langham, Robert. 1983. *A Letter*, ed. R. J. P. Kuin. Leiden: E. J. Brill.

Leicester's Commonwealth. 1985. Ed. D. C. Peck. Athens: Ohio Univ. Press.

Lennon, Colm. 1981. *Richard Stanihurst the Dubliner*. Blackrock, County Dublin: Irish Academic Press.

Lerer, Seth. 1992. "Introduction to 'Cluster on Chaucer.'" *PMLA*, 107:1139-42.

Lessing, Gotthold Ephraim. 1984. *Laocoön: An Essay on the Limits of Painting and Poetry*, trans. Edward Allen McCormick. Baltimore: John Hopkins Univ. Press.

Levy, F. J. 1972a. "Fulke Greville: The Courtier as Philosophical Poet." *Modern Language Quarterly*, 33:433-48.

Levy. 1972b. "Philip Sidney Reconsidered." *English Literary Renaissance*, 2:5-18. Rpt. in *Sidney in Retrospect: Selections from "English Literary Renaissance,"* 3-14. Amherst: Univ. of Massachusetts Press, 1988.

Levy. 1986. "Francis Bacon and the Style of Politics." *English Literary Renaissance*, 16: 101-22.

Lewalski, Barbara. 1990. "patronage." In *The Spenser Encyclopedia*.

Lewis, C. S. 1954. *English Literature in the Sixteenth Century, Excluding Drama*. Oxford: Clarendon Press.

Lievsay, John L. 1961. *Stefano Guazzo and the English Renaissance*. Chapel Hill: Univ. of North Carolina Press.

Loewenstein, Joseph. 1987. "A Note on the Structure of Spenser's *Amoretti:* Viper Thoughts." *Spenser Studies*, 8: 311-23.

Logan, George M., and Gordon Teskey, eds. 1989. *Unfolded Tales: Essays on Renaissance Romance*. Ithaca: Cornell Univ. Press.

Long, Percy W. 1916. "Spenser and the Bishop of Rochester." *PMLA*, 31:713-35.

Long. 1917. "Spenser's Visit to the North of England." *Modern Language Notes*, 32:58-59.

Lupton, Julia Reinhard. 1987. "Home-Making in Ireland: Virgil's Eclogue I and Book VI of *The Faerie Queene*." *Spenser Studies*, 8:119-45.

Lupton. 1993. "Mapping Mutability; or, Spenser's Irish Plot." In Bradshaw et al. 1993, 93-115.

McCabe, Richard A. 1993. "Edmund Spenser, Poet of Exile." *Proceedings of the British Academy*, 80:73-103.

MacCaffrey, Wallace T. 1981. *Queen Elizabeth and the Making of Policy, 1572-1588*. Princeton: Princeton Univ. Press.

MacCarthy-Morrogh, Michael. 1983. "The Munster Plantation, 1583-1641." Ph.D. thesis, Univ. of London.

MacCarthy-Morrogh. 1986. *The Munster Plantation: English Migration to Southern Ireland, 1583-1641*. Oxford: Clarendon Press.

Mace, Thomas. 1676. *Musick's Monument*. London.

McCoy, Richard C. 1985. "Gascoigne's 'Poëmata castrata': The Wages of Courtly Success." *Criticism*, 27:29-55.

McCoy. 1989. *The Rites of Knighthood: The Literature and Politics of Elizabethan Chivalry*. Berkeley: Univ. of California Press.

McKenzie, D. F. 1969. "Printers of the Mind: Some Notes on Bibliographical Theories and Printing-House Practice." *Studies in Bibliography*, 22:1-75.

McKitterick, David. 1981. Review of Virginia F. Stern, *Gabriel Harvey: His Life, Marginalia, and Library*. *Library*, 3:348-53.

McLane, Paul E. 1961. *Spenser's "Shepheardes Calender": A Study in Elizabethan Allegory*. Notre Dame: Univ. of Notre Dame Press.

Maley, Willy. 1994. *A Spenser Chronology*. Lanham, Md.: Barnes and Noble.

Marotti, Arthur F. 1981. "John Donne and the Rewards of Patronage." In *Patronage in the Renaissance*, ed. Guy Fitch Lytle and Stephen Orgel, 207-34. Princeton: Princeton Univ. Press.

Marston, John. 1598. *The Metamorphosis of Pigmalions Image*. London.

May, Steven W. 1991. *The Elizabethan Courtier Poets: The Poems and Their Contexts*. Columbia: Univ. of Missouri Press.

Miller, David Lee. 1979. "Abandoning the Quest." *ELH*, 46:173-92.

Miller. 1983. "Spenser's Vocation, Spenser's Career." *ELH*, 50:197-230.

Miller. 1988. *The Poem's Two Bodies: The Poetics of the 1590 "Faerie Queene."* Princeton: Princeton Univ. Press.

Miller. 1990. "The Writing Thing." *Diacritics*, 20. 4:17-29.

Mohl, Ruth. 1990. "Spenser, Edmund." In *The Spenser Encyclopedia*.

Montrose, Louis Adrian. 1986a. "The Elizabethan Subject and the Spenserian Text." In *Literary Theory/Renaissance Texts*, ed. Patricia Parker and David Quint, 302-40. Baltimore: Johns Hopkins Univ. Press.

Montrose. 1986b. "Renaissance Literary Studies and the Subject of History." *English Literary Renaissance*, 16:5-12.

Montrose. 1988. "Introductory Essay." In Berger 1988, 1-16.

Montrose. 1992. "Spenser's Domestic Domain." Paper given at the Renaissance Subject/Early Modern Object conference at the Univ. of Pennsylvania.

More, Thomas. 1963-. The *Complete Works of St. Thomas More*, ed. Clarence H. Miller et al. New Haven: Yale Univ. Press.

Morgan, Charles. 1944. *The House of Macmillan*. New York: Macmillan.

Morgan, Hiram. 1985. "The Colonial Venture of Sir Thomas Smith in Ulster, 1571-1575." *Historical Journal*, 28:261-78.

Moryson, Fynes. 1903. *Shakespeare's Europe: Unpublished Chapters of Fynes Moryson's Itinerary*, ed. Charles Hughes. London: Sherratt and Hughes.

Mueller, William R., and Don Cameron Allen, eds. 1952. *That Soueraine Light*. Baltimore: Johns Hopkins Univ. Press.

Mulcaster, Richard. 1582. *The First Part of the Elementarie*. London.

Mulcaster ed. 1888. *Positions*, ed. R. H. Quick. London: Longmans, Green.

Mulvey, Laura. 1978. "Visual Pleasure and Narrative Cinema." *Screen*, 16.3:6-18.

Murphy, James J., ed. 1983. *Renaissance Eloquence: Studies in the Theory and Practice of Renaissance Rhetoric*. Berkeley: Univ. of California Press.

Nash, Jerry C. 1991. "The Poetics of Seeing and Showing: Du Bellay's Love Lyrics." In *Lapidary Inscriptions: Renaissance Essays for Donald A. Stone, Jr.*, ed. Barbara C. Bowen and Jerry C. Nash, 45-59. Lexington, Ky.: French Forum.

Nashe, Thomas, ed. 1904-10. *The Works of Thomas Nashe*, ed. R. B. McKerrow. 5 vols. London: Bullen; rev. F. P. Wilson, 1958. Rpt. Oxford: Basil Blackwell, 1966.

Nelson, William. 1963. *The Poetry of Edmund Spenser: A Study*. New York: Columbia Univ. Press.

Neuse, Richard. 1968. "Book VI as Conclusion to *The Faerie Queene*." *ELH* 35:329-53.

Noakes, Susan. 1988. *Timely Reading: Between Exegesis and Interpretation*. Ithaca: Cornell Univ. Press.

Noot, Jan van der. 1569. *Theatre*. London.

Norbrook, David. 1984. *Poetry and Politics in the English Renaissance*. London: Routledge and Kegan Paul.

O'Connell, Michael. 1977. *Mirror and Veil: The Historical Dimension of Spenser's "Faerie Queene."* Chapel Hill: Univ. of North Carolina Press.

O'Rahilly, Alfred. 1938. "The Massacre at Smerwick (1580)." *Historical and Archaeological Papers,* 1 (Dublin and Cork).

Oram, William A. 1983. "Elizabethan Fact and Spenserian Fiction." *Spenser Studies*, 4: 33-47.

Oram. 1989. Introduction to *Mother Hubberds Tale*. In Spenser ed. 1989, 327-33.

Oram. 1990. "Spenser's Raleghs." *Studies in Philology*, 87:341-62.

Oruch, Jack B. 1990. "works, lost." In *The Spenser Encyclopedia*.

Osborn, James M. 1972. *Young Philip Sidney, 1572-1577*. New Haven: Yale Univ. Press.

Ovid. 1916. *Metamorphoses*, trans. Frank Justus Miller. 2 vols. Loeb Classical Library. Cambridge, Mass.: Harvard Univ. Press.

Pagden, Anthony. 1982. *The Fall of Natural Man*. Cambridge: Cambridge Univ. Press.

Parker, Patricia. 1987. "Suspended Instruments: Lyric and Power in the Bower of Bliss." In *Literary Fat Ladies: Rhetoric, Gender, Property*, 54-66. New York: Methuen.

Parry, Adam. 1963. "The Two Voices of Virgil's *Aeneid*." *Arion*, 2.4:66-80. Rpt. 1966 in *Virgil: A Collection of Critical Essays*, ed. Steele Commager, 107-23. Englewood Cliffs, N.J.: Prentice-Hall.

Patterson, Annabel. 1992. "The Egalitarian Giant: Representations of Justice in History/Literature." *Journal of British Studies*, 31:97-132. Expanded in *Reading Between the Lines* (1993), 80-116. Madison: Univ. of Wisconsin Press.

Peacham, Henry. 1612. *Minerva Britanna; or, A Garden of Heroical Devices*..

Pears, Steuart A., trans. 1845. *The Correspondence of Sir Philip Sidney and Hubert Languet*. London: W. Pickering.

Pedantius: A Latin Comedy Formerly Acted in Trinity College, Cambridge. 1905. Ed. G. C. Moore Smith. Rpt. 1963 in *Materialien zur Kunde des älteren englischen Dramas*. Vaduz: Kraus Reprint.

Perkell, Christine G. 1989. *The Poet's Truth: A Study of the Poet in Virgil's "Georgics."* Berkeley: Univ. of California Press.

Peterson, Richard S. "Laurel Crown and Ape's Tail: New Light on Spenser's Career from Sir Thomas Tresham." *Spenser Studies* 12.

Pigman, George, III. 1982. "Du Bellay's Ambivalence towards Rome in the *Antiquitez*." In *Rome in the Renaissance: The City and the Myth*, ed. Paul Ramsay, 321-32. Binghamton, N.Y.: Medieval and Renaissance Texts and Studies.

Pincombe, Michael. 1993. "Some Sixteenth-Century Records of the Words *Humanist* and *Humanism*." *Review of English Studies*, n.s. 44:1-15.

Plomer, H. R. 1923-24. "Edmund Spenser's Handwriting." *Modern Philology*, 21:201-7.

Plomer, Henry R., and Tom Peete Cross. 1927. *The Life and Correspondence of Lodowick Bryskett*. Chicago: Univ. of Chicago Press.

Prescott, Anne Lake. 1978. *French Poets and the English Renaissance: Studies in Fame and Transformation*. New Haven: Yale Univ. Press.

Prescott. 1985. "The Thirsty Deer and the Lord of Life: Contexts for *Amoretti* 67-70." *Spenser Studies*, 6:33-76.

Prouty, C. T. 1942. *George Gascoigne: Elizabethan Courtier, Soldier, and Poet*. Rpt. New York: Benjamin Blom, 1966.

Public Record Office, London, State Papers, Ireland, Elizabeth, S.P. 63/50-106.

Quinn, David Beers. 1945. "Sir Thomas Smith (1513-1577) and the Beginnings of English Colonial Theory." *Proceedings of the American Philosophical Society*, 89.4:543-60.

Quinn. 1976. "Renaissance Influences in English Colonization." *Transactions of the Royal Historical Society*, 5.26: 73-93.

Quint, David. 1992. "Bragging Rights: Honor and Courtesy in Shakespeare and Spenser." In *Creative Imitation: New Essays on Renaissance Literature in Honor of Thomas M. Greene*, ed. David Quint et al., 391-430. Binghamton, N.Y.: Medieval and Renaissance Texts and Studies.

Quitslund, Jon A. 1973. "Spenser's *Amoretti* VIII and Platonic Commentaries on Petrarch." *Journal of the Warburg and Courtauld Institutes*, 36:256-76.

Rambuss, Richard. 1993. *Spenser's Secret Career*. Cambridge Studies in Renaissance Literature and Culture, 3. Cambridge: Cambridge Univ. Press.

Read, Conyers. 1960. *Mister Secretary Cecil and Queen Elizabeth*. New York: Alfred A. Knopf.

Rebholz, Ronald A. 1971. *The Life of Fulke Greville, First Lord Brooke*. Oxford: Clarendon Press.

Ringler, William A., Jr. 1961. "Spenser, Shakespeare, Honor, and Worship." *Renaissance News*, 14:159-61.

Roche, Thomas P., Jr. 1989. "Spenser's Muse." In Logan and Teskey 1989, 162-88.

Rosenberg, Eleanor. 1955. *Leicester: Patron of Letters*. New York: Columbia Univ. Press.

Ruutz-Rees, Caroline. 1910. "Some Notes of Gabriel Harvey's in Hoby's Translation of Castiglione's *Courtier* (1561)." *PMLA*, 25:608-39.

Sale, Roger. 1968. *Reading Spenser: An Introduction to "The Faerie Queene."* New York: Random House.

Saulnier, V.-L. 1968. *Du Bellay*. Paris: Hatier.

Scholes, Robert. 1989. *Protocols of Reading*. New Haven: Yale Univ. Press.

Shepherd, Simon. 1989. *Spenser*. Harvester New Readings. Atlantic Highlands, N.J.: Humanities Press International.

Sherman, William H. 1995. *John Dee: The Politics of Reading and Writing in the English Renaissance*. Amherst: Univ. of Massachusetts Press.

Sidney, Philip, ed. 1973a. *The Countess of Pembroke's Arcadia*, ed. J. Robertson. Oxford: Clarendon, Press.

Sidney ed. 1973b. "Discourse on Irish Affairs." In *Miscellaneous Prose of Sir Philip Sidney*, ed. Katherine Duncan-Jones and Jan Van Dorsten, 7-12. Oxford: Clarendon Press.

Sisson, Charles J., ed. 1933. *Thomas Lodge and Other Elizabethans*. Cambridge, Mass.: Harvard Univ. Press.

Smith, Bruce R. 1991. *Homosexual Desire in Shakespeare's England: A Cultural Poetics*. Chicago: Univ. of Chicago Press.

Spenser, Edmund. 1633. *A View of the Present State of Ireland*. Dublin: Society of Stationers. STC 25067a, part 3.

Spenser ed. 1758. *"The Faerie Queene": A New Edition with a Glossary and Notes Explanatory and Critical*, ed. John Upton. London.

Spenser ed. 1882-84. *The Complete Works in Verse and Prose of Edmund Spenser*, ed. Alexander B. Grosart. 9 vols. London: Hazell, Watson and Viney.

Spenser ed. 1912. *The Poetical Works of Edmund Spenser*, ed. J. C. Smith and E. de Selincourt. Oxford Standard Authors. Oxford: Oxford Univ. Press.

Spenser ed. 1932-57. *The Works of Edmund Spenser: A Variorum Edition*, ed. Edwin Greenlaw et al. 11 vols. Baltimore: Johns Hopkins Univ. Press.

Spenser ed. 1977. *Edmund Spenser: The Faerie Queene*, ed. A. C. Hamilton. New York: Longman.

Spenser ed. 1989. *The Yale Edition of the Shorter Poems of Edmund Spenser*, ed. William A. Oram et al. New Haven: Yale Univ. Press.

Spenser: The Critical Heritage. 1971. Ed. R. M. Cummings. London: Routledge and Kegan Paul.

The Spenser Encyclopedia. 1990. Ed. A. C. Hamilton et al. Toronto: Univ. of Toronto Press.

Stapleton, M. L. 1990. "Spenser, the *Antiquitez de Rome*, and the Development of the English Sonnet Form." *Comparative Literature Studies*, 27:259-74.

Stern, Virginia. 1979. *Gabriel Harvey: His Life, Marginalia and Library*. Oxford: Clarendon Press.

Suzuki, Mihoko. 1989. *Metamorphoses of Helen: Authority, Difference, and the Epic*. Ithaca: Cornell Univ. Press.

Taylor, Gary. 1989. *Reinventing Shakespeare: A Cultural History from the Restoration to the Present*. New York: Oxford Univ. Press.

Teskey, Gordon. 1988. "Milton and Modernity." *Diacritics*, 18:42-53.

Teskey. 1990. "Positioning Spenser's 'Letter to Raleigh.'" In *Craft and Tradition: Essays in Honor of William Blissett*, 35-46. Calgary: Univ. of Calgary Press.

Teskey. 1992. "Benjamin, Allegory, Spenser, Spenserians." Paper given at the 1992 conference of the Modern Language Association of America.

Teskey. 1993. "Mutability, Genealogy, and the Authority of Forms." *Representations*, 41:104-22.

Thomas, Richard F. 1988. "Tree Violation and Ambivalence in Virgil." *Transactions of the American Philological Association*, 118:261-73.

Tottel's Miscellany ed. 1935. Ed. Hyder E. Rollins. Cambridge, Mass.: Harvard Univ. Press. Rev. ed. 1965.

Trimpi, Wesley. 1962. *Ben Jonson's Poems: A Study of the Plain Style*. Stanford: Stanford Univ. Press.

Tucker, George H. 1990. *The Poet's Odyssey: Joachim du Bellay and the "Antiquitez de Rome."* Oxford: Clarendon Press.

van der Noot, Jan. See Noot, Jan van der.

Venuti, Lawrence. 1989. *Our Halcyon Dayes: English Prerevolutionary Texts and Postmodern Culture*. Madison: Univ. of Wisconsin Press.

Vico, Giambattista. 1988. *On the Ancient Wisdom of the Italians Unearthed from the Origins of the Latin Language*, trans. L. M. Palmer. Ithaca: Cornell Univ. Press.

Virgil ed. 1934. *Aeneid*, trans. H. R. Fairclough. 2 vols. Loeb Classical Library. Cambridge, Mass.: Harvard Univ. Press. Rev. ed.

Virgil ed. 1983. *The Aeneid,* trans. Robert Fitzgerald. New York: Vintage.

Wallace, Malcolm W. 1915. *The Life of Sir Philip Sidney*. Cambridge: Cambridge Univ. Press.

Waller, Gary F. 1994. *Edmund Spenser: A Literary Life*. New York: St. Martin's.

Ware, James. 1633a. *Two Histories of Ireland*. Dublin. STC 25067.

Ware. 1633b. *The Historie of Ireland*. Dublin. STC 25067a.

Ware ed. 1971. *Two Histories of Ireland*. The English Experience: Its Record in Early Printed Books Published in Facsimile, 421. Amsterdam: Theatrum Orbis Terrarum; New York: Da Capo.

Weber, Max. 1958. "Science as a Vocation." In *From Max Weber: Essays in Sociology*, ed. and trans. H. H. Gerth and C. Wright Mills, 120-56. New York: Oxford Univ. Press.

Weiner, Seth. 1982. "Spenser's Study of English Syllables and Its Completion by Thomas Campion." *Spenser Studies*, 3:3-56.

Wells, William, ed. 1972. S*penser Allusions in the Sixteenth and Seventeenth Centuries*. Chapel Hill: Univ. of North Carolina Press.

Welply, W. H. 1922. "The Family and Descendants of Edmund Spenser." *Journal of the Cork Historical and Archaeological Society*, 28:22-34, 49-62.

Welply. 1924a. "Edmund Spenser, Some New Discoveries and Corrections of Old Errors." *Notes and Queries*, 146:445-47.

Welply. 1924b. "Spenser Continued." *Notes and Queries*, 147:35.

Welply. 1927. "Spenser's Mistress Rosalind." *Notes and Queries*, 153:389.

Welply. 1932. "Being an Account of Some Recent Researches into His Life and Lineage, with Some Notice of His Family and Descendants." *Notes and Queries*, 162:110-14, 128-32, 146-50, 165-69, 182-87, 202-6, 220-24, 239-42, 256-60.

Welply. 1933a. "More Notes on Edmund Spenser." *Notes and Queries*, 165: 92-94, 111-16.

Welply. 1933b. "Spenser in Ireland." *Times Literary Supplement*, 32 (18 May):348.

Welply. 1940. "Edmund Spenser's Brother-in-Law, John Travers." *Notes and Queries*, 179:74-78, 92-96, 112-15, 180.

Welply. 1941a. "Some Spenser Problems." *Notes and Queries*, 180:56-59, 74-77, 92-95, 120, 151, 248, 436-39, 454-59.

Welply. 1941b. "John Baron Lumley, 1534-1609." *Notes and Queries*, 181:86-88, 104.

Welply. 1944a. "Notes on Spenser." *Notes and Queries*, 186:128-29.

Welply. 1944b. "John Travers: A Correction and Some Additions." *Notes and Queries*, 187:143-44.

West, Michael. 1988. "Spenser's Art of War: Chivalric Allegory, Military Technology, and the Elizabethan Mock-Heroic Sensibility." *Renaissance Quarterly*, 41:654-704.

White, Hayden. 1987. *The Content of the Form*. Baltimore: Johns Hopkins Univ. Press.

Williams, Penry. 1979. *The Tudor Regime*. Oxford: Oxford Univ. Press.

Wilson, Derek. 1981. *Sweet Robin: A Biography of Robert Dudley, Earl of Leicester, 1533-1588*. London: Hamish Hamilton.

Wilson, John Dover. 1936. "The Study of Shakespeare." *University of Edinburgh Journal*, 8:12.

Wofford, Susanne Lindgren. 1992. *The Choice of Achilles: The Ideology of Figure in the Epic*. Stanford: Stanford Univ. Press.

Woudhuysen, H. R. 1981. "Leicester's Literary Patronage: A Study of the English Court, 1578-82." Ph.D. diss., Oxford Univ.

Yeats, W. B. 1961. "Edmund Spenser." In *Essays and Introductions*, 356-83. New York: Macmillan.

Zupko, Ronald E. 1977. *British Weights & Measures: A History from Antiquity to the Seventeenth Century*. Madison: Univ. of Wisconsin Press.